T0294178

TREKKING THE GR7 IN ANDALUCÍA

FROM TARIFA TO PUEBLA DE DON FADRIQUE

TREKKING THE GR7 IN ANDALUCÍA

FROM TARIFA TO PUEBLA DE DON FADRIQUE

by Guy Hunter-Watts

JUNIPER HOUSE, MURLEY MOSS,
OXENHOLME ROAD, KENDAL, CUMBRIA LA9 7RL
www.cicerone.co.uk

© Guy Hunter-Watts 2021
Third edition 2021
ISBN: 978 1 85284 995 5
Second edition 2013
First edition 2007

Printed in China on behalf of Latitude Press Ltd
A catalogue record for this book is available from the British Library.

Route mapping by Lovell Johns www.lovelljohns.com
All photographs are by the author unless otherwise stated.
Contains OpenStreetMap.org data © OpenStreetMap contributors,
CC-BY-SA. NASA relief data courtesy of ESRI

Updates to this guide

While every effort is made by our authors to ensure the accuracy of guidebooks as they go to print, changes can occur during the lifetime of an edition. This guidebook was researched and written before and during the COVID-19 pandemic. While we are not aware of any significant changes to routes or facilities at the time of printing, it is likely that the current situation will give rise to more changes than would usually be expected. Any updates that we know of for this guide will be on the Cicerone website (www.cicerone.co.uk/995/updates), so please check before planning your trip. We also advise that you check information about such things as transport, accommodation and shops locally. Even rights of way can be altered over time.

We are always grateful for information about any discrepancies between a guidebook and the facts on the ground, sent by email to updates@cicerone.co.uk or by post to Cicerone, Juniper House, Murley Moss, Oxenholme Road, Kendal, LA9 7RL.

Register your book: To sign up to receive free updates, special offers and GPX files where available, register your book at www.cicerone.co.uk.

Front cover: The Cortijo de Aute passed on Stage 12A

CONTENTS

Route summary table 8
Author's preface 11

INTRODUCTION 13
The GR7/E4 13
Andalucía. 14
The GR7 in Andalucía 16
Shorter itineraries 18
Historical context 18
Plants and wildlife 21
When to go 23
Getting there 23
Getting back. 24
Luggage transfer 24
Accommodation. 24
Food and drink. 26
Water 27
Equipment 27
Money 28
Language 28
Waymarking. 28
Maps and GPS 29
Staying safe 30
Using this guide 31

THE COMMON ROUTE. 33
Cádiz province. 34
Stage 1   Tarifa to Los Barrios 36
Stage 2   Los Barrios to Castillo de Castellar 43
Stage 3   Castillo de Castellar to Jimena de la Frontera 48
Stage 4   Jimena de la Frontera to Ubrique 52
Stage 5   Ubrique to Montejaque via Villaluenga del Rosario 58
Málaga province 66
Stage 6   Montejaque to Arriate via Ronda 68
Stage 7   Arriate to Ardales 73
Stage 8   Ardales to El Chorro. 78
Stage 9   El Chorro to Valle de Abdalajís 82
Stage 10   Valle de Abdalajís to Antequera 85
Stage 11   Antequera to Villanueva de Cauche 90

THE NORTHERN VARIANT 95
Stage 12A Villanueva de Cauche to Villanueva del Trabuco 96
Stage 13A Villanueva del Trabuco to Villanueva de Tapia 100
Stage 14A Villanueva de Tapia to Villanueva de Algaidas 104
Stage 15A Villanueva de Algaidas to Cuevas de San Marcos 108
Córdoba province 113
Stage 16A Cuevas de San Marco to Rute 114
Stage 17A Rute to Priego de Córdoba 118
Stage 18A Priego de Córdoba to Almedinilla 124
Stage 19A Almedinilla to Alcalá la Real 127
Jaén province 132
Stage 20A Alcalá la Real to Frailes 134
Stage 21A Frailes to Carchelejo 137
Stage 22A Carchelejo to Cambil 142
Stage 23A Cambil to Torres 146
Stage 24A Torres to Bedmar 150
Stage 25A Bedmar to Jódar 155
Stage 26A Jódar to Quesada 158
Stage 27A Quesada to Cazorla 163
Stage 28A Cazorla to Vadillo Castril 167
Stage 29A Vadillo Castril to Coto Ríos 170
Stage 30A Coto Ríos to Pontones 175
Stage 31A Pontones to Santiago de la Espada 180
Stage 32A Santiago de la Espada to Puebla de Don Fadrique 184

THE SOUTHERN VARIANT 189
Stage 12B Villanueva de Cauche to Riogordo 190
Stage 13B Riogordo to Ventas de Zafarraya 193
Granada province 197
Stage 14B Ventas de Zafarraya to Alhama de Granada 200
Stage 15B Alhama de Granada to Arenas del Rey 204
Stage 16B Arenas del Rey to Jayena 207
Stage 17B Jayena to Albuñuelas 211
Stage 18B Albuñuelas to Nigüelas 217
Stage 19B Nigüelas to Lanjarón 222
Stage 20B Lanjarón to Soportújar 226
Stage 21B Soportújar to Pitres 230
Stage 22B Pitres to Trevélez 236
Stage 23B Trevélez to Cádiar 242
Stage 24B Cádiar to Yegen 247
Stage 25B Yegen to Laroles 253
Stage 26B Laroles to Puerto de la Ragua via Bayárcal 259
Stage 27B Puerto de la Ragua to La Calahorra 264

Stage 28B   La Calahorra to Narváez via Charches 269
Stage 29B   Narváez to Zújar 278
Stage 30B   Zújar to Benamaurel 283
Stage 31B   Benamaurel to Cúllar 288
Stage 32B   Cúllar to Orce 291
Stage 33B   Orce to Huéscar 295
Stage 34B   Huéscar to Puebla de Don Fadrique 301

Appendix A   Facilities table 306
Appendix B   Spanish–English glossary 310
Appendix C   Further information 312
Appendix D   Further reading 313

Acknowledgements

My first and most trusted reference when researching this book was the original Cicerone guide, *Walking the GR7 in Andalucía*, by Kirstie Shirra and Michelle Lowe with additional help from Miguel Angel Santaella.

While I walked the route in sections with a day pack and a hotel room at the end of many days, Kirstie and Michelle walked the route in one go with a tent and cooking gear. I couldn't be more grateful for their pioneering, meticulous research.

The second edition of their guide benefitted from feedback from many readers as well as from Jonathan and Lesley Williams who walked sections of the route for that update.

I also owe a big *gracias* to Mick Borroff who kindly helped sort out a number of issues with my original GPX files. Your help was invaluable and much appreciated.

ROUTE SUMMARY TABLE

Stage	Start	Distance	Ascent	Descent	Highest point	Time	Page
The common route							
Cádiz province (167.6km, 6–9 days)							
1*	Tarifa	47.1km	800m	795m	244m	12hr 30min	36
2(*)	Los Barrios	33.3km	790m	550m	255m	9hr 40min	43
3	Castillo de Castellar	21.3km	210m	375m	255m	6hr 15min	48
4*	Jimena de la Frontera	37.7km	1200m	970m	840m	10hr 30min	52
5(*)	Ubrique	28.2km	1205m	835m	1029m	7hr 40min	58
Málaga province (117.2km, 7–8 days)							
6	Montejaque	19.8km	605m	695m	752m	5hr 30min	68
7(*)	Arriate	34.5km	895m	1085m	894m	9hr 30min	73
8	Ardales	16km	690m	885m	583m	5hr	78
9	El Chorro	10.6km	595m	475m	681m	3hr	82
10	Valle de Abdalajís	19.5km	740m	565m	770m	5hr 40min	85
11	Antequera	16.8km	555m	370m	942m	4hr 40min	90
Total for common route		**284.8km**	**8285m**	**7600m**	**1029m**	**13–17 days (79hr 55min)**	
The northern variant							
Málaga province (97.4km, 5–6 days)							
12A	Villanueva de Cauche	16.6km	345m	355m	813m	4hr 15min	96
13A(*)	Villanueva del Trabuco	31.2km	590m	610m	951m	8hr 45min	100
14A	Villanueva de Tapia	17.2km	465m	580m	896m	4hr 45min	104
15A	Villanueva de Algaidas	18.8km	550m	675m	702m	5hr 10min	108
Córdoba province (63km, 3 days)							
16A	Cuevas de San Marcos	13.6km	540m	340m	681m	3hr 40min	114

Stage	Start	Distance	Ascent	Descent	Highest point	Time	Page
17A	Rute	25.9km	905m	875m	979m	7hr 30min	118
18A	Priego de Córdoba	12.1km	310m	315m	768m	3hr 10min	124
19A	Almedinilla	25km	965m	700m	1104m	7hr	127

Jaén province (292.9km, 13–15 days)

Stage	Start	Distance	Ascent	Descent	Highest point	Time	Page
20A	Alcalá la Real	10.2km	310m	265m	1012m	2hr 30min	134
21A	Frailes	35.2km	1415m	1580m	1491m	10hr	137
22A	Carchelejo	13km	520m	565m	833m	3hr 45min	142
23A	Cambil	27.7km	1105m	980m	1659m	8hr 30min	146
24A	Torres	16.4km	660m	900m	1164m	4hr 45min	150
25A	Bedmar	9.2km	550m	545m	1127m	2hr 50min	155
26A	Jódar	35.3km	605m	580m	677m	9hr 45min	158
27A	Quesada	18.1km	845m	720m	1198m	4hr 50min	163
28A	Cazorla	16km	950m	770m	1380m	5hr 30min	167
29A	Vadillo Castril	33.8km	1180m	1485m	1443m	8hr 30min	170
30A	Coto Ríos	30.3km	1585m	930m	1733m	8hr	175
31A	Pontones	13.4m	450m	455m	1639m	3hr 45min	180
32A	Santiago de la Espada	34.3km	755m	910m	1600m	8hr 15min	184
Total for northern variant		**453.3km**	**15,600m**	**15,135m**	**1733m**	**21–24 days (125hr 20min)**	

The southern variant

Málaga province (52.4km, 2 days)

Stage	Start	Distance	Ascent	Descent	Highest point	Time	Page
12B	Villanueva de Cauche	23.8km	580m	885m	927m	5hr 30min	190
13B	Riogordo	28.6km	1040m	520m	943m	7hr 30min	193

Granada province (433.1km, 22–23 days)

Stage	Start	Distance	Ascent	Descent	Highest point	Time	Page
14B	Ventas de Zafarraya	20.4km	410m	440m	1093m	5hr 45min	200
15B	Alhama de Granada	22.3km	550m	555m	1137m	6hr	204
16B	Arenas del Rey	17.2km	595m	630m	1081m	6hr	207

Stage	Start	Distance	Ascent	Descent	Highest point	Time	Page
17B(*)	Jayena	31km	765m	945m	1327m	8hr 30min	211
18B	Albuñuelas	14.9km	680m	480m	931m	4hr 30min	217
19B	Nigüelas	18.8km	745m	1020m	1287m	5hr 15min	222
20B	Lanjarón	12.7km	945m	650m	1118m	4hr 10min	226
21B	Soportújar	12.6km	1020m	720m	1537m	3hr 45min	230
22B	Pitres	17.4km	1105m	815m	1733m	5hr 40min	236
23B	Trevélez	20.5km	625m	1245m	1761m	5hr 50min	242
24B	Cádiar	17.1km	1025m	910m	1457m	5hr 10min	247
25B	Yegen	17.9km	660m	675m	1254m	5hr 15min	253
26B	Laroles	16.2km	1395m	375m	2041m	6hr	259
27B	Puerto de la Ragua	11.6km	65m	910m	2041m	3hr 20min	264
28B*	La Calahorra	54.6km	1600m	1430m	2037m	14hr	269
29B	Narváez	24.2km	270m	870m	1370m	6hr	278
30B	Zújar	22km	495m	540m	885m	5hr 30min	283
31B	Benamaurel	14.1km	290m	120m	905m	3hr 20min	288
32B	Cúllar	23.9km	330m	290m	1063m	5hr 30min	291
33B	Orce	17.7km	260m	230m	960m	4hr 10min	295
34B	Huéscar	26km	580m	375m	1481m	6hr 45min	301
Total for southern variant		**485.5km**	**16,030m**	**15,630m**	**2041m**	**22–25 days (133hr 25min)**	
GR7 total (common route + northern variant)		**738.1km**	**23,885m**	**22,735m**	**1733m**	**34–41 days (205hr 15min)**	
GR7 total (common route + southern variant)		**770.3km**	**24,315m**	**23,230m**	**2041m**	**35–42 days (213hr 20min)**	

* It is recommended that you split these stages into two days either by leaving the route or by camping. (An asterisk in brackets indicates an optional two-day section.) You will need to camp if you want to break Stage 17B.

AUTHOR'S PREFACE

Limestone outcrops at the heart of the Sierra de Mágina park (Stage 23A)

When Spain and long-distance treks come to mind, the thoughts of many walkers will invariably turn to the Camino and the network of paths leading to Santiago de Compostela. It's a walk which somehow seems greater than the sum of the parts, an inner as well as an outer journey and, for many, a life-changing experience. The GR7 footpath receives far less press and sees far fewer walkers yet the 1250 kilometres of its trail as it passes through Andalucía easily vies in beauty with those of the Camino while offering one of Europe's most challenging and inspirational on-foot adventures.

In the course of trekking the two variants of the GR7 I saw red and roe deer, wild boar, ibex, mongoose, foxes, a badger and, perhaps the most magical of many special sightings, an imperial eagle rising metres away from me in the Sierra de Mágina. I swam in river pools, bathed in thermal springs and beneath waterfalls and took a dip in the Atlantic. I met with shepherds, olive pickers, a beekeeper, park rangers, resin collecters and cork cutters. And, astonishingly, in the entirety of the trail I met with no more than two dozen walkers and, on many stages, not a soul.

Walking the route proved to be more challenging than I'd anticipated. Some stages involve 1000m ascents while others can only be comfortably negotiated by splitting them in two. If much of the original waymarking is damaged or illegible, marker posts long gone and paint flashes faded, new signage and more durable posts have recently been added on several sections. With the previous Cicerone guide that this one replaces, a map, a compass and a keen eye, it still proved easy enough to find the way. And a most wonderful way at that.

Looking back towards Lanjarón (Stage 20B)

INTRODUCTION

Looking back towards Montejaque from Ronda on Stage 6

Andalucía is home to an astonishing variety of natural habitats. Grandiose peaks rise to almost 3500 metres, there are windswept beaches with the highest dune formations in Europe, forests of cork and holm oak, vast groves of olives and almond along with subtropical valleys dotted with citrus, persimmon and avocado. Jagged outcrops of karst are cut through by deep gorges, semi-desert regions are reminiscent of those of Colorado or New Mexico, irrigated terraces cling to precipitous slopes, fields of wheat are contrasted by those of cotton and sunflowers; it seems as if there's a wonder of nature around every corner.

The GR7 introduces you to these myriad landscapes as it runs west to east across southern Spain linking several of the region's most beautiful protected areas. You pass hilltop fortresses dating back to the Moorish times, troglodyte dwellings, churches and palaces built during Spain's Golden Age, ancient olive mills and isolated convents and chapels. Walking by way of Roman roads, Berber footpaths, drovers' routes and country lanes the trail links towns and villages that feel a world away from the busy resorts of the southern Spanish coast.

THE GR7/E4

GR7/E4, a pan-European hiking trail, was created in the early 1970s by The European Ramblers Association.

The ERA's mission statement reads:
'E-paths connect people and are the paths for peace, understanding and unity'.

GR comes from the French *grande randonnée* – in Spanish, *gran recorrido* – which means 'long distance path' and GR7 refers to the Spanish, Andorran and French sections of the E4.

The E4 is the longest of 12 E-paths in Europe. It originally ran from Tarifa in southern Spain to Delphi in Greece. After crossing Andalucía and running up the eastern side of Spain via Murcia, Valencia and Catalonia the GR7 enters France via Andorra. Leaving France, now waymarked as simply E4, it passes through Switzerland, Germany, Austria, Hungary, Serbia and Bulgaria before running south into Greece.

Variants have recently been added that extend the E4 further south into Morocco, Crete and Cyprus and, at the other end, west along the Algarve to Cabo São Vicente in Portugal. The total length of the route is now approximately 12,000 kilometres.

The Andalucían section of the GR7, which includes a northern and southern variant, was waymarked by FEDAMON (The Andalucían Federation of Mountaineering) in the late 1990s. The path links footpaths and country tracks as well as a few sections of minor road to create a trail that totals 1225 kilometres. It's this section of the E4 – the GR7 in Andalucía with both variants – that's described in this guide.

ANDALUCÍA

Andalucía occupies around one-fifth of the Spanish mainland, flanked by the Mediterranean Sea and the Atlantic Ocean. It encompasses eight provinces that stretch from the Portuguese border in the west to its border with Murcia in the east. The region takes its name from Al Andalus, the name the Arabs gave to an area that saw eight centuries of Muslim rule between the eighth and 15th centuries. With rich agricultural lands irrigated by abundant mountain waters, groves of almonds, olives and citrus, vineyards, wheatlands, mountain pastures and a benign climate it's not hard to see why the Moors considered Andalucía to be an earthly paradise.

The mightly Baetic system of mountains occupies about half of the Andalucían territory, running west to east like a mighty sabre, separated from the Sierra Morena by the broad valley of the Guadalquivir. As it crosses the provinces of Granada and Jaén the massif spilts into two branches: the Subbetic range to the north and the Penibetic range to the south. The latter is home to mainland Spain's highest peaks with El Mulhacén rising to 3457m in the Sierra Nevada.

Andalucía is one of 17 autonomous regions within Spain with its own regional government based in Seville, the region's largest city. There are excellent communications via road and rail including a high speed link with Madrid while Málaga is one of Europe's busiest regional airports with links to every major airport in the UK. Several smaller airports also have flights to and from the UK.

This is one of Europe's most popular holiday destinations. Some 30 million tourists visit every year and this is reflected in the vast range of hotel accommodation, along with a huge numbers of restaurants and bars, on offer. If sun, sea and sand remain the main magnet for travel, the past 30 years have seen a huge increase in the number of visitors exploring inland regions.

The gorge and Puente Nuevo in Ronda (Stage 6)

Many visitors now come on walking holidays. Just two decades ago there were few waymarked paths, the GR7 being among the first. Things are now very different with an extensive network of short distance routes along with several new GR trails. Walking tourism has become an important part of many a mountain village's economy while the regional government is now taking an active part in promoting Andalucía as a top walking destination.

The people of Andalucía

Anyone who's travelled to other parts of the Iberian peninsula will be aware of the huge differences between the regions of Spain and its peoples. If Franco sought to impose a centralist and authoritarian system of government on his people, in the new Spain, ushered in with his departure and the advent of liberal democracy, most Spaniards actively celebrate the country's diverse, multilingual and multi-faceted culture.

If Spain is different, as the marketing campaigns of the 1990s and noughties would have us believe, then Andalucía is more so. It is, of course, about much more than those stereotypical images of flamenco, castanets, flounced dresses and bullfighting: any attempt to define what constitutes the *andaluz* character must probe far deeper. But what very quickly becomes apparent on any visit to the region is that this is a place of ebullience, joie de vivre, easy conversation and generous gestures. One of the many attractions of the GR7 is acquainting yourself with untouristy villages and towns that are way off piste and where the welcome you're given is likely to be both warm and genuine.

15

THE GR7 IN ANDALUCÍA

The GR7 is made up of 3 sections: the initial common stages, the northern variant and the southern variant. The common stage totals 285km and can be walked in 13 to 17 days. The complete northern variant – that's with the common stage added on – is 738km and takes between 34 and 41 days. The complete southern variant is 770km and requires between 35 and 42 days of walking.

	Distance	Time	Days
Common route	284.8km	79hr 55min	13–17
Northern route	453.3km	125hr 20min	21–24
Southern route	485.5km	133hr 25min	22–25
Common + northern route	738.1km	205hr 15min	34–41
Common + southern route	770.3km	213hr 20min	35–42

This is a challenging long-distance trail that can be broken up into shorter sections: few of us have the luxury of being able to take the five to six weeks that walking the whole of one variant requires. The more detailed descriptions that follow, along with the summaries of the individual stages, will help you decide which parts of the trail to hike. The Shorter itineraries section, below, also offers suggestions as to how you might break the route.

Stages 1, 4, and 28B are between 37.7km and 54.6km and are therefore too long to complete in one day for all

but the most hardened walkers. When tackling these you'll need to choose between wild camping or diverting off-route to a nearby town or village to find accommodation then rejoining the trail the next day (more details are provided in all the individual stages).

Wild camping is not permitted in the natural parks through which the walk passes while in all other places you will always find a quiet and beautiful place to pitch a tent. That said, with forward planning, there's no need to carry camping gear. Villages at the end points of all stages apart from two have accommodation and restaurants. Those stages both end at remote mountain refuges which are no longer open and where no public transport is available. So you'll need to take a taxi to your accommodation or wild camp.

The common route: Stages 1–11
Via Cádiz and Málaga provinces (285 km, 13–17 days)
For the initial 11 stages of the walk the northern and southern variants share a common trail. Departing from Tarifa, one of Andalucía's most enchanting ocean-side towns, the trail runs close to the Atlantic before climbing inland through the forested hillsides of the Alcornocales Natural Park. Passing some of Spain's most beautiful hilltop villages, the GR7 next cuts through the stunning sierras of the Grazalema Natural Park before reaching Ronda where you enter the town close to its plunging cliff face.

From Ronda the route adopts a northeasterly course via little-known towns and villages, traversing the mountains just north of the Sierra de las Nieves Natural Park before reaching the spectacular gorge of El Chorro. Here you could take time out to hike the Caminito del Rey, a footpath suspended high above the gorge (www.caminitodelrey.info/en/). Reaching more open countryside the GR7 passes through Antequera, the largest town on the route, before dividing into its northern and southern variants at the tiny hamlet of Villanueva de Cauche.

The northern route: Stages 12A–32A
Via Málaga, Córdoba and Jaén provinces (453km, 21 to 24 days)
Running north from Villanueva de Cauche before adopting an easterly tack, the northern route crosses the vast olive belt that stretches from Antequera to the eastern reaches of Andalucía. In spite of a long section through seemingly endless olive groves, each day of hiking has its own beauty, linking towns and villages that see few other travellers besides those walking the GR7.

After crossing the vast plain north of Villanueva de Trabuco you reach the magnificent limestone ranges of the Subbetica Natural Park. Olive groves still cover the lower slopes of the mountains but much of the trail is via higher footpaths and tracks where the hand of Man on the landscape is much less marked.

The northern route gathers in momentum and beauty as it leads on through the wild landscapes of the Sierra de Mágina Natural Park before traversing the mountains of the Sierra de Cazorla Natural Park to reach Puebla de Don Fadrique, the end point of the GR7 in Andalucía.

The southern route: Stages 12B–34B
Via Málaga and Granada provinces (485km, 22 to 25 days)
The GR7's southern variant sticks to the Penibetic range as you pass through the northern Axarquía and the Sierras de

Poppies close to Cuevas del Engarbo (Stage 32A)

Tejeda, Almijara and Álhama Natural Park. Running on east along the Lecrín Valley it reaches the Sierra Nevada, home to mainland Spain's highest mountains and villages.

This is one of the GR7's most beautiful sections as the trail threads its way along the southern flank of the Sierra Nevada. Crossing a 2040m pass – that's about 700m higher than the summit of Ben Nevis – you descend to a high plain before climbing into the eastern reaches of the Subbetic range and the Sierra de Baza Natural Park. Remote mountain tracks and paths then lead to the flatter, semi-desert landscapes surrounding Orce, Galera and Huéscar before reaching the trail's end point at Puebla de Don Fadrique.

Given that few walkers will have the opportunity to walk the entire northern or southern variant in one go, you might consider tackling a week or a fortnight-long section of the GR7. Details of local transport links along the route are provided in the provincial chapter introductions and in the individual village boxes to facilitate planning.

The author's top choices for a week of hiking would be:

• **Stages 1-7, Tarifa to Ronda:** challenging trails through three natural parks passing through some of Andalucía's most beautiful villages. Good transport links at the start and end point to and from Seville and Málaga.

• **Stages 19B-25B, Nigüelas to Laroles:** a stunning and challenging section of the trail across the southern flank of the Sierra Nevada via the beautiful villages of Las Alpujarras with good transport links with Granada.

• **Stages 28B-34B, La Calahorra-Puebla de Don Fadrique:** the final section of the GR7's southern variant leads through the wild mountains of the Sierra de Mágina Natural Park before passing through the semi-desert landscapes of eastern Andalucía. Limited transport links with Granada.

And for a fortnight of hiking:

• **Stages 17A-31A, Rute to Santiago de la Espada:** a challenging section of the northern variant of the GR7 passing through the little-known yet beautiful Sierra de Mágina Natural Park before you undertake a stunning traverse of the Cazorla Natural Park. Limited transport links with Córdoba and Jaén.

• **Stages 15B-27B, Alhama de Granada to La Calahorra:** a wonderful section of trail leading through a wild swathe of the Sierra de Almijara then on through the fertile terraces of the Lecrín Valley before a stunning traverse of the Sierra Nevada National Park via the high villages of Las Alpujarras. Limited transport links with Granada.

Pre-history, Phoenecians and Romans
Many vestiges throughout Andalucía – burial sites, cave paintings, flint-knapping sites and countless axes, arrow heads and pottery shards – bear witness to the area having seen constant human

The ruins of Mata Bejíd passed on Stage 23A

passage and settlement during the pre-historical era. There's substantial evidence to suggest that it was along the valleys leading north into Andalucía that man first passed from Africa into Europe.

These early inhabitants of the Iberian peninsula would later be dominated by waves of population from the north, giving rise to the Celtiberian culture. These early pastoralists established fortified settlements throughout the peninsula and began to work the land between its many chains of mountains.

A thousand years before Christ, the minerals and rich agricultural lands of Andalucía had attracted the interest of the Phoenicians, who established trading posts in Málaga and Cádiz. But it was under the Romans, who ruled Spain from the third century BC to the fifth century AD, that the region began to take on its present-day character. They established copper and silver mines,

planted olives and vines, cleared land for agriculture and built towns, roads, aqueducts, bridges, theatres and baths while imposing their native language and customs. Incursions by Vandals and then Visigoths ended their rule, but its legacy was to be both rich and enduring.

The Moorish period

If Rome laid the foundations of Andalucían society in its broadest sense, these were shallow in comparison to those that would be bequeathed in the wake of the expeditionary force that sailed across the Strait in 711 under the Moorish commander Tariq whose army decisively defeated the ruling Visigoths in their first encounter. What had been little more than a loose confederation of tribes, deprived of their ruler, offered little resistance to the advance of Islam across Spain. It was only when Charles Martel defeated a Moorish army close

19

to the banks of the Loire in 732 that the tide began to turn and the Moors looked to consolidate their conquests rather than venture deeper into Europe.

A first great capital was established at Toledo before the centre of power shifted south to Córdoba: Andalucía would become part of an Islamic state for almost eight centuries. Moorish Spain's golden age took hold in the 10th century when Jews, Christians and Moors established a *modus vivendi*, the likes of which has rarely been replicated, and which would yield one of the richest artistic periods Europe has known. Philosophers, musicians, poets, mathematicians and astronomers from all three faiths helped establish Córdoba as a centre for learning second to no other in the West, at the centre of a trading network that stretched from Africa to the Middle East and through Spain to northern Europe.

The Moorish Kingdom was always under threat and the Reconquest – a process that was to last more than 800 years – gradually gained momentum as the Christian kingdoms of central and northern Spain became more unified. Córdoba fell in 1031, Seville in 1248, and the great Caliphate splintered into a number of smaller taifa kingdoms. The Moors clung on for another 250 years, but the settlements along la frontera fell in the early 1480s, and finally Granada in 1492. The whole of Spain was once again under Christian rule.

Spain's Golden Age

If ever anybody was in the right place at the right time, it was the Genoese adventurer Cristóbal Colón, aka Christopher Columbus, who was in the Christian camp at Santa Fe when Granada capitulated. His petition to the Catholic monarchs for funding for an expedition to sail west in order to reach the East fell on fertile soil.

The discovery of America, and along with it the fabulous riches that would make their way back to a Spain newly united under Habsburg rule, was to usher in Spain's *Siglo de Oro* (Golden Age). Spain's empire would soon stretch from the Caribbean through Central and South America and on to the Philippines; riches flowed back from the colonies at a time when Seville and Cádiz numbered among the wealthiest cities in Europe. The most obvious manifestation of this wealth, and nowhere more so than in Andalucía, were the palaces, churches, monasteries and convents that were built during this period: never again would the country see such generous patronage of the Arts.

However, by the end of the 16th century, Spain's position at the centre of the world stage was under threat. A series of wars in Europe depleted Spain's credibility as well as the state coffers: by the late 17th century Spanish power was in freefall. It remained a spent force into the 19th century, and yet further violent conflict in the early 20th century led to General Francisco Franco ('El Caudillo') sweeping into power in 1936.

The modern era/new challenges

Franco embarked on a crusade to re-establish the traditional order in Spain. The ensuing conflict – the Spanish Civil War – lasted for three years, during which an estimated 500,000 Spaniards lost their lives. The eventual victory of the Nationalists in 1939 led to Franco's consolidation and centralisation of power and the establishment of an authoritarian state that remained until his death in 1975.

Franco had hoped that King Juan Carlos, whom he'd appointed as his successor prior to his death, would continue to govern much in his image; but the young king knew which way the tide was running and facilitated the creation of a new constitution for Spain and, along with it, parliamentary democracy. Andalucía, as was the case for several other regions of Spain, saw the creation of an autonomous *junta*, or government, based in Seville.

The 1980s, 1990s and 2000s were very good years for Andalucía after Spain became part of the European Community during which it saw its infrastructure rapidly transformed. New roads, schools, hospitals and hotels were built, along with a high-speed train lines linking the country's major cities. A huge construction boom put money into many a working person's pocket; Andalucía had never had it so good at a time when it became one of the world's most popular holiday destinations.

Tourism continues to be a major motor of the Andalucían economy along with the construction industry, fuelled by ex-pats setting up home in the south and other foreigners buying holiday homes and flats. But the economic downturn that began in the late noughties hit the region hard and the deadly spread of Covid-19 decimated the tourist sector in 2020 and 2021. The region has Spain's highest unemployment rate among its adult workforce: more than 20% of the working population are currently out of work while that percentage is almost double among young people. At the time of writing, the building industry – a yardstick for the rest of the Andalucían economy – is beginning to bounce back and there are encouraging signs that the worst of *la crisis* is over.

Spain still faces deep internal problems in the present era as populist politics gain momentum in Catalonia and other parts of the country. The dual party system that characterised the post-Franco era has given way to the more troubled waters of coalition government while a series of financial scandals at both ends of the political spectrum have nurtured a deep distrust of political representatives. Yet in spite of all of the bad stuff you'll meet few Andalucíans who'd want to live anywhere else and it's not hard to see why many northern Europeans have chosen southern Spain as their new home.

PLANTS AND WILDLIFE

Two major highlights of hiking the GR7 come in the form of the flowers and birds you see along the way.

Andalucía numbers among the finest birding destinations in Europe. The best time for birdwatching is during the spring and autumn migrations between Europe and Africa – you walk directly beneath the main migratory route at the beginning of the GR7 – but at any time of year you can expect rich avifauna. If you'd like a list of the more common species, visit www.cicerone.co.uk/995/resources.

As well as seasonal visitors there are more than 250 species present throughout the year. Several species of eagle are commonly seen and you're guaranteed sightings of soaring griffon vultures – sometimes a hundred or more – which nest in the deep gorge at El Chorro, close to Ubrique and Ronda as well as in the Cazorla Park. You might even be lucky enough to spot the Spanish Imperial Eagle which has been recently reintroduced to the Sierra de Mágina.

The mountains and valleys through which the GR7 passes also offer rich rewards for botanists. 40% of all species found in Iberia are present in Andalucía including a number of endemic species. The annual wildflower explosion in late spring is as spectacular as anywhere in southern Europe, especially in areas where the rural exodus has ensured that much of the land has never seen the use of pesticides. For a list of 300 of the more common species to be found in Andalucía, with common and Latin names, visit www.cicerone.co.uk/995/resources.

Vertebrates are less easy to spot, leaving dogs aside. Along with the grazing goats, sheep, cattle and Iberian pigs

Pink butterfly orchid, Orchis papilionacea

you may see squirrels, hares, rabbits, stoat, wild boar, otters and mongoose. Ibex (*Capra pyrenaica hispanica*) are making a rapid comeback in Andalucía while the dense oak forests of Los Alcornocales are home to large numbers of red and roe deer. In the Cazorla Park, a former hunting reserve, you'll almost certainly encounter ibex, boar and deer.

Inquisitive ibex on the flanks of the Sierra de Huma (Stage 9)

Appendix D includes details of guide-books that will help you to identify the plants and wildlife of the region.

Andalucía has a long roll call when it comes to reptiles. Of its many species of snakes just one is poisonous, the Lataste's Viper (easily identified by the distinctive zigzag stripe that runs the length of its back with a line of black dots to each side). Iberian and Wall lizards are common, as are came-leons, while the much larger ocellated lizard often be seen near the coast. Invertebrates are potentially far more of a nuisance and health risk than snakes. Always give processionary caterpillars a wide berth – their barbs are highly toxic – be sure to have mosquito repellant in your pack, keep an eye out for scorpions and ants when you rest up in rocky terrain and acquaint yourself via a quick google with the Megarian Banded Centipede (*Scolopendra cingulata*). This easily recognised centipede has a very painful sting and is very aggressive: the author writes from experience.

WHEN TO GO

As a general rule the best time to walk in Andalucía is from March through to mid June and from September to late October. This is when you're most likely to encounter mild, sunny weather: warm enough to eat al fresco meals midday yet not so hot as to make temperature an additional challenge. Wildflowers are at their brilliant best in late April/early May.

The months most walkers avoid are July and August when temperatures that regularly reach the high thirties make walking far more of a challenge.

If you're prepared to risk rain then winter can be wonderful time to hike, especially from December to February when rainfall is generally less than in November, March and April. Hotel prices also tend to be less in the low season.

But bear in mind that Las Alpujarras and the Sierra Nevada as well as the Sierras of Mágina and Cazorla can see heavy snowfall during this period. If you plan to walk in these areas in winter always check the long-term weather forecast.

GETTING THERE

By air
Gibraltar is the closest airport to the GR7's start point and has regular flights from several cities in the UK with British Airways and Easyjet. A taxi from the Spanish side of the border in La Línea to Tarifa costs about €60. The bus transfer – there are six buses daily – takes an hour and costs €5.

Jerez is about an hour's drive from Tarifa and also has charter flights with Easyjet and Ryanair from a number of UK airports. From Jerez, a taxi to Tarifa costs €150. There are two daily buses from the centre, which take two hours and cost around €15.

You can get to Tarifa in about two hours by taxi from both **Seville** and **Málaga**. The latter has by far the greatest number of flights. There are buses from Málaga to La Línea from where you'd need to take a second bus to Tarifa. There are also direct buses from Seville to Tarifa. The journey takes three hours and costs about €20. A taxi to

Tarifa from either Málaga or Seville costs about €175.

From **Madrid** there are regular flights to Seville with Iberia and Air Europa, to Jerez with Iberia and to Málaga with Iberia and Air Europa.

For the middle to end sections of the walk, Málaga or **Granada** would be the nearest airports.

By train

The nearest train station to Tarifa is at **Algeciras**, which has two direct trains daily from Madrid (5hr 30min–6hr 30min). There are also connections via Antequera-Santa Ana from Granada (4hr 30min–5hr 45min) and Málaga (3hr 30min–4hr). For international rail travel, refer to www.raileurope.com or www.seat61.com.

Intermediary access

For details of all local rail, bus and flights, www.omio.es is a good source of information, along with the individual company websites listed in the provincial chapter introductions. Information on local transport links along the route is provided in the provincial chapter introductions and in the individual village boxes.

GETTING BACK

Most towns and villages through which the walk passes have connections with their regional capital, that's to say Cádiz, Málaga, Jaén and Granada. All of these cities, in turn, have connections via bus or train to the other major cities in Andalucía where airports are located. More details of transport are included in the regional sections of this guide.

From Puebla de Don Fadrique, where the northern and southern variants of the GR7 end, there are two buses to Granada each weekday, and one on Sundays. The journey time is about 3hr 30min.

LUGGAGE TRANSFER

One option for walking the route is to have your main luggage moved on by taxi, allowing you the luxury of walking from village to village with just a day pack.

You'll find taxi contact numbers listed in village boxes while hotel owners will often be happy to help out.

In 2021 the cost of this service would average about €30 per transfer with just a couple of the longer stages where this would rise to about €50. Shared two or more ways this wouldn't add too much to the overall cost of your hike.

Unlike the Camino de Santiago, there are currently no companies offering luggage transfers along the GR7.

ACCOMMODATION

Thanks to the rapid growth of inland tourism, nearly every small village in Andalucía now has accommodation on offer. For €50–€75 you should find a decent hotel room or apartment for two with its own bath or shower room while a more basic hostel would cost between €30 and €50.

In Spain the principal difference between a hotel and a 'hostal' is that hotels always have private rooms with en suite bathrooms. A 'hostal' equates more to what in the UK is referred to as a 'hostel' – that's to say a place that

Montejaque, one of the many pueblos blancos on the GR7 (Stage 5)

offers some rooms that are shared with other guests and where bathrooms might also be communal. That said, many hostals have rooms that are for the exclusive use of couples, many with their own private bathroom.

The € symbol beside each hotel gives an idea of what you should expect to pay for a double room:

€ – less than €50
€€ – between €50 and €100
€€€ – more than €100

Contact details of recommended hotels, hostels and B&Bs are listed at the end of each village box. Most offer breakfast while many can prepare evening meals and picnics, given prior warning. Bear in mind that some self-catering places that are listed may sometimes only accept two-night bookings, depending on season/circumstances.

Where no accommodation is available in the villages through which the GR7 passes, nearby alternatives are mentioned. In these cases the distance quoted to the accommodation is by road, not on foot.

The Booking.com (www.booking.com) and Tripadvisor (www.tripadvisor.co.uk) websites can also be good starting points for planning your walk. If you find a hotel on Booking.com, by calling the property direct you may well get a cheaper price and save the owners the commission they pay to receive reservations via the site. If the recommended hotels/B&Bs are fully booked, consider staying in an apartment. In this case, Airbnb (www.airbnb.es) is a good initial reference. Town hall websites often have a list of the accommodation on offer in their particular village.

25

Horaltic griffons atop La Mocha en route to Vadillo Castril (Stage 28A)

Camping

There are a handful of campsites along the route, which are listed along with hotels in the village sections but it isn't possible to do the GR7 as a campsite-to-campsite trek. If you wish to use a tent for the whole route this will entail wild camping most nights.

Wild camping is generally tolerated in Andalucía and you can always find places to pitch a tent close to the end point of all stages. I'd look for a spring then search for a secluded spot nearby so you have drinking and washing water to hand.

Several stages of the walk lead through natural parks and protected areas where wild camping is prohibited. That said, with ingenuity and common sense you'll always find a secluded spot to camp. Should you ask permission to camp at farms along the way the chances are the answer will be *sí* (yes).

When wild camping, never light fires and take great care if using a gas or kerosene stove: for much of the year Andalucía becomes a vast tinder box.

FOOD AND DRINK

Although it may not be known as a gourmet destination, you can eat well in Andalucía if you're prepared to leave a few preconceptions at home. Much of the food in village restaurants is deep frozen then microwaved when ordered while tapas are freshly prepared and displayed in glass cabinets in bars and restaurants. These can provide a delicious meal in themselves.

A *tapa* has come to mean a saucer-sized plate of any one dish, served to accompany an apéritif before a meal. If you wish to have more of any particular *tapa* order a *ración* (plateful) or a *media ración* (half plateful). Two or three *raciónes* shared between two, with a salad, would make a substantial and inexpensive meal.

When eating à la carte, don't expect there to be much in the way of vegetables: they just don't tend to figure in Andalucían cuisine. However, no meal is complete without some form of salad and fresh fruit is always available as a dessert.

Bear in mind there's always a *menú del día* (set menu) available at lunchtime. Although you have less choice, set menus are often prepared on the day using fresh rather than frozen ingredients.

Expect to pay around €10 for a set menu, which normally includes one drink. When eating à la carte, €20-€30 should buy a three-course meal including beverages while a tapas-style meal would be less. In the village descriptions you'll find listings for the best places to eat.

The southern Spanish eat later than is the custom in northern Europe. Lunch isn't generally available until 1.30pm while restaurants rarely serve dinner before 7.30pm. A common lament among walkers is that breakfast is often not served at hotels until 9am although village bars are open from 8am, or earlier.

Village shops are generally open from 9am–2pm then from 5.30pm–8.30pm. Many smaller shops will make you up a *bocadillo* (sandwich) using the ingredients of your choice.

WATER

During the hotter months in southern Spain the greatest potential dangers are heat exhaustion and dehydration. Wear loose-fitting clothing, a hat and keep drinking – and try to do so before you get thirsty.

If you're tackling the longer stages of the GR7 in summer you could find yourself drinking 5 litres or more in a single day.

Springs marked 'no potable' mean that the water is untreated and unchlorinated. In 30 years of drinking from these springs the author has never been affected by the water and it will almost certainly taste better than that from a tap. There's no need to buy bottled water.

Water springs are sometimes mentioned in the route description but bear in mind that during dry periods they may not be running.

EQUIPMENT

I'd recommend taking the following items with you:

- Water: carry a minimum of 1 litre, preferably more
- Broken-in walking boots
- Waterproof daypack
- Hat/sun block
- Map and compass
- Swiss army knife/multi-purpose pocket tool
- Torch and whistle
- Fully charged phone with numbers of all emergency services and those of destination hotels
- Juice pack/USB charger lead
- Solar charger (especially useful if you plan to wild camp or use navigation apps which eat up battery power)
- Waterproofs, according to season
- Fleece or jumper: temperatures can drop rapidly at the top of the higher passes
- First aid kit to include antihistamine cream, plasters, bandage, blister-plasters
- Water purification tablets
- Emergency food supplies for at least 24 hours
- Credit card/cash (euros)
- Photocopies of all credit cards, passport and travel documents
- Walking poles which can also help fend off dangerous-looking dogs

- Binoculars
- Liquid detergent for clothes

And I'd highly recommended the following for the GR7's remoter, wilder stages:

- Tablet, phone or handheld device with GPS tracks uploaded along with relevant map tiles

If you're planning to camp, you will also need:

- Waterproof rucksack
- Sleeping bag, mat and tent
- Gas stove and cooking utensils

MONEY

Most travellers to Spain still consider that the cost of their holiday essentials – food, travel and accommodation – is lower than in northern Europe. You can still find a decent meal for two, with drinks, for around €40 while €60 can buy you a comfortable hotel room for two.

Nearly all villages along the GR7 have an ATM and nearly all shops, restaurants and hotels accept payment with a credit card. Be aware that you'll often be asked for your card details when booking a hotel room by phone.

LANGUAGE

Visitors to inland Andalucía often express surprise at how little English is spoken: even in restaurants and hotels, a working knowledge of English is the exception rather than the norm. In addition, the Spanish spoken in southern Spain – *andaluz* – can be difficult to understand even if you have a command of basic Spanish. It's spoken at lightening speed with the ends of many words left unpronounced.

But if you're patient and prepared to gesticulate you'll get there in the end and you can always fall back on a language app like Itranslatevoice or Sayhi. Better still, pick up a phrasebook before you travel and learn a few basic phrases. Any effort to communicate will be amply rewarded.

WAYMARKING

The trail was waymarked in the late 1990s with signs indicating village names and timings, red-and-white banded marker posts and paint flashes along with a number of signboards showing the complete route. 20 years on, much of this original waymarking is damaged, faded or missing.

Sections of the GR7 coincide with other newly-created GR paths like the GR249 Gran Senda de Málaga, the GR240 Ruta Sulayr and the GR247 Bosques del Sur trails. On some trails signage for these new routes includes the GR7, too. In several other places – like the early sections through the province of Cádiz – new GR7 waymarking has been added that differs slightly from the old signage.

New waymarking can cause confusion where the GR7 and the new GR routes diverge so bear in mind that marker posts and paint flashes might be marking a different GR. Remember, too, that some faded marker posts might be indicating 'not this way' even if the original 'X' is no longer distinguishable.

When reaching forks where there's no waymarking be prepared to check out both branches: you'll often find a marker post placed – puzzlingly – 20m or 30m along one branch of the path.

New GR7 waymarking; illegible GR7 signboard; GR7 waymarking near Arriate

The sections where waymarking is most scant (in 2021) is on the southern variant as the trail passes through Las Alpujarras while on some more remote sections of the northern trail it's almost non-existent. These sections require more time and patience and a certain amount of navigational nous. On these stages some form of GPS back up could prove both useful and reassuring, whether on a phone, tablet or handheld device.

MAPS AND GPS

Paper maps

The best maps that cover all stages of the GR7 in Andalucía are the 1:25,000 series of the Centro Nacional de Información Geográfico (CNIG). But,

practically, you're unlikely to want to carry the large number of maps you'll need to cover all stages.

If you opt for the 1:50,000 series and are walking the GR7's southern variant you'll need 26 maps; for the northern variant, 24. They make for extra weight but I'd be loathe to be without them if not carrying digital maps on a handheld device.

In Andalucía, the best places to order maps are LTC in Seville (www. ltcideas.es/index.php/mapas) and Mapas y Compañia in Málaga (www. mapasycia.es).

In Madrid, the best places to order maps are La Tienda Verde (www.face-book.com/latiendaverde) and Centro Nacional de Información Geográfica (www.cnig.es).

In the UK, the best sources for maps are Stanfords (www.stanfords.co.uk) and The Map Shop (www.themapshop.co.uk).

Digital maps/GPS and GPX files

Using a tablet or smartphone with a hiking app, with the relevant 1:25,000 quadrants uploaded along with the GPX files for the stages you plan to hike, is highly recommended due to the scant and damaged waymarking on some sections of the GR7.

The free app, Maps.me, has a map with nearly all of the GR7 clearly visible.

The Gaia GPS app, free for Android and iPhone, has a pretty decent map – for more detailed maps you'll need to subscribe – while the Viewranger app is also free and you can buy and upload the 1:25,000 tiles of the CNIG. Buying the digital 1:25,000 tiles is far less expensive then buying all the paper maps.

Even without the tiles, Viewranger, with the relevant GPX files uploaded, will give you your position within a few metres relevant to the trail.

GPX files for all stages of the GR7 in Andalucía are available as free downloads from Cicerone (www.cicerone.co.uk/995/GPX) or via the author's website (www.guyhunterwatts.com).

By using a program such as Garmin's BaseCamp you can download the files to your desktop, import them into the program then transfer them to your handheld device/phone. You can download Basecamp for Mac and PC at www.garmin.com/en-GB/software/basecamp/.

GPX files are provided in good faith but neither the author nor Cicerone can accept responsibility for their accuracy. Your first point of reference should always be the walking notes, map and the visual references that surround you.

STAYING SAFE

When heading off on any stage of the GR7, always let one person know where you're heading, the time you expect to arrive and the route you intend to follow. Be ready for intermittent phone coverage in valley floors and on more remote paths. Coverage in towns and villages is generally excellent and virtually all hotels, hostels and campsites have fast Wi-Fi.

Log the following numbers into your mobile:
- 112 Emergency services general number
- 062 Guardía Civil (police)
- 061 Medical emergencies
- 080 Fire brigade

In addition to the usual precautions there are a few things to remember when walking in Andalucía:
- **Water** – see earlier section.
- **Fire** – in the dry months the hillsides of Andalucía become a vast tinderbox. Be very careful if you smoke or use a camping stove.
- **Hunting areas** – signs for 'coto' or 'coto privado de caza' designate an area where hunting is permitted in season and not that you're entering private property. Cotos are marked by a small rectangular sign divided into a white-and-black triangle. **You might consider having a reflective safety waistcoat in your day pack when walking in these areas to make yourself more visible to hunters.**

- **Close all gates** – you'll come across some extraordinary gate-closing devices. They can take time, patience and effort to open and close.

- **Dogs** – when walking the GR7 you're bound to experience the occasional close encounter of the canine kind. Hunting is popular in Andalucía and most remote farms will have at least one hunting or guard dog chained up or within a fenced enclosure. If you walk swiftly on by the chances of being bitten are infinitessimally small. In 30 years of walking past hundreds of farms in Andalucía with barking dogs the author has never been attacked or bitten. If you feel nervous about dogs, having walking poles to hand could be reassuring.

USING THIS GUIDE

The walking notes that make up the main body of this book describe the GR7 stage by stage, beginning at its most southwesterly point then following it from the west to east across Andalucía.

The first section of the guide describes the 11 stages that are common to both the northern and southern variants of the route. The second section describes the 21 stages of the northern variant of the walk (stages 12A-32A). The third section describes the 23 stages of the southern variant (stages 12B-34B).

The walking notes include an introduction to each of the provinces through which the GR7 runs. Thus the common route section gives an overview of Cádiz and Málaga provinces, the northern variant section those of Córdoba and Jaén, and the southern variant an overview of the province of Granada with a short

31

reference to Almería (through which the walk passes for only a few kilometres) You'll also find descriptions of the different natural and national Parks through which the route passes, along with notes about points of cultural, geographical and historical interest.

The information box at the start of each stage description gives you the nitty-gritty: start point, distance covered, total ascent and descent, highest point and the estimated walking time. Timings are based on an average walking pace, without breaks. On all routes build in additional time for food, photography and rest stops. This box also lists en-route refreshment options. The subsequent introduction gives you a feel for what that particular stage of the GR7 involves.

The route description, together with the individual stage map, should allow you to follow each stage without difficulty. Places and features that appear on the map are highlighted in **bold** in the route description to aid navigation. A handheld GPS device – ideally with the relevant 1:25,000 map tiles uploaded – is always an excellent second point of reference: free GPX tracks for all stages of the GR7 in Andalucía can be downloaded from www.cicerone.co.uk/995/GPX.

The route description also includes brief descriptions of the towns and villages through which the GR7 passes. In these sections you'll also find information about accommodation, restaurants and local sources of information.

Planning your walk

When it comes to choosing which section of the GR7 to walk the best course of action is to read the provincial introductions and summary paragraphs of the

individual stages. Of the 55 stages of the GR7 in Andalucía, 52 can be covered in a single day of walking. Three stages, between 37.7km and 54.6km, would be beyond the capabilities of most walkers to complete in a day. When tackling these stages you'll need to wild camp or leave the route, taking a taxi, hitching or walking to the nearest accommodation. The walking notes include suggestions as to the best points to break up these longer stages.

A further nine stages are between 30.3km and 35.3km. Suggestions are also provided for shortening/dividing these stages even though they're manageable in a longish day of walking. The Route summary table gives a résumé of all 55 stages of the GR7, and in Appendix A, there is a table showing the facilities on offer in the towns and villages through which the route passes.

53 of the 55 stages end in towns or villages where accommodation is available. The two exceptions are Stage 26B which ends at Puerto de la Ragua and Stage 28B which ends in Narváez, where hostels at the end points are now closed. Here, the best solution is to take a taxi to a nearby village where accommodation is available.

Terminology and abbreviations

The terms used in this guide are intended to be as unambiguous as possible. In walk descriptions, 'track' denotes any thoroughfare wide enough to permit vehicle access while 'path' is used to describe any that are wide enough only for pedestrians and animals.

'TO' is used as an abbreviation for tourist office, 's/c' for self-catering and 'PO' for post office.

THE COMMON ROUTE
Stages 1–11: from Tarifa to Villanueva de Cauche

Approaching El Chorro (Stage 8)

CÁDIZ PROVINCE

The track beside the railway en route to Jimena (Stage 3)

From Tarifa, at the confluence of the Atlantic and the Mediterranean, the GR7 hugs the Atlantic coast before running north into the Alcornocales Natural Park, home to one of Europe's largest stands of cork oaks. Passing through Los Barrios the route continues north via the hilltop villages of Castillo de Castellar then Jimena de la Frontera.

Reaching Ubrique after one of the GR7's most challenging and remote stages the trail enters the Grazalema Natural Park where it links some of Andalucía's most beautiful villages. Passing through the Pueblos Blancos of Benaocáz and Villaluenga it reaches Málaga province where you descend to Montejaque via a remote, rocky-sided valley.

HIGHLIGHTS OF THE GR7 IN CÁDIZ PROVINCE

Some of the many highlights of this section include:

• The walled town of Tarifa
• Ocean-side walking beside the beach of Los Lances
• Hilltop villages, including the citadel fortress of Castillo de Castellar
• Remote trails through the cork oak forests of the Alcornocales Natural Park
• The karst landscapes of the Grazalema Natural Park
• Abundant bird life including eagles, vultures, storks and sea birds

Approaching Ubrique on Stage 4

GETTING THERE/BACK

See the general introduction at the start of this book for the most common points of arrival if you're starting the route in Tarifa – that's to say Gibraltar, Jerez, Seville and Málaga.

The Algeciras to Ronda train stops at stations close to three villages on the early part of the GR7: San Roque for Los Barrios, La Almoraima for Castillo de Castellar and Estación de Jimena for Jimena de la Frontera (www.renfe. com). Algeciras is served by two direct trains daily from Madrid (5hr 30min–6hr 30min). From Granada there are three daily departures via Antequera-Santa Ana (4hr 30min–5hr 45min). There's one direct bus from Madrid to Algeciras (9hr) while arriving from Granada entails a change in Málaga after two hours or in Seville after three hours.

Nearly all villages along the route have local bus services in operation. In Cádiz province the major companies are Comes (www.tgcomes.es) and Damas (www.damas-sa.es).

Most villages through which the GR7 passes have taxi services. These are listed within the village information boxes.

GENERAL INFORMATION

Cádiz tourist office, www.cadizturismo. com, tel 956 807 061/807 223

STAGE 1
Tarifa to Los Barrios

Start	Tourist office, Ada Fuerzas Armadas, Tarifa
Distance	47.1km
Ascent	800m
Descent	795m
Time	12hr 30min
Highest point	Puerto de Ojén, 244m
Refreshments	Hotels/bars at end of Playa de Los Lances
Notes	The section linking two tracks shortly before Los Barrios is tricky. You can avoid it by sticking to the main track.

Ocean-side walking, a wild tract of the Alcornocales Park and views of Morocco are all part of this challenging initial stage. The stage can be split by diverting to Facinas or shortened by 8.5km by staying at the end of Los Lances beach leaving a manageable (38km/10hr 30min) walk to Los Barrios.

TARIFA (ALTITUDE 15M, POPULATION 18,169)

Accommodation, campsite, restaurant/bar/café, food shop, ATM, post office (PO), pharmacy, tourist office (TO), transport

Facing Morocco across the Strait of Gibraltar at the confluence of the Mediterranean and the Atlantic, the walled town of Tarifa is the southernmost point of continental Europe. Thanks to the levante winds which are funnelled through the strait, Tarifa became the wind then later the kitesurfing capital of Europe.

The town is infused with a young, cosmopolitan spirit. Along with shops selling surf gear there's a big choice of accommodation as well as numerous bars and restaurants: listings here can only scratch the surface of what's on offer.

Don't miss the lively municipal market and – if you have time – the Roman ruins at the nearby village of Bolonia.

Accommodation: Hostal Asturiano €, www.hostalelasturiano.es, tel 618 385 301, is a good budget option close to the GR7's start point. Hostal Alameda €€, www.hostalalameda.com, tel 956 681 181, is a mid range option with rooms overlooking the palm-lined *paseo* (park/promenade) and port. Casa La Favorita, www.lacasadelafavorita.com, tel 690 180 253, is at the heart of the walled town, a quiet up-market option. The best local campsite is Camping Río Jara €€, www. campingriojara.com, tel 956 680 570. Set just back from the beach 4km into stage 1 of the GR7, it's open all year with shop and restaurant (Tent+2ppl €27–€33).

Food: Tarifa's restaurant scene reflects its multi-ethnic fabric. There are Sushi bars, Moroccan and Italian eateries, veggie and vegan options as well as traditional tapas bars and restaurants.

Transport: Bus to/from Cádiz, Jerez, Seville and Algeciras. The bus station is 500m north from the centre. Taxi, tel 956 799 077

Town hall: www.aytotarifa.com, tel 956 684 186

Tourist office: www.turismodetarifa.com, tel 956 680 993. Next to the start point of the GR7 on Paseo de la Alameda.

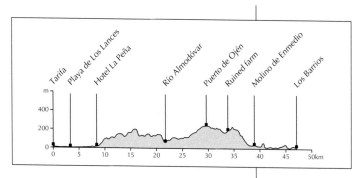

Tarifa to Los Barrios (47.1km/12hr 30min)
From a GR7 signboard next to the tourist office walk towards the sea. Turning right at the entrance to the port you reach the causeway separating the Atlantic and the Mediterranean. Here go right along a road between apartment blocks and a wall above the beach. Where the road arcs right, continue straight ahead along a planked walkway, left of a high wall. Crossing a car park the walkway runs through marshland behind the beach of **Los Lances**. Angling right to merge with a track you reach the **N-340**. Turn left and continue along a narrow path left of the road. Passing the entrance to **Camping Río Jara** a section of tarmac road leads across the Río Jara.

Continue parallel to the N-340 to reach a track and a sign, 'Playa de Los Lances Norte'. Here go left then bear right

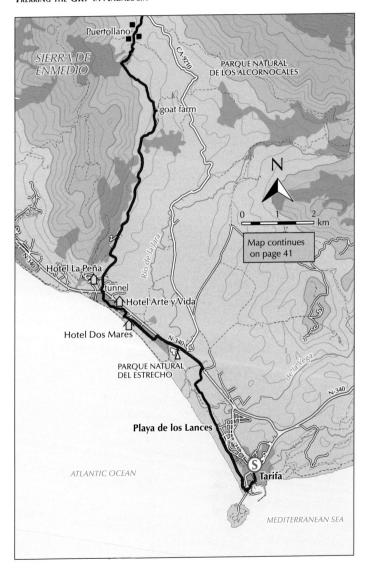

Puertollano

SIERRA DE
ENMEDIO

CA-9210

PARQUE NATURAL
DE LOS ALCORNOCALES

goat farm

N

0   1   2
km

Map continues
on page 41

Río de la Jara

Hotel La Peña

tunnel

Hotel Arte y Vida

N-340

Hotel Dos Mares

N-340

PARQUE NATURAL
DEL ESTRECHO

de la Vega

N-340

Playa de los Lances

ATLANTIC OCEAN

S **Tarifa**

MEDITERRANEAN SEA

Leaving Tarifa along the beach of Los Lances

at a car park. Continue parallel to the beach past **Hotel Dos Mares** then turn back inland at waymarking. Bearing left through a picnic area you come to a track. Turn left then continue past **Hotel Arte y Vida** to pick up a path once more. Passing a caravan site you reach a fork. Keep right then pass through a **tunnel** beneath the N-340. Angle left to come to a road in front of **Hotel La Peña**. Here, turn right following a sign, 'GR7 Puerto de Ojén 21.3km'. ▶

You'll see both GR7 and GR145 waymarking on this section.

The road gently climbs along the eastern flank of the Sierra de Enmedio. Tarifa and a group of wind turbines are now visible. Cross an open swathe of land past a farm with a green hopper, then follow the track as it descends towards the valley floor. Be ready to cut left, away from the track, up a path which shortly passes left of a **goat farm**. You're now entering the **Alcornocales Natural Park**.

LOS ALCORNOCALES NATURAL PARK

Bordering to the south with the Estrecho Park and to the north with that of Grazalema, El Parque Natural de los Alcornocales encompasses a 170,000 hectare slice of the province of Cádiz and is home to Spain's largest expanse of cork oak (*Quercus suber*) forest. The harvesting of cork has long been part of the local economy and despite the arrival of synthetic corks its growing use as insulation in eco-construction has ensured it remains a thriving industry.

Los Alcornocales is also home to the only sub-tropical forest or *laurisilva* in Europe. Characterised by narrow, fern-filled *canutos* (ravines) shaded by slender alders the park's diverse plant life is born of the moist, mild conditions arising from the interplay of Atlantic and Mediterranean weather systems. Given doubly-protected status within the natural park, the *canutos* offer a unique insight into how the forests of Europe might have looked during the Tertiary period.

39

The park is one of Spain's prime birding locations, lying to one side of the principal migratory route between Western Europe and Africa. Much of the bird-life is non-migratory including several colonies of griffon vultures. Other raptors include kites, goshawks, kestrels, Egyptian vultures, buzzards as well as short-toed, booted, Bonelli's and golden eagles. At the last count there were more than 220 species within the protected area.

Among the typical species of the park's extensive forests are cork, holm and gall oak, arbutus, wild olive, carob and rhododendron while a dense, lower-forest level – where the predominant species are cistus, lavender, rosemary, heather and fern – is home to abundant animal life. This includes wild boar, genets, martens, ferrets, otters, badgers, Egyptian mongoose, red and roe deer and ibex while half of Iberia's reptile species are also found in the park.

The natural park's **visitor centre** is in Cortes de la Frontera (tel 951 154 599).

On reaching a track beyond the farm maintain your course, signed 'GR7 Puerto de Ojén 5hr'.

Continue for 1.6 kilometres until you reach a sign, 'GR7 Puerto de Ojén 14km'. Here turn right down a track which crosses a river then a water channel to reach the houses of **Puertollano** and a gravel track. Turning right then, at the next fork right again, you come to the **CA-9210**. Go left and continue over the **Puerto de la Torre del Rayo** pass. Views open out towards the north and more wind generators.

1km beyond the pass bear right, away from the CA-9210, along a track signed 'GR7 Puerto de Ojén 3hr'. ◀

You can continue down the CA-9210 to Facinas, 6km away, where there's accommodation.

Pass a farm with solar panels while the track descends. Eventually it arcs right then left and crosses the **Río Almodóvar** via a concrete bridge. Pass through a gate, climb past a farm building then follow the path as it arcs right to reach a tarmac road. Follow it left then after 50 metres turn right along a road that loops round the **Cerro de Torrejosa** before running along the north side of the **Embalse de Almodóvar** (reservoir).

Pass through a gate, and you'll soon pass a sign for 'Puerto de Ojén 4.3km'. Stick to the track to eventually reach the **Puerto de Ojén** where you pass the **Venta de Ojén** (a *venta* is a roadside bar/restaurant; this one is rarely open) then a *mirador* (viewpoint).

Continue along the main track, ignoring any side turnings. Signs appear for the Eurovelo 8 del Mediterráneo cycle route. The track runs past a signboard and an old bread oven. Looping past a **ruined farm** you pass a spring then a pond

The road leading up to Puerto de Ojén

where a sign warns of amphibians crossing. 5.7 kilometres beyond Puerto de Ojén, at a point where the track angles left, go right through a **gate** at a sign, 'Los Barrios 10.9km'. ▶

Beyond the gate, continue down an indistinct path that shortly angles right then left, descending with a streambed to its right. Upon reaching open ground, look for red-and-white paint flashes and cairns which lead down across the hillside, passing close to three wireless telegraph poles on a NE course.

The next section is tricky. You can avoid it by continuing down the track on the waymarked Med' 8 route.

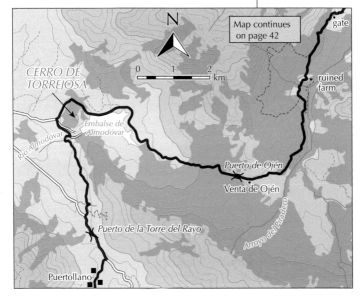

Map continues on page 42

N

gate

CERRO DE TORREJOSA

ruined farm

Embalse de Almodóvar

Río Almodóvar

0   1   2 km

Puerto de Ojén

Venta de Ojén

Puerto de la Torre del Rayo

Arroyo del Piladero

Puertollano

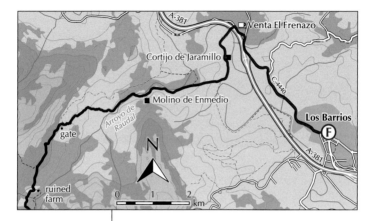

Cross a streambed to reach more open ground. Bear right, continue down to the valley floor then go through a gate. The path becomes clearer, running parallel to the Arroyo del Raudal. Passing through a second gate you reach GR7 'Not this way' paint flashes on a rock. Here, turn right and cross the streambed by a damaged wooden bridge then go left along a track that leads through a gate before passing **Molino de Enmedio**.

When you reach a junction, turn left. The track climbs then merges with the cycle way of the El Corredor Verde Dos Bahias. After passing **Cortijo del Jaramillo** farm, cross a bridge over the **Río de las Cañas or Palmones** then pass beneath the **A-381**. At a Stop sign, turn right past **Venta El Frenazo** to reach a roundabout and petrol station then follow the C-4440 into **Los Barrios** to a roundabout with a fountain at its midst.

LOS BARRIOS (ALTITUDE: 10M, POPULATION 25,513)

Accommodation, restaurant/bar/café, food shop, ATM, PO, pharmacy, TO, transport

A quiet town at the confluence of the rivers Palmones, Cañas and Guadarranque, Los Barrios dates from the early 18th century when Spaniards, ousted from Gibraltar by the British, formed a small settlement. The forested hillsides west of the town stand in contrast to the industrial sprawl of the nearby Bay of Algeciras which is home to a steelworks and an oil refinery.

Toros bravos (fighting bulls) are bred in the area and the town forms part of the recently created Ruta del Toro.

Accommodation: Hotel Real €€, www.hotelreallosbarrios.es, tel 956 620 024, is a modern 1-star hotel in the town centre with a popular restaurant. Hotel Montera Plaza €€, www.hotelmontera.com, tel 856 220 220, is an inexpensive 4-star hotel at the southern edge of town with quiet rooms and a pool.

Food: Bodeguita La Iberica, tel 956 621 122, for traditional Spanish cuisine. There are several restaurants near the main square as well as numerous tapas bars.

Transport: Bus to/from Algeciras via Jimena de la Frontera. Taxi in main rank, tel 956 574 444 or 608 548 354

Town hall/tourist info: www.losbarrios.es, tel 956 582 500

STAGE 2
Los Barrios to Castillo de Castellar

Start	Roundabout with fountain at centre of Los Barrios
Distance	33.3km
Ascent	790m
Descent	550m
Time	9hr 40min
Highest point	255m
Refreshments	In San Roque/Castellar de la Frontera

The second stage of the GR7 can be shortened by 6km by ending the walk in Castellar de la Frontera at the hotel of La Almoraima. Stunning views and a final section of ancient footpath compensate for a long stretch of road walking.

Los Barrios to Castellar de la Frontera (26.5km, 7hr 40min)
Retrace your footsteps northwest along the CA-440a to the roundabout and petrol station. Take the first exit signed 'Venta El Frenazo' then the first turn to the right. Continue up a wide road past an entrance to the military camp of **Charco Redondo**.

Reaching a second entrance to Charco Redondo turn right up a track to a gate marked 'Camino Cortado'.

A recycling plant you'll pass later is visible on a hilltop to your right.

Go through a smaller gate to its right then follow a track up across open countryside past a line of corrals. ◀ Pass through another gate, cross a cattle grid then climb to a junction. Here angle right and continue climbing. Pass through another gate to reach a junction with a wide track. Turn right following a sign, 'Sendero GR7'.

The track runs southeast along a ridgetop towards Gibraltar, now visible up ahead. Pass the buildings of **Ventorillo de Malpica** then a quarry to reach the recycling site of **Gamasur**. Continue along its fence to a junction at the plant's entrance. Here go left, immediately passing a hut with four green doors. 20 metres beyond a weighbridge, angle right through a gate then bear left. When you reach a fork after 100 metres keep right, downhill. Passing through two gates you descend to a track running along the valley floor. Here, go right at a sign 'GR7 Castellar 4hr 30min'.

Cross a streambed then a cattle grid to meet the **CA-9207**. Turn left along the road which climbs, levels, then descends past an electricity substation. Crossing the **Río Guadarranque**, you come to a Stop sign. Turn left and follow a cycle path parallel to the A-405 past two restaurants. Bearing right then left the path rejoins the A-405.

After 6km the cycle path merges with the road just before a roundabout at the outskirts of **Castellar de la Frontera**.

CASTELLAR DE LA FRONTERA (ALTITUDE 30M, POPULATION 3013)

Accommodation, restaurant/bar/café, food shop, ATM, PO, pharmacy, transport

A quiet, grid-plan village built in the 1960s to house the former inhabitants of Castillo de Castellar.

Accommodation: Hotel Convento La Almoraima €€/€€€, www.laalmoraimahotel.com, tel 956 693 002. 18th-century convent hotel and restaurant within the vast estate of La Almoraima next to the GR7.

Food: Restaurante Virgil, tel 956 693 150, and Origen Castellar, tel 956 742 024, offer friendly service and good food.

Transport: Bus to/from Jimena de la Frontera and Algeciras. Train to/from Algeciras and Ronda via Estacíon de Jimena. For taxi, tel 666 951 439

Town hall/tourist info: www.castellardelafrontera.es, tel 956 693 001

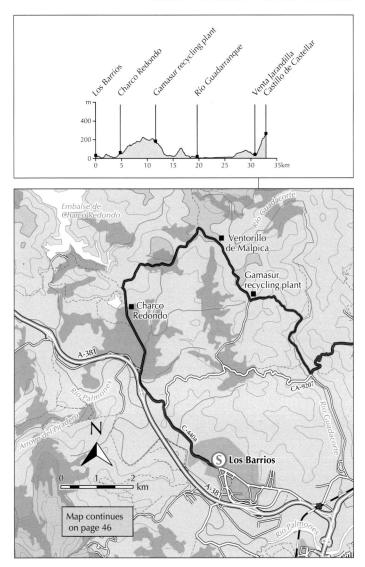

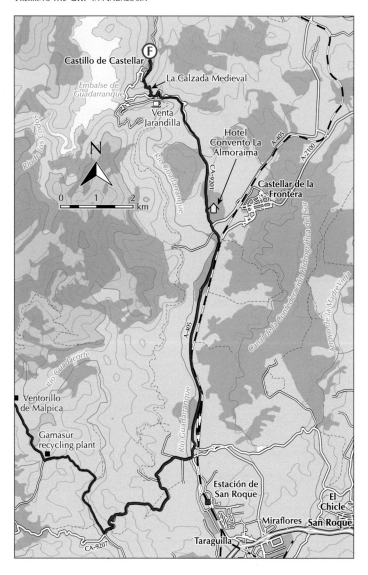

Castellar de la Frontera to Castillo de Castellar (6.8km, 2hr)

Continue along the A-405 past Venta La Cantina to a second roundabout. Here turn left for Castellar de la Frontera along the CA-9201. To your right is the entrance of **Hotel Convento La Almoraima**. 500 metres beyond the km2 post, turn right at a sign, 'La Jarandilla'. Continue along the old road to Castellar which passes beneath the CA-9201 before rejoining it just before **Venta Jarandilla**. 30 metres past the restaurant take a path that cuts down left. After crossing a streambed, go left at a fork then climb back to the road. Head straight across then climb a cobbled path, **La Calzada Medieval**. ▶

Passing a *mirador*, you reach a fork. Keep right to rejoin the CA-9201 where, turning right, you come to the Punto de Información. Turn left then pass beneath two archways to reach the tiny square of Plaza La Posada of **Castillo de Castellar**.

The medieval path leading up to Castillo de Castellar

The path is said to date from the Moorish period.

CASTILLO DE CASTELLAR (ALTITUDE 255M, POPULATION 103)

Accommodation, restaurant/bar/café, TO

Few places in Andalucía are as enigmatically evocative as Castillo de Castellar. The citadel fortress, wrapping round a cluster of tiny houses, was built by the Moors soon after the conquest of Gibraltar.

When the Guadarranque reservoir was created in the 1960s, the villagers were moved to Castellar de la Frontera. A few years later hippies squatted in the abandoned houses and Castellar became synonymous with drugs and off-piste living. The opening of the Hotel El Alcázar along with several self-catering houses has attracted a different type of visitor.

Accommodation: La Posada Travellers Inn €, tel 625 533 642. Simple B&B with evening meals if pre-arranged. Hotel El Alcázar €€, www.tugasa.com, tel 956 693 150. Housed within the old castle with restaurant, bar and rooms-with-views. Also manages nine self-catering houses in the village.

Food: Venta Carmen, tel 956 693 055, a short walk down the hill, has excellent home cooking. A couple of bars within the castle walls also serve food.

Transport: No bus connections. Taxi in Castellar de la Frontera (6km), tel 666 951 439

Tourist office: www.castillodecastellar.es, tel 633 538 930

STAGE 3
Castillo de Castellar to Jimena de la Frontera

Start	Plaza La Posada, Castillo de Castellar
Distance	21.3km
Ascent	210m
Descent	375m
Time	6hr 15min
Highest point	255m
Refreshments	None en route

A gentle day of walking along the Hozgarganta Valley, sticking close to the river and the Ronda/Algeciras railway line.

Castillo de Castellar to Jimena de la Frontera (21.3km/6hr 15min)
From the square retrace your steps to the Punto de Información then turn left along the CA-9201 signed 'Jimena 5hr 45min'. After passing the cemetery then the entrance to Finca La Boyal, the tarmac ends. Continue past a chain down a sandy track between fences.

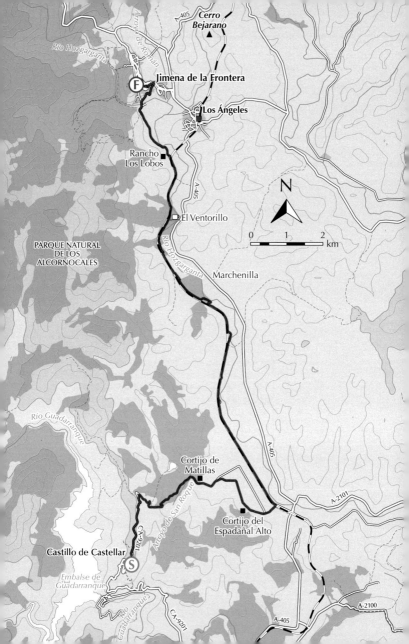

Cerro
Bejarano

Río Hozgarganta

Arroyo de Román

Jimena de la Frontera

F

Los Ángeles

Rancho
Los Lobos

A-405

El Ventorillo

N

0   1   2
                          km

PARQUE NATURAL
DE LOS
ALCORNOCALES

Río Hozgarganta

Marchenilla

Río Guadarranque

A-405

Cortijo de
Matillas

Arroyo de San Roque

Cortijo del
Espadañal Alto

A-2101

CA-9201

Castillo de Castellar

S

CA-9201

Embalse de
Guadarranque

Río Guadarranque

CA-9201

A-405

A-2100

Passing a second chain the track shortly loops right across the streambed of **Arroyo de San Roque** then descends to the valley floor where you pass above **Cortijo de Matillas**. Continue along the southern edge of a vast, cultivated field. Pass **Cortijo del Espadañal Alto** to reach a junction. Here bear left, cross the railway line, then turn left, parallel to the tracks.

At the end of a large field the track loops left to cross the railway line. You, however, should continue straight ahead. After passing through a pine plantation continue to the end of another field. Here go right for 20 metres then turn left into a copse. After crossing a stream via stepping stones, bear back up left. Stick close to the east side of the railway and you'll eventually reach a fork. Continue straight ahead, ignoring a track cutting right towards the A-405. Passing a sheep farm

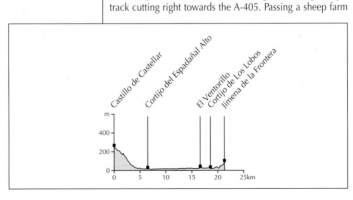

the track arcs right towards the river. Continue past a rusting level crossing sign then turn left, cross a wooden bridge and bear up to the left.

Stick to the east side of the line then pass the buildings of the **El Ventorillo** country house, and you'll eventually cross the railway beyond which you pass **Rancho Los Lobos**. When you reach a tarmac road, bear right and cross the **Río Hozgarganta**. The road angles right then climbs to a junction by Bar Cuenca. Here go left and follow the road up to the Plaza de la Constitución and the clock tower.

JIMENA DE LA FRONTERA (ALTITUDE 91M, POPULATION 9773)

Accommodation, restaurant/bar/café, food shops, ATM, PO, pharmacy, TO, transport

The land around Jimena has been populated since prehistoric times: Palaeolithic rock paintings were discovered west of the village at Laja Alta and burial sites close to the Hozgarganta river. During the Roman period a town developed of sufficient importance to have minted its own coins whilst the Moors established a settlement where the castle now stands, naming it Xemena.

In the 18th century a foundry was constructed to manufacture cannon balls, many of which were fired across the water during the Siege of Gibraltar. The old foundry now houses an excellent B&B (see Accommodation). The town suffered extensive damage during the Peninsular War when its municipal archives were destroyed by Napoleonic troops.

Nowadays Jimena has the feel of a crossroads between coast and mountain. The arrival of foreign residents – they number a tenth of the present population – has helped boost the local economy.

Accommodation: Casa Henrietta €€, www.casahenrietta.com, tel 956 648 130. A beautifully decorated, warmly welcoming hotel with great food. El Estanque y El Almendro €€, www.elestanqueyelalmendro.com, tel 617 714 267. Riverside B&B housed within the old artillery factory. Hostal El Anon €€, www.hostalanon.com, tel 956 640 113. Characterful rooms and restaurant with terrace plunge pool.

Food: Restaurante La Tasca, tel 956 641 123, has al fresco dining on the main square while El Ventorillo, tel 956 640 997, has an imaginative menu that follows the seasons.

Transport: Bus to/from Ronda and Algeciras. Train station (2km) with connections to Ronda and Algeciras. Taxi, tel 607 383 590

Town hall/tourist info: www.jimenadelafrontera.es, tel 956 640 254

STAGE 4
Jimena de la Frontera to Ubrique

Start	Plaza de la Constitución, Jimena de la Frontera
Distance	37.7km
Ascent	1200m
Descent	970m
Time	10hr 30min
Highest point	840m
Refreshments	None en route
Notes	You can shorten the route by taking a taxi from the point you meet the A-373 at Peñon del Berrueco, 27.2km into the walk.

Another demanding stage if undertaken in one go. Remote paths and tracks lead through stands of cork oak and pine via some of the Alcornocales Park's most grandiose limestone scenery. Approaching Ubrique you pass into the Grazalema Natural Park.

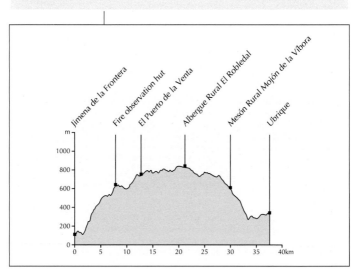

Sandstone outcrops en route to Ubrique

Jimena de la Frontera to Ubrique (37.7km/10hr 30min)
Exit the square towards the Unicaja bank then turn left and head all the way through the village. Continue past the Los Alcornocales **campsite** then cross the **CA-3331**. Passing a sign, 'Ubrique 9hr 45min', climb a cobbled path, which narrows then levels before reaching a gate. Beyond the gate, turn right then after 20 metres left through a second gate. Climb close to a wall to your right; after 150 metres, you'll pass a sign pointing uphill for Ubrique.

Bear left at sandstone boulders and follow the path as it arcs back right before passing through a metal gate. Continue up an eroded track through scrubby terrain to a junction. Here go left. The track bears right then leads through another gate to reach a broad track. Turn right following a sign, 'Ubrique 8hr 45min'. When you reach an unmarked fork, take the right branch. The track loops up past a sign for Monte Benazanilla then another for 'Mirador'. ▶

As the track levels, you'll pass two more signs for Monte Benazanilla before looping left then back right where you should ignore a track left signed 'Depósitos'. Leave the track at the next fork by bearing up right, past a trig post marked 'AMP5'. Climb close to a wall up an indistinct path marked by cairns to reach a gate in the wall to your right. Go through the gate then angle down left to a track where you need to bear

It's worth diverting 25 metres to the *mirador* for the views back down towards Jimena.

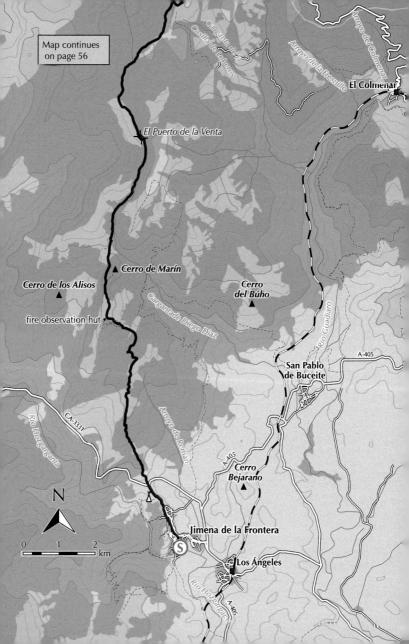

Map continues
on page 56

El Colmenar

Arroyo del Colmenar

Arroyo de la Fresnillo

Gargante d...a

Casilla de...oderos

El Puerto de la Venta

▲ Cerro de Marín

Cerro de los Alisos ▲

Cerro
del Búho ▲

fire observation hut

Garganta de Diego Díaz

Río Guadiaro

**San Pablo
de Buceite**

A-405

Río Hozgarganta

CA-3331

Arroyo de Ramón

A-405

Cerro
Bejarano ▲

N

Jimena de la Frontera

Ⓢ

Los Ángeles

Río Hozgarganta

A-405

0   1   2 km

up left for 200 metres before coming to a fork. Ignore a track cutting in towards a **fire observation hut** and keep right. ▸

The track passes through a wire-and-post gate then descends through oaks. Continue through a metal gate and pass a sign, 'Monte Majada del Lobo'. Cross more open ground to reach a crossroads. Turn right following a sign, 'Ubrique 6hr 45min', then descend 250 metres to a fork. Here bear left, along a less distinct track that narrows to become a path. Cross a narrow bridge as the path climbs, close to a streambed. Crossing to the stream's right bank, the path shortly passes back to its left bank. ▸

Cross the stream once again as the path climbs to a sandy track. Turn left, uphill, then bear slightly right across an open area then go through a gate in a stone wall. From here a narrow path leads down to a track, and a GR7 sign pointing back towards Jimena. Turn right, continue past a chain across the track, then cross a streambed.

Running high above a ruined farm the track leads to a junction at **El Puerto de la Venta** (764m) where you should go left. Running fairly level, the track leads through a stand of pines. Ignore tracks off to the right or left. Enter the cork forest, cross a cattle grid to come to a junction. Here, turn right. ▸

Crossing another cattle grid, you'll reach another junction where you should keep left. At the next junction, as the trees thin out, you reach **Albergue Rural El Robledal** refuge. Continue straight on, following a sign, 'Ubrique 4hr 15min'.

Angling left then right the track runs up to a crossroads. Again, carry on straight ahead. At the next fork go left then after 550 metres, at a sign, 'Reserva Andaluza de Caza', cut left along a narrower track blocked to vehicles by boulders. After 1km the track rejoins the one you left earlier, which descends to the A-373 opposite the rocky, southern flank of the **Peñon del Berrueco**. ▸ Turn left and you'll shortly cross from the province of Málaga into Cádiz as Ubrique comes into sight.

Follow the **A-373** to **Mesón Rural Mojón de Víbora**. A few metres beyond the bar, turn right down a track which narrows, descending just east of the road. In 1.8km, you'll cross the A-373 three times in succession then descend to a junction. Head straight on up a section of Roman road to another junction. Here go right, cross a bridge over the **Garganta de Barrida** then turn left. When you reach a tarmac road at the edge of **Ubrique**, turn right then take the next left

From here there are magnificent vistas out east to the Costa del Sol and the Sierra Bermeja.

20 metres beyond this crossing look for a tiny shrine to the Virgin in a rock face to your right.

The Sierra de Grazalema now comes into view to the north.

This could be your taxi pick-up point.

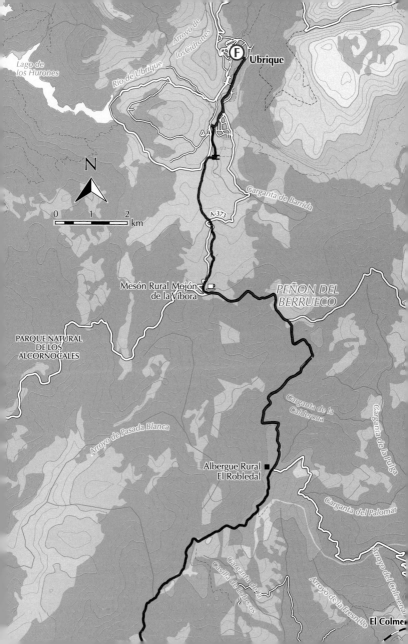

STAGE 4 – JIMENA DE LA FRONTERA TO UBRIQUE

to reach a roundabout by a petrol station on the A-373. From here head north into the village to the Santander bank then turn left to reach the tourist office.

UBRIQUE (ALTITUDE 330M, POPULATION 16,615)

Accommodation, restaurant/bar/café, food shop, ATM, PO, pharmacy, TO, transport

Ubrique is one of the largest of the *pueblos blancos* (white villages) and lies on the border of the Grazalema and Los Alcornocales Natural Parks. The town is famous for its leather goods with several factories manufacturing belts, shoes, handbags and purses along with equine accoutrements. The industry attracted workers from surrounding villages and the town's population doubled between 1930 and 1990. El Museo de la Piel is housed within a 17th century Capuchin Convent and worth a visit.

The Roman settlement of Ocuri can be visited on a hilltop just north of the village. The GR7 follows a section of the Roman road that once linked Ubrique with the garrison town of Acinipo near Ronda.

Accommodation: Hotel Ocurris €€, www.hotelocurris.com, tel 956 463 939. Smart rooms and restaurant with terrace dining. Pensión Rosario €, tel 670 522 642. Friendly, more basic option, some rooms sharing bathrooms. Hotel Sierra de Ubrique €€, www.hotelsierradeubrique.com, tel 956 466 805. Swish 3-star with pool and restaurant 2km from centre.

Food: Bar La Herradura, tel 673 467 594, is a steak house with al fresco dining. El Laurel de Miguel, tel 956 115 109, is more upmarket with a more imaginative menu. And several lively tapas bars to choose from close to the main drag through town.

Transport: Bus to/from Cádiz and Málaga via Grazalema and Ronda. Taxi, tel 610 909 777 or 617 484 832

Town hall/tourist info: www.ayuntamientoubrique.es, tel 956 461 290

SIERRA DE GRAZALEMA NATURAL PARK

Leaving Ubrique, the GR7 enters the Parque Natural de Grazalema. The park straddles the provinces of Cádiz and Málaga and encompasses the tail end of the Subbaetic System. It was the first natural park to be created in southern Spain after gaining UNESCO biosphere status in 1977. Its rugged massif, predominantly composed of limestone and dolomite, rises dramatically from the rolling farmlands around Jérez to a height of nearly 1700m.

The park covers an area of just 50,000 hectares yet its terrain is extraordinarily varied. Rugged formations of karst give way to poplar-lined valleys while stands of cork and evergreen oaks alternate with groves of olives and almonds and fields of wheat and barley.

The park's exceptional botanical variety – one-third of Spain's plants are found here – is the result of a complex climatic conjunction. Continental, Mediterranean and Atlantic influences are all present while Grazalema, at the centre of the park, has a higher annual rainfall than anywhere else in Spain. This high precipitation explains the existence of a large stand of rare Spanish firs (*Abies pinsapo*) on the northern slopes of the Sierra del Pinar.

The park is an ornithological wonderland. Most notable is the raptor population: booted, short-toed and golden eagles are easily spotted and the largest colony of griffon vultures in Europe inhabit the high ledges of Garganta Verde close to Zahara de la Sierra. The griffon population is thriving thanks to a number of feeding sites in the Sierra while one of the major migratory routes between Europe and Africa runs along the western flank of the park.

Within the Grazalema Natural Park are a number of *pueblos blancos*. Their abrupt mountain perches are testimony to their having been built with defence in mind: this was the area of the ever-changing *frontera* (border) between Muslim and Christian Spain.

There are endless hiking possibilities within the natural park. Cicerone's *The Mountains of Ronda and Grazalema* lists 40 local walks.

Park office (issues permits for hikes with restricted access): Centro de Visitantes, PN Sierra de Grazalema, C/ Federico García Lorca 1, El Bosque, tel 956 709733.

STAGE 5
Ubrique to Montejaque via Villaluenga del Rosario

Start	Tourist office in Ubrique
Distance	28.2km
Ascent	1205m
Descent	835m
Time	8hr 30min
Highest point	1029m
Refreshments	In Benaocáz and Villaluenga del Rosario
Notes	You could divide the stage by breaking your journey in Villaluenga del Rosario.

After climbing the old Roman road from Ubrique to Benaocáz as you enter the Grazalema Natural Park a track leads along the valley floor to Villaluenga del Rosario. From here the trail leads through some of the park's most stunning karst formations before descending to Montejaque.

Ubrique to Benaocáz (4.5km/1hr 10min)
From the tourist office, head west along Avenida Solís Pascual. Turn right at Hotel Ocurris along Avenida Fernando Quiñones, which becomes Avenida de Manuel de Falla. At the end of the street bear right then after 100 metres turn left at signs for 'Sendero Calzada Romana' and 'GR7 Benaocáz 3.4km'.

The surface of the dirt track becomes cobbled as you climb the old **Roman road**, passing through two wire-and-post gates. Beyond the second gate angle left up a path to meet the **A-374**. ▶ Head straight on past a bus stop and a GR7 signboard. At the next junction turn right to reach the Plaza de las Libertades in **Benaocáz**.

By turning right at the gate you could cut a corner, avoiding Benaocáz.

The Roman Road leading out from Ubrique

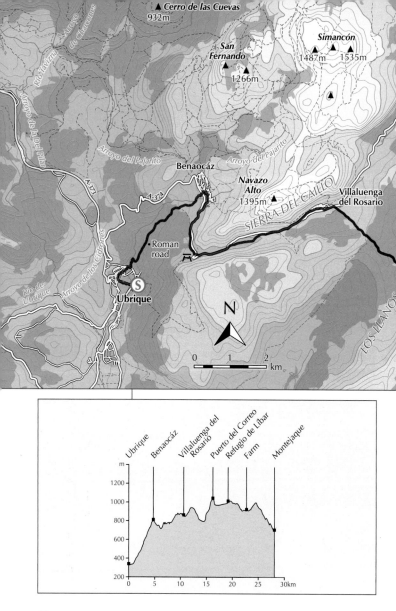

▲ Cerro de las Cuevas
932m

San Fernando
1266m

Simancón
1487m 1535m

Arroyo de Charcones

Río Tavizna

Arroyo de la Del Pilar

Arroyo del Pajarito

A-371

A-374

Benaocáz

Arroyo del Pajarito

Navazo Alto
1395m

Villaluenga del Rosario

SIERRA DEL CAILLO

Roman road

Río de Ubrique

Arroyo de los Cíntares

S Ubrique

LOS LLANOS

N

0   1   2
km

Ubrique
Benaocáz
Villaluenga del Rosario
Puerto del Correo
Refugio de Líbar
Farm
Montejaque

m
1200
1000
800
600
400
200

0   5   10   15   20   25   30km

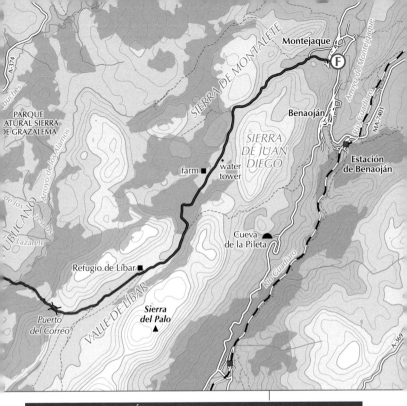

BENAOCÁZ (ALTITUDE 790M, POPULATION 694)

Accommodation, restaurant/bar/café, food shop, ATM, PO, pharmacy, transport

Backed by the stark cliffs of the Sierra del Endrinal, at the southern tip of the Grazalema Natural Park, Benaocáz is one of the least visited *pueblos blancos* with a sleepy, out-of-time vibe.

Climb north from its pretty square to see the partially restored Moorish quarter. Its museum – Ecomuseo, Calle Jabonería 7, tel 956 125 500 – gives an insight into life in the region from Prehistoric times through to the present day.

Accommodation: Posada El Parral €€, www.posadaelparral.weebly.com, tel 956 125 565. Characterful hostel on northern tip of village with pool and excellent food. Hotel Apartamento San Antón €, tel 956 125 564. Simple doubles in village centre. No breakfast but close to bars/restaurants.

Food: Bar Las Vegas, tel 626 565 411, serves tapas as well as full meals, to one side of main square with valley views. Bar Nazarí, tel 653 275 320, has a terrace with panoramic views.

Transport: Bus to/from Ubrique, Villaluenga, Grazalema and Ronda. Taxi in Ubrique (7km), tel 610 909 777 or 617 484 832

Town hall/tourist info: www.benaocaz.es, tel 956 125 500

Benaocáz to Villaluenga del Rosario (6.1km/1hr 30min)

Exit the square along Calle Lavadero. Continue past the old wash house to the A-374 then turn left at a sign, 'GR7 Villaluenga 1hr 20min'. Just past a warning sign for cattle, branch right at a sign, 'GR7 Villaluenga 4.3km', then at the next fork keep left down a rough track. Passing a spectral, unfinished hotel you rejoin the A-374 at a **picnic area**. Cross the road then climb a track which merges with the A-374. Continue along the road's left side on a narrow path.

Just beyond a cattle warning sign, cross the road then branch right along a track that leads through a gate by a signboard, 'La Calzada Medieval de La Manga'. Pass through a second gate to reach a fork. Keep left and follow a cobbled track back up left to the A-374. Continue along a path parallel to the road. When you come to a fork 100 metres before the village, angle left to enter **Villaluenga del Rosario** along a tree-lined avenue then bear right down Calle Carazola to rejoin the A-374 opposite a chapel.

VILLALUENGA DEL ROSARIO (ALTITUDE 843M, POPULATION 438)

Accommodation, restaurant/bar/café, food shop, ATM, PO, pharmacy, transport

To one side of the Roman road that ran along 'La Manga' (the flat valley floor), Villaluenga is surrounded by some of Spain's most dramatic karst formations. The mountains are riddled with potholes and cave systems and the village is home to the Andalucían Caving Federation (FAE). The tortured terrain once provided safe refuge to some of Andalucía's most notorious *bandoleros* (highway brigands/smugglers).

After the successful establishment of a cheese cooperative in the 1990s, several small-scale businesses followed suit and the village now hosts an annual cheese festival.

Accommodation: Hotel la Posada €€, www.tugasa.com/hotel14_1.php, tel 956 305 611. Small hotel decorated in rustic style with restaurant, Los Llanos. Also manages adjacent s/c apartments.

Food: Mesón Rural Los Caños, tel 956 126 134. On main drag through village, excellent set meals and very friendly.

Transport: Bus to/from Ubrique, Villaluenga, Grazalema and Ronda. Taxi in Ubrique (13km), tel 610 909 777 or 617 484 832

Town hall/tourist info: www.villaluengadelrosario.es, tel 956 460 001

Villaluenga backed by the Sierra del Caillo

The Líbar Valley close to Montejaque

Villaluenga del Rosario to Montejaque (17.6km/5hr)

Continue northeast along the A-374 to a roundabout with a sculpture of a cheese at its midst. Here go right along a track, passing between a pool and a sports ground. The track crosses a rise where you pass between a farm and a parking area. Continue through a metal gate then after 200 metres branch right at a sign, 'Puerto del Correo 2hr'. Follow the track down through oak forest then pass through a second gate. After 375 metres turn left at a sign, 'GR7 Puerto del Correo 1hr 30min'.

Cross to the far side of the valley floor of **Los Llanos del Republicano**, heading towards a pass in the ridge to your east. Go through a metal gate then after 5 metres turn right up a path that climbs parallel to a wall.

The path levels as you cross the pass of **Puerto del Correo** and reach the province of Málaga. Descend past a signboard and sign, 'Montejaque 11.2km', then pass through a metal gate as the path arcs right towards a wall and a gate. Don't go through the gate but bear left and descend with a wall to your right to the **Valle de Líbar**. Where the wall cuts right, maintain your course, passing through a gate to reach a sign, 'Fin de Sendero, Llanos del Republicano'. ◀

Bear slightly right to reach a track. Angle left here and you'll soon merge with a more clearly defined track that runs left of a wall topped by a fence. A few metres before the

If you go right here you'll reach a pond where artesian waters well up throughout the year. It is home to hundreds of frogs or tadpoles, depending on the season.

Refugio de Líbar (a mountain refuge, now closed) the track cuts right through a gate then back to the left. Follow the track to the valley's far end where, crossing a cattle grid, it arcs left then right before descending past a ruin. After passing through a gate with GR7 waymarking the track runs past a **farm** then a **water tower**.

Cross a pass as the track descends for 2.4 kilometres to a fork by a signboard depicting local birds. Here, continue straight ahead to reach the first houses of **Montejaque**. At the bottom of the street turn right to reach La Plaza de la Constitucíon.

MONTEJAQUE (ALTITUDE 690M, POPULATION 970)

Accommodation, restaurant/bar/café, food shop, ATM, PO, pharmacy, TO, transport

The village's name is derived from Monte Xaquez meaning 'sacred mountain'. A fortress once stood on the site of the present village, which was a vital link in Nasrid Granada's western line of defence. During La Guerra de la Independencía (aka The Peninsular War), the village would gain fame when a force of 250 villagers defeated a French army of 600 foot soldiers and 90 cavalry.

The limestone peaks surrounding the village are home to some of the most extensive cave systems in Andalucía and the village has a museum dedicated to *espeleología* (caving). The nearby Pileta cave contains some of Europe's finest cave paintings.

Accommodation: Posada del Fresno €€, www.posadadelfresno.com, tel 649 972 979. Friendly inn close to square with six small rooms. Hotel Palacete de Mañara €€, tel 623 174 903. Attractive hotel on main square. Casas de Montejaque €€, www.casasdemontejaque.net, tel 952 168 120. An arc of s/c houses round a pool and garden. Apartamentos Sierra del Hacho €€, tel 952 118 688. S/c apartments for 2, 3 and 4 above a small breakfast/tapas bar.

Food: Entre Ascuas, tel 623 174 903, is on main square and specialises in grilled meats. La Casita, tel 632 548 489, has good food and al fresco dining in its garden.

Transport: Bus to/from Ronda via Benaoján. Taxi Alonso, tel 607 919 352

Town hall: www.montejaque.es, tel 952 167 196

Tourist info: www.montexaquez.org lists all accommodation options in village. Pileta cave visits and info: www.cuevadelapileta.org, tel 952 167 343

MÁLAGA PROVINCE

Ronda seen from El Puerto de las Muelas (Stage 6)

After leaving Villaluenga del Rosario and crossing the Puerto del Correo pass, the GR7 enters Málaga province. Descending past some of Andalucía's most stunning karst landscapes to Montejaque, the route next traverses the Guadiaro Valley to reach Ronda, one of Europe's most spectacular mountain towns.

Running north through the villages of Arriate and Ardales the GR7 follows a snaking path down to the extraordinary gorge of El Chorro. From here it adopts a northeast course to Antequera before splitting into its northern and southern variants, still within Málaga province.

The northern variant runs northeast through Andalucía's vast olive belt via little-known villages towards Córdoba province. The southern variant adopts a higher course through the mountains of La Axarquía, running east towards the higher mountains of Sierra Nevada.

HIGHLIGHTS OF THE GR7 IN MÁLAGA PROVINCE

Some of the many highlights of this section include:

- The hilltop town of Ronda with its bridge and gorge
- Montejaque, one of the most beautiful *pueblos blancos*
- The Chorro gorge and surrounding mountains
- The elegant civic and religious buildings of Antequera
- Little-known villages in Andalucía's vast olive belt

Descending to the plain from Sierra Gorda (Stage 13A)

GETTING THERE/BACK

The two largest towns on part 1 of the GR7 – Ronda and Antequera – are easily accessed from all major cities in Andalucía by both bus and train. Either town would be a good place to begin or end walking (see links, below).

For bus/train connections with other villages refer to the individual village boxes that accompany each stage.

Train: Ronda lies on the Madrid to Algeciras line while trains from Madrid to Málaga stop at Santa Ana and Bobadilla, close to Antequera. The two lines have links with Seville and Granada (www. renfe.com, tel 912 320 320).

Bus: Ronda to/from Málaga – Damas (www.damas-sa.es) or Portillo (http:// malaga.avanzagrupo.com/en); Ronda to/from Jerez/Cádiz – Comes (www. tgcomes.es); Antequera to/from Málaga and Granada – Alsa (www.alsa.com).

Taxis: Ronda main rank, tel 952 872 316 or 670 207 438; Antequera main rank, tel 687 597 500

GENERAL INFORMATION

Regional tourist office in Málaga: www. malagaturismo.com, tel 951 926 020.

STAGE 6
Montejaque to Arriate via Ronda

Start	Plaza de la Constitución, Montejaque
Distance	19.8km
Ascent	605m
Descent	695m
Time	5hr 30min
Highest point	752m
Refreshments	Bars and restaurants in Ronda
Notes	You may be tempted to break your journey in Ronda, one of Europe's most beautiful mountain towns.

A steep ascent leads past a mountain chapel before you cross into the Guadiaro valley as Ronda comes into view. After another climb you reach the town's mesmerising gorge and bridge before a gentler section leads on to Arriate via quiet country lanes.

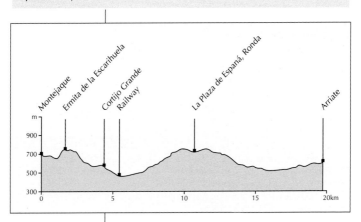

Montejaque to Ronda (10.8km/3hr 15min)
From the square head north along Avenida Andalucía. When you reach a fork follow the **MA-8402** right towards Ronda for 400 metres then go left at a sign, 'Ermita de la Escarihuela'.

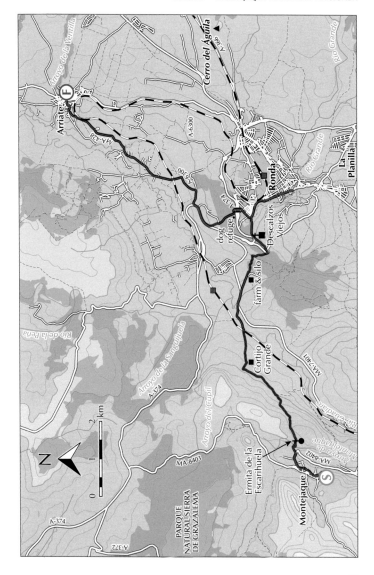

Continue past the village cemetery then climb a cobbled track that loops up to the **Ermita de la Escarihuela**.

Upon reaching the chapel, bear left across a meadow for 400 metres. Pass to the left of a farm with a small shrine, and the path widens to become a track as Ronda comes into view. Descend through broom and groves of olive and almond until the path braids then reconnects before passing two houses.

Carry on across open farmland towards **Cortijo Grande** farm, visible ahead on a bluff, as the track gently climbs then arcs right and descends. 50 metres before the farm it angles left then drops down to the **Ronda-Algeciras railway line**. Cross the track, turn left along a narrow lane parallel to the **Río Guadiaro** then continue past a row of houses to the **MA-7401**.

Go left along the road for 160 metres then turn right along a track, shortly passing to the left of a row of houses. When you reach a **farm** and a **silo**, turn left up a narrow track that climbs past a line of cottages. Passing Villa Mimosa, you reach a junction with another track.

Turn right, and follow GR7/GR249 waymarking. The track arcs left then climbs through pine forest to a junction. Here, go right then after 10 metres turn left up a path that hugs the cliff edge. The path widens as you pass the **Descalzos Viejos**, a winery housed within a 16th century monastery. Reaching a junction in front of a row of houses, bear right to merge with a road. Head on, parallel to the cliff, then continue down Calle Jerez past the Hotel Reina Victoria to La Plaza de España and the Puente Nuevo at the centre of **Ronda**.

RONDA (ALTITUDE 725M, POPULATION 33,978)

Accommodation, campsite, restaurant/bar/café, food shop, ATM, PO, pharmacy, TO, transport

Ronda's physical setting is without rival in southern Spain. The town occupies a high plateau through which, over the millennia, the Río Guadalevín has cut a deep gorge. This plunging abyss is spanned by the Puente Nuevo, its most famous landmark.

A favoured destination on the Grand Tour, the town became a magnet for poets, painters and aesthetes: Rilke, David Roberts, Orson Welles, Hemingway and Bomberg were among its illustrious visitors.

The town saw westward expansion when the Puente Nuevo was completed in 1793. The same decade saw the opening of its Plaza de Toros where the rules of the modern fight were laid down by Pedro Romero then later refined by the great maestro Antonio Ordoñez.

Accommodation: Dozens of hotels and hostels. Hotel San Francisco €€, www. hotelsanfrancisco-ronda.com, tel 952 873 299. Spruce, well-priced hotel in town centre. Hotel Plaza de Toros €€, www.hotelplazadetoros.net, tel 952 872 721. At the edge of gorge in a pedestrian street. Alavera de los Baños €€€, www.alaveradelosbanos.com, tel 952 879 143. Next to the Arab baths with garden and pool. Camping El Sur, www.campingelsur.es, tel 952 875 939. Excellent campsite 2km from the centre with pool, laundry, shop and restaurant (tent+2ppl €18).

Food: For traditional tapas, Bar Lechuguita, tel 952 878 076, or Bar Faustino, tel 952 190 327. For more elaborate, innovative tapas, try De Locos Tapas, tel 951 083 772, or El Almacén, tel 951 489 818. For more formal dining, Restaurante Almocabar, tel 952 875 977, and for superb food and wines, try Carmen La de Ronda, tel 952 878 735.

Transport: Bus to/from Seville, Cádiz and Málaga as well as with all local villages (refer to Málaga province section). Train links with all major cities via Bobadilla or Santa Ana. Taxi, main rank, tel 952 872 316 or 670 207 438

Town hall: www.ronda.es, tel 952 873 240

Tourist office: www.turismoderonda.es, tel 952 187 119

The old town of Ronda

Ronda to Arriate (9km/2hr 15min)

From the bridge retrace your steps past the Reina Victoria hotel to the point where Descalzos Viejos is signed left. Ignore this sign and follow the road as it angles right along Calle Zahara de la Sierra then Calle Prado del Rey. Keep left when you reach a fork, and cross a roundabout then a bridge over the A-374 to a second roundabout. Continue past a metal barrier then follow a track down past a **dog refuge**. Ignore a waymarked path to the left to reach the A-374. Turn right along a narrow path, parallel to the road. Where the road arcs left turn right at a sign, 'Hotel Fuente de la Higuera'.

Continue along a lane which angles left, passes beneath a railway line then bears right before running up to a fork. Keep right and follow the lane past Venta El Polvorilla then Venta El Pelistre. Reaching a fork just before **Arriate**, where the train line is to your right, bear left and follow the road into the village to reach Café Albarra on Calle Ronda in the village centre.

ARRIATE (ALTITUDE 602M, POPULATION 4,147)

Accommodation, restaurant/bar/café, food shop, ATM, PO, pharmacy, transport

A dormitory village to Ronda, Málaga's smallest municipality takes its name from *Arriadh*, which means 'fertile garden' in Arabic. The village lies amidst the irrigated orchards of the Guadalcobacín Valley. Its lively square is a great spot for al fresco dining.

Accommodation: Hotel and Spa Plaza Arriate €€, www.hotelspaplazaarriate. com, tel 678 518 730. In village centre with in-house spa. Hotel Rural Villa Ignacia €€, www.hotelvillaignacia.es, tel 654 110 368. Friendly B&B close to GR7 1km NE of village. Arriadh Hotel €€, www.arriadhhotel.com, tel 952 114 370. Top-notch rooms with valley views, 500m from centre.

Food: Taberna Manolo, tel 619 57 89 96, for traditional Andalusian cuisine is on the main square, with outside dining. El Chozo, tel 952 165 244, is a friendly, untouristy tapas bar in village centre.

Transport: Bus to/from Ronda. Train to/from Algeciras and Antequera. The station is 300m from village centre. Taxi, tel 646 955 622

Town hall/tourist info: www.arriate.es, tel 952 165 096

STAGE 7
Arriate to Ardales

Start	Calle Ronda, Arriate
Distance	34.5km
Ascent	895m
Descent	1085m
Time	9hr 30min
Highest point	894m
Refreshments	Bars and shops in Serrato
Notes	You could divide the day by staying at Cortijo Nuevo or by diverting a short distance to Cuevas de Becerro.

After climbing away from Arriate, the route adopts a northeasterly course across open farmland, passing close to Cuevas de Becerro (a possible diversion if you plan to split this stage). Descending through more rugged terrain to Serrato, a steep ascent leads you over the Puerto de las Cruces before a second, long section of downhill walking leads on to Ardales.

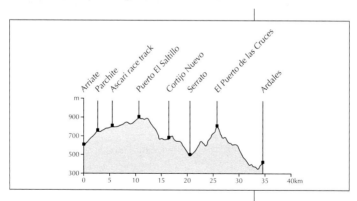

Arriate to Serrato (20.2km/5hr 20min)
From the town centre, head north following signs for Setenil. The road descends steeply then climbs back to the outskirts of the village. Here, go right at a sign, 'Urbanización Los Arroyos', along a quiet lane. Ignore turnings left or right to come to a railway line and the hamlet of **Parchite**. Bear left,

parallel to the track for 100 metres then pass over a level crossing. Angle right then left and continue along a sandy track flanked by drystone walls to the **A-367**. Cross the road and turn left along a track that narrows to become a path that runs just right of the A-367.

Passing the entrance to the **Ascari race track**, the path widens to become a track. Follow the track until, to your left, you see the km29 post of the A-367. The old GR7 path ahead is blocked by landscaping for an abandoned golf development. Angle left over a bank and continue along a narrow path beside the A-367 for 2.5km. When you reach a sign, 'Puerto El Saltillo 885m', turn right along a track. This was part of the old drover's route that ran from Ronda to Córdoba. The track climbs across open countryside punctuated by limestone outcrops.

At a fork, keep right. Crossing a ridge, **Cuevas del Becerro** comes into view to your left. At the next fork, where a sign, 'Cordel del Nacimiento', points down left, keep right. ◀ After running fairly level, the track drops down to reach a narrow lane. Turn right following a sign, 'Cañada de Serrato'. After climbing, you pass the farmhouse of **Cortijo Nuevo**. It's an ideal place to break journey if you're happy to self-cater (see Ardales box).

Turn left for Cuevas del Becerro, where food and accommodation is available, to divide this stage.

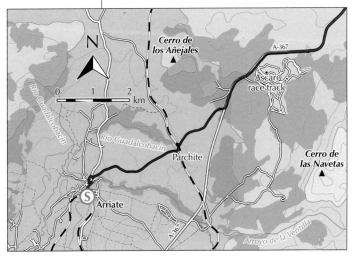

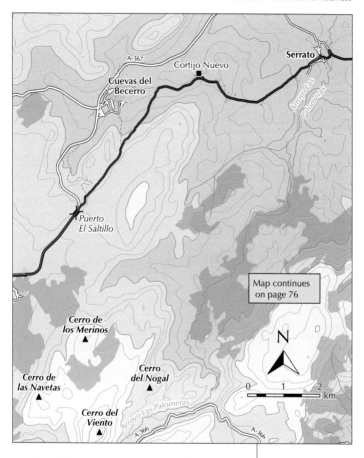

Beyond Cortijo Nuevo, continue to a fork just before the ridgetop where the lane's tarmac surface ends. Keep left, cross the ridge then continue down through open fields and olive groves. The track merges with a broader one which descends to **Serrato**. ▶ Passing the cemetery, you'll reach a junction. Take the lower, left fork and head down into the village where, following the road as it arcs left, you reach the town hall.

Serrato has a couple of bars and shops but no accommodation.

75

Ardales, backed by a line of wind turbines

Serrato to Ardales (14.3km/4hr 10min)

At the town hall, turn right then take the second left down Calle Andalucía. At the bottom of the street, continue across a bridge then bear left along a track signed 'GR7 Ardales 4hr'. At the next junction turn up right. After levelling the track runs past the southern flank of the **Sierra de Ortegicar** as you pass through scrubby *monte bajo* (low growing, shrubby vegetation) and low-growing pines. The track then climbs again to **El Puerto de las Cruces** (806m) where you reach a sign, 'GR7 Ardales 3hr'. As you descend, the rugged mountains surrounding El Chorro come into view out east.

Upon reaching a junction after 200 metres, continue straight ahead. The track becomes rougher underfoot before you reach a better surfaced track where, turning left, you pass a farm building, and the terrain is now more open. Passing

more farm buildings, the track levels then merges with another track. Maintain your course. ▶

Crossing a ridge, Ardales comes into sight as the track descends steeply through pines. Approaching the village past small holdings then a **solar farm**, the track merges with another that runs in from the left. Continue for 400 metres, cross a bridge over the **River Turón**, go through an underpass then climb to the top of Calle Nueva. Bear right along Calle Fray Juan to reach the main square, La Plaza de la Constitución, of **Ardales**.

Views open out south towards the Sierra de Ojén.

ARDALES (ALTITUDE 413M, POPULATION 2493)

Accommodation, restaurant/bar/café, food shop, ATM, PO, pharmacy, transport

A friendly and attractive village close to the Guadalhorce reservoir and the start point of El Caminito del Rey (see Stage 8). During the Moorish period the village fell under the sway of rebel chieftain Omar Ben Hafsun before the Caliphate of Córdoba reconquered the area.

La Cueva de Ardales was discovered nearby when an earthquake in 1821 revealed its entrance. The cave has Palaeolithic paintings and unusual rock formations. To visit (as part of group), tel 952 458 046.

Accommodation: Apartamentos Ardales €€, www.apartamentosardales.com, tel 952 459 466. Spruce apartments in village centre with patio pool. Hotel Restaurante El Cruce €/€€, www.ardaleselcruce.com, tel 952 459 012. Roadside hotel with pool and restaurant passed as you leave Ardales on the GR7. Passed on route: Cortijo Nuevo €, tel 670 602 350. S/c apartments in farm 16km from start point close to Cuevas del Becerro.

Food: Bar El Millán, tel 652 072 542, is a cheap-and-cheerful tapas bar. Mesón La Alternativa, tel 952 458 305, offers traditional Spanish cooking with veggie options as does Restaurante Falco, tel 952 459 066.

Transport: Bus to/from Ronda and Málaga. Taxi, tel 610796 043

Town hall/tourist info: www.ardales.es, tel 952 458 087

STAGE 8

Ardales to El Chorro

Start	Plaza de la Constitución, Ardales
Distance	16km
Ascent	690m
Descent	885m
Time	5hr
Highest point	583m
Refreshments	None en route
Notes	You could build in extra time to hike El Caminito del Rey but book several weeks in advance.

Ridge-top tracks with views to all points of the compass, the archaeological site of Bobastro and a snaking path down to El Chorro make for another memorable stage of the GR7.

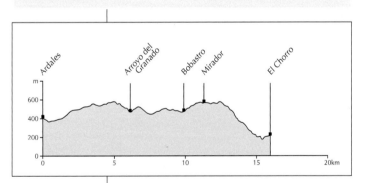

Ardales to El Chorro (16km/5hr)

Exit the square down Calle Fray Juan. When you reach a fork keep left, cross a roundabout then a bridge. At a second roundabout turn right past **Hostal El Cruce**. 100 metres after passing beneath the A-367 turn left at a sign, 'Estación El Chorro 14.9km'. The road climbs, loops right then levels. The surface reverts to dirt as it runs on through groves of almond and olive. Views open out back towards Ardales.

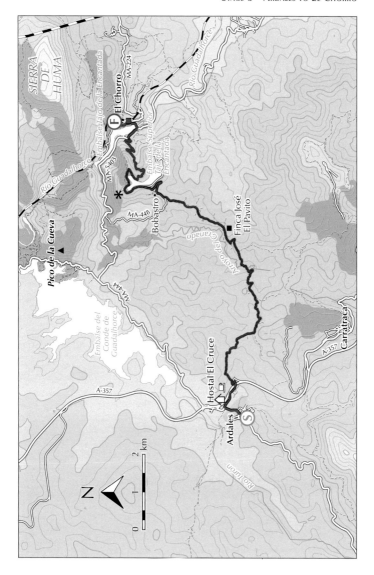

To the south is a high ridge topped by a line of windmills while out east, on clear days, the Sierra Nevada is visible.

The steep cliff faces of the gorge of El Chorro come into view.

Passing through a breach in the hillside you'll reach a fork where you should keep left. Continue through sparse pine forest until you come to another fork. Here, keep left again. Cross a streambed and follow the track as it climbs to the top of a rise before reaching a junction where **Carratraca** is signposted right on the GR249. Here keep left, signed 'GR7 El Chorro 11.6km'. ◄

The dirt track, eroded in sections, loops down through pine forest then crosses the **Arroyo del Granado**. Climbing steeply once more it levels as you pass right of a graffiti-daubed hut. At the top of the next rise ignore a track cutting right. ◄

After descending the track arcs left then right before you pass a farm marked **Finca José El Pavito**. Passing above of a group of the farm buildings the track levels then descends, waymarked at intersections, to the **MA-448**. Turn right to pass the ticket office of the **Bobastro** archaeological site.

Looping right then back left past sculptural sandstone formations the road hairpins right. Here, leave the MA-448 to its left along a track which arcs round the retaining wall of the **Embalse Superior Tajo de la Encantada**. As the track bears round east through pine forest you pass a *mirador* (viewpoint).

A signboard details the birds found in and around the **Desfiladero de los Gaitanes**. Its cliff face, as well as the jagged slopes of Pico La Huma, are visible to the northeast. Parts of the Caminito del Rey are also visible.

After passing the *mirador* then a chain across the track, you come to a junction. Here turn right. After 200 metres pass left of a metal gate along a narrow path that hugs a fence. The path merges with a track beneath the dam wall. Follow the track for 150 metres then turn left at a marker post down a rocky path. The path loops down to a rough track that leads to the MA-5403 and the reservoir of El Chorro.

Turn right along the road then at the next junction left at a sign, 'El Chorro/Valle de Abdalajís'. Cross the retaining wall of the reservoir as the road bears left then climbs to reach a junction beside a ceramic map of **El Chorro**.

El Chorro seen on the approach from the west

EL CHORRO (ALTITUDE 220M, POPULATION 245)

Accommodation, campsite, restaurant/bar/café, food shop, transport

The railside village at the entrance to the Chorro gorge has seen a huge boost to its fortunes since the inauguration of El Caminito del Rey in 2015. The suspended walkway along the side of the gorge was built in the early 20th century, giving access to a water channel powering HEP turbines. A second pathway above the damaged, original cakewalk is now open to walkers and makes for a great diversion of approximately three hours. The walk's popularity means you need to book several weeks in advance via www.caminitodelrey.info.

Climbers from all over Europe pit themselves against the cliff faces around El Chorro and local hostels all cater to the vertically-mobile community.

Accommodation: Complejo Turístico La Garganta €€/€€€, www.lagarganta.com, tel 952 495 000. Converted flour factory overlooking the reservoir with excellent restaurant. Finca la Campaña €, www.fincalacampana.com, tel 626 963 942. S/c cottages and campsite (€9pp) with climbing gear for hire, 1km from village. The Olive Branch €, www.olivebranchelchorro.co.uk, tel 686 669 359. B&B, bunkhouse and s/c apartments 2km from village with pool and camping (€11pp).

Food: Bar Estación El Chorro, tel 658 525 171, next to the station has good tapas.

Transport: Bus to/from Málaga. Train to/from Málaga and Antequera from where there are connections with all major cities. Taxi in Valle de Abdalajís (10km), tel 679 423 635

Town hall/tourist info: www.ardales.es, tel 952 458 087

STAGE 9
El Chorro to Valle de Abdalajís

Start	The ceramic map at the centre of El Chorro
Distance	10.6km
Ascent	595m
Descent	475m
Time	3hr
Highest point	681m
Refreshments	None on route
Notes	You could expand a short day of walking by walking El Caminito del Rey before you depart or diverting up to the Sierra de Huma whose trailhead you pass 40min into the walk.

A stiff climb through pine forest east of El Chorro leads past the towering flank of the Sierra de Huma before the walk levels then breaks out into open terrain from where farm tracks lead eastwards to Valle de Abdalajís.

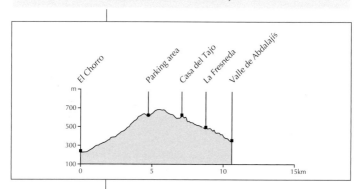

El Chorro to Valle de Abdalajís (10.6km/3hr)
From the ceramic map, follow the **MA-5403** up past the old **railway station** for 200 metres. Reaching a sign, 'Barriada El Chorro', turn hard left. The road becomes a track as you pass a ruin then a sign indicating you're on the Haza del Río route. The track loops up through pine and eucalyptus,

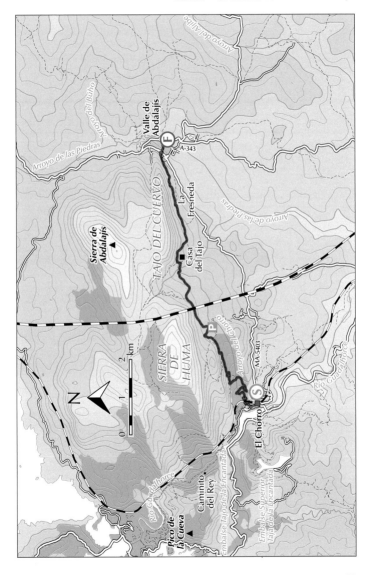

Vultures will almost certainly be riding the thermals up above you and you may spot ibex among the rocks.

twice crossing the **Arroyo del Chorro** then running close to the southern face of the **Sierra de Huma**, which is to your left. Reaching a junction bear hard left. ◄

After levelling the track leads to another junction by twin signboards. Keep left then, at the next junction, turn right. The track to your left leads up to the Sierra de Huma.

At the next junction keep right. The track descends through olive and almond groves to a **parking area** with signboards detailing the Sierra de Huma ascent. Maintain your course and at the next intersection, signed 'Abdalajís 3hr 30min', turn left. The track climbs before bearing right past a farmhouse. Views open out to the east and south to the Sierra de Mijas.

Passing beneath a spring then a farmhouse you reach a junction. Bear right, following GR7 waymarking. Reaching the next fork turn left, uphill, passing the **Casa del Tajo** farm then at the next junction go right, signed 'Valle de Abdalajís 4.1km'. Descend parallel to the flank of the **Tajo del Cuervo** rocky outcrop to reach the hamlet of **La Fresneda**. At its far end, turn left at a GR7 sign. Upon entering **Valle de Abdalajís**, you come to two metal benches. Here turn right then take the next, sharp left. After 40 metres go right down a flight of steps then descend to La Plaza de San Lorenzo and the municipal market.

The track leading up the flank of Las Pedreras

VALLE DE ABDALAJÍS (ALTITUDE 337M, POPULATION 2568)

Accommodation, restaurant/bar/café, food shop, ATM, PO, pharmacy, TO, transport

The eponymous Valle de Abdalajís has long served as thoroughfare to the rich farmlands of the *vega* (plain) of Antequera. During the Roman period Seneca referred to a settlement here called Nescania. The Moors under Abid Al-Aziz founded a new settlement from which the village takes its name. Two elegant buildings dating back to the 16th century are worth a look: El Palacio del Conde de los Corbos and La Antigua Posada.

Accommodation: Hostal Vista a la Sierra €, tel 699 649 477. Pleasant hostel with views across the valley. Refugio de Alamut €/€€, www.refugioalamut.com, tel 952 489 064. Friendly rural hotel with restaurant 1km north of village. La Sorpresa €€/€€€, www.la-sorpresa.com, tel 473 650 566. Swish, Belgian-run B&B 1.8km east of the village with evening meals available 3 times a week.

Food: Rincón del Tapeito, tel 685 417 331, for tapas in village centre. Venta los Atanores, tel 952 488 068, is a roadside restaurant just north of the village close to Vista a la Sierra.

Transport: Bus to/from Antequera. Taxi, tel 679 423 635

Town hall/tourist info: www.valledeabdalajis.es, tel 952 489 100

STAGE 10
Valle de Abdalajís to Antequera

Start	Plaza de San Lorenzo, Valle de Abdalajís
Distance	19.5km
Ascent	740m
Descent	565m
Time	5hr 40min
Highest point	770m
Refreshments	None on route

After an initial steep climb tracks and quiet roads lead round the western flank of the Torcal then down into Antequera, the largest town on the GR7 path through Andalucía.

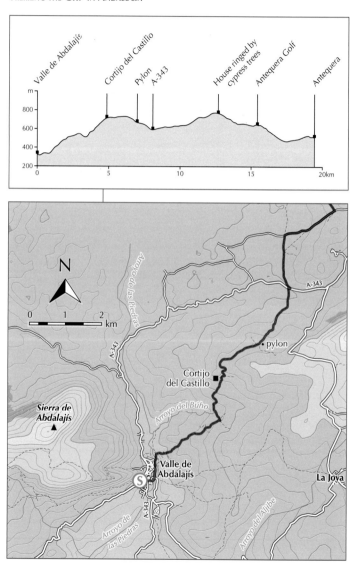

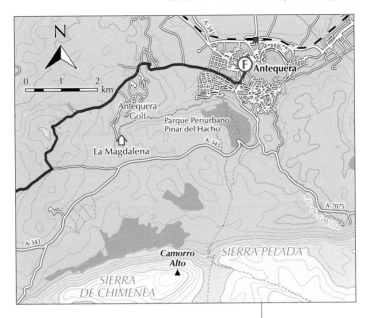

Valle de Abdalajís to Antequera (19.5km/5hr 40min)
From the square head down Callejón de los Molinos. Bear left to reach a junction with the **A-343**. Follow it left then just before a petrol station turn right down a tarmac road. The road angles left, descends past a damaged GR7 signboard then fords the **Arroyo de las Piedras**.

Follow the track steeply up, passing beneath three sets of power lines. After levelling it climbs again, arcs left then descends and crosses a streambed to the right of another damaged track. Climb steeply to reach a junction. Turning right, continue round a rocky outcrop past **Cortijo del Castillo** farm and a white silo.

1.7km beyond Cortijo del Castillo, when you reach a **pylon** left of the track, turn left down a less distinct track. The track descends, angles right then peters out. Maintain your course down the left side of a field then clamber across a streambed where you may spot GR7 paint flashes. Continuing along the left side of the next field the track improves as you pass right of a house with a pine tree at its eastern side.

Fording a stream, the track meets with the A-343. Turn right then after 35m left up a steep track. Upon reaching a junction, head straight on. Passing left of a ruin, you'll reach a second junction. Here go right and continue to the top of a rise. Passing an 8T weight limit sign, with a white hut to your right, turn left up a track which levels before descending past a house ringed by cypress trees.

Continue down past the entrance to **La Magdalena** hotel then that of **Antequera Golf** (golf course). When you reach a roundabout, head straight on past Hotel Antequera and at the next roundabout, continue straight ahead. Pass the Plaza de los Capuchinos to reach a junction. Turn left then go right at a fork down Calle del Picadero to reach the statue of Vicente Moreno Baptista on the Alameda de Andalucía in **Antequera**.

ANTEQUERA (ALTITUDE 510M, POPULATION 41,154)

Accommodation, restaurant/bar/cafe, food shop, ATM, PO, pharmacy, TO, transport

Antequera and its Moorish fortress in the evening light

In spite of being the largest town on the GR7, Antequera feels both intimate and welcoming. Dominated by its castellated Moorish fortress the town lies beside the fertile plain between the Sierra del Torcal and the Guadalhorce river, which for centuries served as bread basket to Málaga.

To the north of the city, three of Europe's largest dolmens, a UNESCO World Heritage Site, make for a fascinating excursion (www.museosdeandalucia.es), while south of the town, El Torcal de Antequera encompasses some of Europe's most stunning karst formations (see Paraje Natural Torcal de Antequera box). It is a 3.5km diversion from the Boca del Asno pass (Stage 11).

El Peñon de los Enamoradas ('Lover's Peak') rises steeply above the plain a few kilometres east of the town. Legend tells that Tello, a young Christian soldier, and Tazgona, a Moorish girl, eloped from Archidona before being pursued to the edge of the mountain-top by Moorish troops. Rather than give themselves up and face certain separation they threw themselves to their death.

Accommodation: Coso Viejo €/€€, www.hotelcosoviejo.es, tel 952 705 04. Characterful rooms in converted 17th century town house on a pretty square. Hotel Manzanito €, www.hotelmanzanito.com, tel 951 994 165. Budget option in quiet side street. Hospedería Colon €€, www.hostal-colonantequera.com, tel 902 902 749. On main drag through town with simple twins and doubles. El Parador de Antequera €€, www.parador.es, tel 952 840 261. Modern *parador* (hotel group owned and managed by the state) with rooms overlooking manicured gardens.

Food: Mesón Las Hazuelas, tel 952 704 582, next to Coso Viejo has superb food and wines with al fresco dining in season. Recuerdos Tapas Bodega, tel 951 356 365, serves both tapas and meals and feels refreshingly untouristy.

Transport: Train to/from Málaga, Seville, Granada and Madrid. Bus to/from Seville, Málaga and Granada. Taxi, tel 952 845 530

Town hall: www.antequera.es, tel 952 708 100

Tourist office: https://turismo.antequera.es, tel 952 702 505

PARAJE NATURAL TORCAL DE ANTEQUERA

A 15 minute drive south from Antequera, the Torcal de Antequera, a UNESCO World Heritage Site, numbers among Andalucía's most remarkable inventions of nature. This is one of the largest swathes of karst in Europe, covering some 17 square kilometres.

The limestone plateau was a seabed during the Jurassic period before being uplifted during the Tertiary era to 1300m when the African plate collided with that of Europe. Dissolution by the action of wind and rain, along with freeze-thaw splitting, created its extraordinary, sculptural rock formations.

The Torcal is home to a huge variety of rock-dwelling wildflowers including 30 varieties of orchid. Marked routes snake their way through the fantasia of rock and the protected area draws thousands of visitors every year.

Visitor Centre at the entrance to park: www.torcaldeantequera.com, tel 952 243 324.

STAGE 11
Antequera to Villanueva de Cauche

Start	Alameda de Andalucía, Antequera
Distance	16.8km
Ascent	555m
Descent	370m
Time	4hr 40min
Highest point	942m
Refreshments	Restaurant close to end of the walk
Notes	There's little to see in Villanueva de Cauche so you could break your journey at Hotel Las Piedras, just before the village.

After passing through Antequera's historic centre the walk follows a river past a number of old textile mills. After a spell of road walking, farm tracks lead on across open countryside to the point just before Villanueva de Cauche where the GR7 divides into its northern and southern variants.

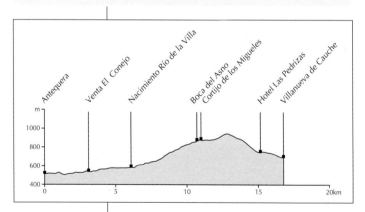

Antequera to Villanueva de Cauche (16.8km/4hr 40min)
From the Alameda de Andalucía head east along Calle
Infante Don Fernando. Cross Plaza San Sebastián then

continue round the eastern side of the **Alcazaba** via Cuesta Los Zapateros, Calle del Río, La Plaza del Carmen, Bajada del Río then Calle Río del Rosal. Upon reaching a junction, go left and continue parallel to the river past a number of old textile mills following signs for Sendero Verde.

Reaching the **A-7075** and Venta El Conejo, turn left. After passing the **Molino Blanco** restaurant then the km49 post, turn right away from the road then bear left along a quiet lane to a fork just before El Paraje Natural Nacimiento de Río de la Villa. Here, bearing right, you will rejoin the A-7075.

Follow the road up to the **Boca del Asno pass**. After two hairpin bends, 30 metres beyond the km44 post, leave the A-7075 at the point where it's met by two tracks next to **Cortijo de los Migueles**. Take the track to the right then at the first fork branch left and continue along the western slopes of the **Sierra de las Cabras**.

Antequera's alcazaba with its Moorish portal to the right

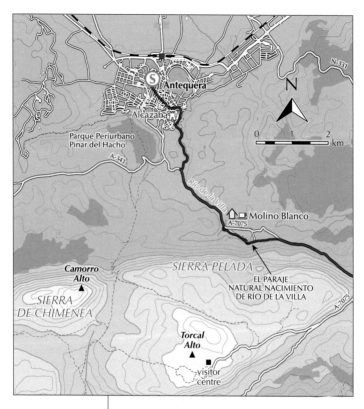

Hotel Las Pedrizas is the only accommodation option close to Villanueva de Cauche.

The track descends to a slip road onto the **A-45** motorway. Bear left then right through a tunnel to reach **Hotel Las Pedrizas**. ◄ Bearing left at a Stop sign, follow the road to the right through a second tunnel beneath the A-45. Bear right then left, and you'll come to a junction. This is the point where GR7 splits into its southern and northern variants. Turn right, cross a roundabout then the A-7204 to reach the hamlet of **Villanueva de Cauche**.

Heading east towards Villanueva del Cauche after autumn ploughing

VILLANUEVA DE CAUCHE (ALTITUDE 695M, POPULATION 65)

Accommodation, restaurant/bar/café, food shop, transport

A tiny hamlet of 65 inhabitants next to the A-45 motorway. The sleepy church square, with its starkly *andaluz* architecture, has been used for filming period dramas. The tiny Bar La Peña serves simple food and opens between 1pm and 11pm. It doubles as a shop.

Accommodation: Hotel Las Pedrizas €, tel 952 730 850. Budget hotel and restaurant close to the motorway passed on the GR7 just before Villanueva de Cauche. Hotel La Sierra €€, www.hotellasierra.com, tel 952 845 410. A 5-minute drive north of Villanueva de Cauche, comfortable roadside hotel and restaurant.

Food: None available apart from at recommended hotels and Bar La Peña.

Transport: Bus to/from Málaga. Taxi in Villanueva de la Concepción (12km), tel 670 766 787 or El Colmenar (13km), tel 625 836 089

Town hall: www.antequera.es, tel 952 708 100

Tourist office: https://turismo.antequera.es, tel 952 702 505

THE NORTHERN VARIANT

Stages 12A-32A: from Villanueva del Cauche to Puebla de Don Fadrique

Heading east en route to Hornos de Peal (Stage 26A)

STAGE 12A

Villanueva de Cauche to Villanueva del Trabuco

Start	The church, Villanueva de Cauche
Distance	16.6km
Ascent	345m
Descent	355m
Time	4hr 15min
Highest point	813m
Refreshments	Bars/restaurants in Villanueva del Rosario

A short and gentle stage, the first of the GR7's northern variant follows minor roads and farm tracks across open farmland to Villanueva del Trabuco.

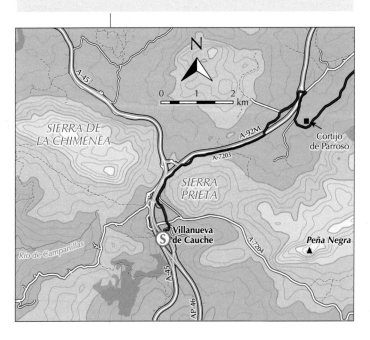

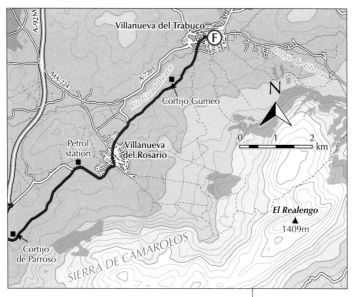

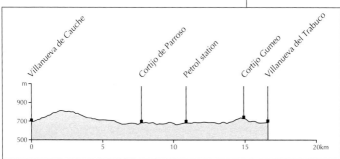

Villanueva de Cauche to Villanueva del Rosario
(11.7km/3hr)

Exit Villanueva de Cauche along Calle Granada then bear
left and head north out of the village. At a junction, head
straight across the **A-7204** then continue straight on at a
roundabout. After 100 metres, you pass the point where the
southern and northern variants of the GR7 divide. At the

On through the olive groves en route to Villanueva del Rosario

next junction, turn left along the **A-7203**. Passing the km18 post, just before reaching the A-45, bear right and continue along the A-7203, parallel to the motorway.

After passing the km16 post, the road angles left and passes beneath the **A-45** then, after 1.6km, passes back to its eastern side. After 100 metres, where the road arcs left, turn right at a sign, 'Parroso'. Head south along a broad track and in 800 metres, you'll reach a fork. Here, go left at another sign for Parroso along a track that runs beneath the north-western slopes of the **Sierra de Camarolos**. Passing a farm, **Cortijo de Parroso**, continue through open fields and olive groves. The track merges with the MA-231. Continue past a **petrol station**, Hotel Las Delicias then Hostal El Cerezo to reach the centre of **Villanueva del Rosario**.

VILLANUEVA DEL ROSARIO (ALTITUDE 697M, POPULATION 3373)

Accommodation, restaurant/bar/café, food shop, ATM, pharmacy, transport

Lying north of the Sierra de Camarolos, away from major roads, Villanueva del Rosario sees little in the way of passing traffic. The village dates from the 16th century when the region was repopulated after the Reconquest. It was originally called Puebla de Saucedo or 'Village of the Willows' and the trees still line some of its streets. Local legend tells that a stash of Roman treasure lies hidden beneath the nearby Peñon de Solis peak.

Accommodation: Venta las Delicias €, tel 952 742 094. Next to A-7203 arriving in village, simple rooms and restaurant. Hotel El Cerezo €, tel 952 742 129 or 697 130 176. On GR7 at entrance to village, basic rooms above restaurant. Cortijo Sabila €€/€€€, www.boutiquehotel-spain.com, tel 685 177 739. Swish, *cortijo*-style hotel close to end of stage with pool, friendly British owners and superb food.

Food: Bar Los Mellizos, tel 685 692 197, is a good choice for cosy, inexpensive dining.

Transport: Bus to/from Málaga and Archidona. Taxi in Archidona (12km) tel 658 405 683

Town hall/tourist info: www.villanuevadelrosario.es, tel 952 742 008

Villanueva del Rosario to Villanueva del Trabuco (4.9km/1hr 15min)

Head straight through the village then on along the A-7203. Passing the km9 post, as the road angles left, go right up a broad track. After 1km, you pass **Cortijo Gumeo**. Reaching **Villanueva del Trabuco**, cross the **Río Guadalhorce** then at the A-7203 turn right to reach the village centre and La Plaza del Prado.

VILLANUEVA DEL TRABUCO (ALTITUDE 683M, POPULATION 5300)

Accommodation, restaurant/bar/café, food shop, ATM, PO, pharmacy, transport

With the wooded slopes of the Gordo and San Jorge sierras as backdrop, olive groves and irrigated orchards stretching away to the north and east and narrow streets of whitewashed houses, Villanueva del Trabuco could not feel more *andaluz*.

Abundant spring waters, including those of La Fuente de los Cien Caños ('The 100-spouted spring') feed the Guadalhorce river, which rises close to the village before passing through its centre spanned by four bridges. At the midst of its attractive plaza, La Fuente de los 3 Caños is reputed to have never run dry.

Accommodation: Hotel El Capricho €, www.salonrestauranteelcapricho.com, tel 650 403 702. Roadside hotel 4km north of village. El Paneque €€, www.restaurantepaneque.com, tel 951 904 716. Facing El Capricho on other side of motorway with plush rooms and restaurant. In 2021, a new hostel with pool is due to open at the top of the village. Information via the town hall.

Food: El Ventero del Trabuco, tel 685 541 286, offers traditional Andalucían fare. Venta Talilla, tel 952 751 895, is a cosy choice for local cuisine.

Transport: Bus to/from Málaga, Antequera and Archidona. Taxi in Archidona (8km), tel 658 405 683

Town hall/tourist info: www.villanuevadeltrabuco.es, tel 952 751 021

STAGE 13A

Villanueva del Trabuco to Villanueva de Tapia

Start	Plaza del Prado, Villanueva del Trabuco
Distance	31.2km
Ascent	590m
Descent	610m
Time	8hr 45min
Highest point	951m
Refreshments	None en route
Notes	You can avoid the large loop out east by following the A-7203 north out of Villanueva to reach the second olive oil mill described in the text or follow a track due east out of the village to El Chorillero.

A long, beautiful stage leads past the western end of the Sierra de Caramolos before passing through the flatter farmlands surrounding Villanueva de Tapia.

Villanueva del Trabuco to Villanueva de Tapia (31.2km/8hr 45min)

Exit the square to the southeast along Calle Pilar del Prado then cross the Río Guadalhorce and continue along Calle Miguel Induraín. At a junction at the edge of the village, continue straight ahead. After 100 metres, at a fork, bear slightly right and continue steeply up towards the **Sierra Gorda** along a tarmac road. Just beyond a pylon, as the road bears right, turn left at a GR7 post passing behind the peak of **Eulogio** (974m). ◄

There are superb views out west and up to the flanks of the Sierra de Camarolos.

Passing **Cortijo de Fuente de Borreguero** the track descends along lower edge of a stand of pines. Descending more steeply past a rocky outcrop you reach a junction. Keep right following a sign, 'Camino Sierra Gorda'. At the next junction, by a round water deposit, turn left.

Bearing right then left you reach the **MA-400**. Turn left and continue through the hamlet of **Morales** to the houses of **El Chorillero**. Here go right, climb past a spring then continue up a broad track. When you reach the MA-4100, head straight across, following a sign, 'Vereda de Archidona a Alfarnate'. As you pass an **olive mill**, the track crosses open farmland before reaching the **A-7203**. Here turn right then after 300 metres, at a second **olive oil mill**, bear left along a gravel track which after 2.4km passes beneath the **A92-M** motorway.

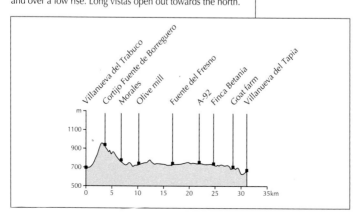

The track levels after climbing from Villanueva del Trabuco

At the next crossroads, turn right. After 3 kilometres you'll reach a junction where, up to the right, you'll see **Cortijo Alto**. Turn left then pass through the hamlet of **Fuente del Fresno**.

Follow the tarmac road on across the plain, heading straight on at a junction with a minor road. Reaching the A-7200 again head straight on. Entering a stand of oaks follow the track as it cuts right then left as you cross the **A-92** motorway then a railway line via an unmanned crossing. Angling left then right after 350 metres you pass beneath the **AVE railway line**. You now pick up GR249 waymarking, which leads up and over a low rise. Long vistas open out towards the north.

Hotel Rural Carlos Astorga (see Villanueva de Tapia box) is signposted right just before the A-333. It's 2km from this point.

Continue along the track for 700 metres until, to your right, you see a sign, 'Prohibido arrojar basuras y escombros'. Here, go right, ignoring GR249 waymarking pointing straight ahead. Pass the entrance gates to **Finca Betania** then bear right then left to reach the A-333. ◄

Turn left along the road then branch left again at a sign, 'GR7 Villanueva de Tapia 5.25km', along a quieter road. When you reach the A-333 once again continue for 75 metres

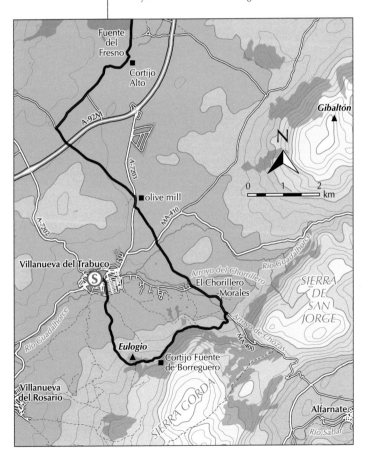

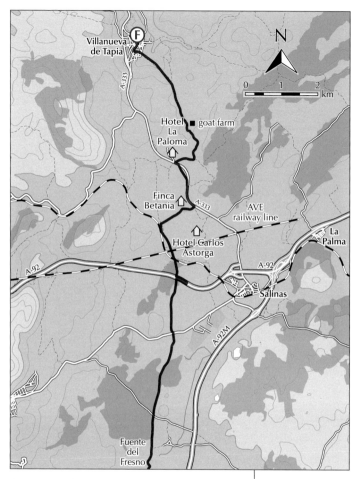

then go right along a track signed 'Camino de Entredicho' where you again pick up GR249 waymarking. ▸ Bear left as the track runs along a ridgetop. Pass a **goat farm** and follow the track as it descends to the eastern edge of **Villanueva de Tapia**. Here, head up Calle Nueva to a junction. Turn right after 275 metres to reach the Plaza de España.

Continue along the A-333 for 100 metres for Hotel La Paloma (see box).

VILLANUEVA DE TAPIA (ALTITUDE 660M, POPULATION 1490)

Restaurant/bar/café, food shop, ATM, PO, pharmacy, transport

At the fringe of Andalucía's vast olive belt, at the northeastern tip of Málaga province, Villanueva de Tapia is a pretty yet little-visited village with whitewashed houses fanning out from its wafer-bricked church. South of the village the Sierra del Pedrosa rises to 1000m while to the north the landscape is characterised by undulating olive groves and fields of wheat.

Accommodation: None in village but good options nearby. Hotel Rural La Paloma €€, www.hotelrurallapaloma.com, tel 952 750 409. Just off the GR7 3km before Villanueva de Tapia, a roadside hotel with garden, pool and great food. Hotel Rural Carlos Astorga €€, tel 608 982 576. Rustic-style rooms with pool and restaurant signposted right (1km) just before the GR7 meets the A-333.

Food: Half a dozen bars offer tapas and simple meals.

Transport: Bus to/from Málaga, Antequera and Archidona. Taxi in Archidona (15km), tel 658 405 683

Town hall/tourist info: www.villanuevadetapia.es, tel 952 757 007

STAGE 14A
Villanueva de Tapia to Villanueva de Algaidas

Start	Plaza de España, Villanueva de Tapia
Distance	17.2km
Ascent	465m
Descent	580m
Time	4hr 45min
Highest point	896m
Refreshments	None on route

An initial steep climb then on through olive groves following a clearly waymarked route in which the GR7 and GR249 run together.

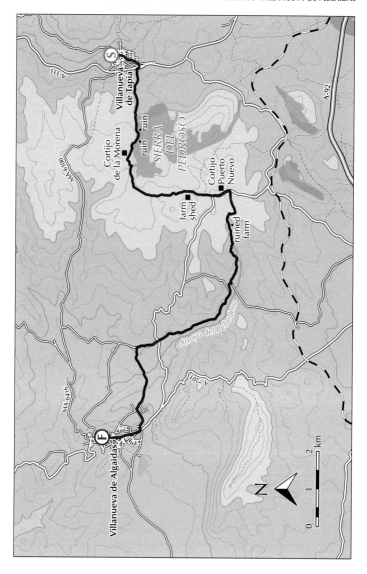

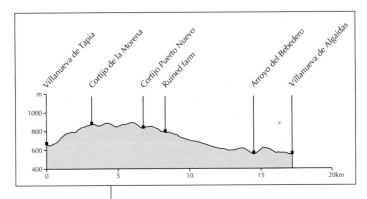

Villanueva de Tapia to Villanueva de Algaidas (17.2km/4hr 45min)

Leave the square to the south along Avenida de la Constitución. At a roundabout head straight on, pass beneath a bridge then turn right up a track passing a signboard detailing the route you're following, 'La Colada de Entredicho'. The track climbs steeply along the northern slopes of the **Sierra del Pedroso**.

Passing two ruins the track descends before passing **Cortijo de la Morena**, beyond which you reach a junction. Go left following a sign, 'V de Algaidas 12.1km'. ◄ At the next junction turn left at another sign, 'V de Algaidas 11.2km', and continue through olive groves on a southerly course.

There are now panoramic views out north.

The track leads past a farm shed with green doors. Descend past a number of farmsteads to reach a tarmac road. Here turn left. After passing **Cortijo Puerto Nuevo**, cut right along a dirt track signed 'V de Algaidas 8.3km'.

After 600 metres, at the end of a fenced enclosure, turn right then at the next farm go hard left. The track descends, crosses a streambed then climbs, passing above a **ruined farm**. Views now open out towards the south. The track passes right of two houses then just past a third house reaches a crossroads. Here, go left and continue down through the olives. Bearing right the track adopts a course parallel to the Arroyo del Bebedero, passing a small house. Swing left at a ruin to cross the stream via a concrete bridge to reach a road.

Here turn right. Follow the road round left then after 200 metres turn left and continue down a track that runs parallel once more to the Arroyo del Bebedero. Eventually the

track reverts to tarmac before reaching a Stop sign. Continue straight on, signed 'V de Algaidas 2.3km', along a quiet road. At the next crossroads turn left. The track descends, crosses the **Arroyo del Bebedero** then climbs to the outskirts of **Villanueva de Algaidas**. Pass an olive mill, take the second turning left then at the next junction turn right to reach the village square.

Olive groves in the evening light

VILLANUEVA DE ALGAIDAS (ALTITUDE 545M, POPULATION 4218)

Accommodation, restaurant/bar/café, food shop, ATM, PO, pharmacy, TO, transport

Surrounded by rolling olive groves Villanueva de Algaidas dates from the 16th century when the founding of the monastery of Nuestra Señora de la Consolación attracted settlers to the area.

The renowned sculptor Miguel Ortiz Berrocal was born in the village where a museum contains a number of his works. Berrocal created the first Goya statuette, the Spanish equivalent of the Oscar. It was considered vulgar and replaced soon after.

Accommodation: Hostal Algaidas €, tel 952 743 308. Basic hostel at the south side of village with restaurant. Hostal Restaurante Chovi €/€€, www.facebook.com/RestauranteChovi, tel 952 743 451. In village centre by the park with inexpensive rooms and restaurant.

Food: Bar Beatas, tel 952 74 4107, has good burgers and outside dining.

Transport: Bus to/from Málaga, Antequera, Archidona and Cuevas de San Marcos. Taxi, tel 952 743 339 or 659 656 149

Town hall/tourist info: www.villanuevadealgaidas.es, tel 952 743 002

STAGE 15A

Villanueva de Algaidas to Cuevas de San Marcos

Start	Plaza Miguel de Miguel Berrocal next to Cajasur bank
Distance	18.8km
Ascent	550m
Descent	675m
Time	5hr 10min
Highest point	702m
Refreshments	Shops and bars in Cuevas Bajas
Notes	The GR7 has recently been re-routed between Cuevas Bajas and Cuevas de San Marcos, initially following the same route as the GR249 and GR245.

On through the olive belt, passing a ruined convent before picking up a new variant of the GR7 which avoids the overgrown path beside the Arroyo de Burriana.

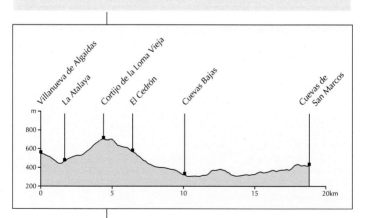

Villanueva de Algaidas to Cuevas Bajas (10km/2h 50min)
From the square, head north out of the village along the **A-7201**. Reaching a fork go left at a sign for Cuevas Bajas along the **MA-203**. After 200 metres turn right at a sign, 'Camino Mozárabe de Santiago'.

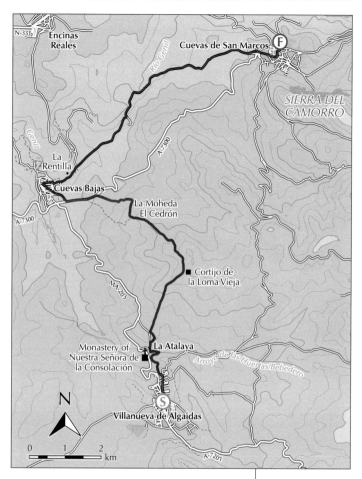

The Camino Mozárabe de Santiago pilgrimage route links five of Andalucía's major towns – Jaén, Málaga, Granada, Almería and Córdoba – with the Vía de la Plata which it joins at Mérida. From here the route runs up through western Spain to Santiago de Compostela.

The monastery was founded in 1566 by an order of Franciscan monks.

Where the road ends, just past a row of houses, bear right to pick up a path which descends, crosses a streambed then loops left. Descend once again as the path hugs the fenced ruins of the **Monastery of Nuestra Señora de la Consolación**. ◄

The airy ceiling of Nuestra Señora de la Consolación

Angling right the path levels then drops down to cross a bridge, built in the Middle Ages by monks from the **monastery**, spanning the **Arroyo de las Huertas**. Angling right the path runs up to a fork. Go left following a sign, 'Cuevas Bajas 7.9km', then climb to a row of houses at the edge of **La Atalaya**.

Here, go right and at the next junction right again, signed 'Cuevas Bajas 7.2km'. Reaching a bus stop turn right then take the first left, uphill. At the next junction turn right along Calle Ventilla. The road bears left and climbs. Immediately past house number 30 turn right along a track, El Camino de las Algaidas. As you gain height views open out across the sea of olives stretching out to the west.

At a fork at the threshing floor of the ruined farm **Cortijo de la Loma Vieja**, branch left. As you descend Cuevas Bajas comes into view before you pass through the hamlet of **El Cedrón**. ▶ Continue along the track and pass through a second hamlet, **La Moheda**, then come to a junction. Here go left. When you reach the A-7300 turn left then turn right after 600 metres at a sign for 'Cuevas Bajas'. Passing the cemetery, continue down through the village to the church, La Iglesia de San Juan Bautista, at the centre of **Cuevas Bajas**.

A sign points off right to El Cedrón's old communal bread oven.

CUEVAS BAJAS (ALTITUDE 327M, POPULATION 1482)

Restaurant/bar/cafe, food shop, ATM, PO, pharmacy, transport

A sleepy village on the banks of the Río Genil at the heart of the olive belt, Cuevas Bajas sees few visitors. During the Roman period it lay close to the Via Antoniana, a major route of communication across southern Spain, and the remains of a number of villas and a bathhouse were found close to the present settlement.

Accommodation: Nearest place to stay in El Tejar @ 9km from village, Hostal Restaurante Reina €, tel 957 53 06 55, a roadside hostel with great home cooking or in Cuevas de San Marcos (see listings).

Transport: Bus to/from Antequera and Cuevas de San Marcos. Taxi, tel 658 188 515

Town hall/tourist info: www.cuevasbajas.es, tel 952 727 501

Cuevas Bajas to Cuevas de San Marcos (8.8km/2hr 20min)
Turn right at the church along Calle Real, signed 'Camino del Río'. Heading east past the *ayuntamiento* (town hall) you'll reach a mini roundabout. Maintain your course then,

At this point you leave the Camino Mozárabe.

at a junction, take the lower of two right turns, passing a signboard, 'El Camino Mozárabe de Santiago', then a sports ground. Passing an olive mill **La Rentilla** you reach a signed path cutting left. Carry on straight ahead following a sign, 'Sendero Europeo GR7/E4'. ◀

The track runs on through olive groves. Descending towards the **Río Genil** you come to a fork. Maintain your course, signed 'Cuevas de San Marcos 4.5km'. At the next fork keep right. The track runs close to the poplar-lined course of the river, heading towards the flank of the **Sierra del Camorro**. At the next junction continue straight ahead. The track descends then crosses a bridge over the Arroyo de los Puercos. Reaching the next fork keep left and climb to another junction. Turning right you come to a roundabout. Go left following a sign for Cuevas de San Marcos. Continue past a petrol station along Avenida Pablo Picasso then cut left down Calle Molinos. Turn right down Calle Cervantes to reach the church and the main square of **Cuevas de San Marcos**.

CUEVAS DE SAN MARCOS (ALTITUDE 420M, POPULATION 3671)

Accommodation, restaurant/bar/café, food shop, ATM, PO, pharmacy, TO

A pretty village at the foot of the Sierra del Camorro, just south of the Río Genil and a few kilometres from the Iznájar reservoir. In the nearby Cueva de Belda arrow and axeheads were discovered dating back to the Neolithic era, which can be seen in the Senda de los Milenios museum (visits arranged via town hall, see below). Olive growing is the mainstay of the local economy.

Accommodation: Casa Bob Guest House €, www.casa-bob.com, tel 690 217 055. British-run guesthouse with smallish rooms, some en-suite, others sharing bathrooms. Hostal Vista Bella €, tel 952 728 123. Basic hostel at top of town where the GR7 enters village. No meals but close to bars and restaurants.

Food: Mesón Mangas, tel 952 728 427, for inexpensive, *andaluz* cuisine.

Transport: Bus to/from Málaga, Archidona and Villanueva de Algaidas. Taxi, tel 610 072 133

Town hall/tourist info: www.cuevasdesanmarcos.es, tel 952 728 102

CÓRDOBA PROVINCE

Faded GR7 sign en route to Priego (Stage 18A)

Crossing the Río Genal over the Armiñan Bridge the GR7 enters the province of Córdoba before adopting a northeasterly course through the olive belt towards the workaday town of Rute.

From Rute a long and beautiful day of hiking leads to Priego de Córdoba as the walk adopts a high and beautiful course along the flank of the Sierra de Rute and the Sierra de la Horconera. Priego's historic centre, with narrow streets flanked by geranium-clad balconies and the extraordinary Fuente del Rey, is ample reward for a long day of hiking.

Leaving Priego's lofty plateau the trail descends to the tiny village of La Concepción before running on through more olive groves to Almedinilla and the provincial boundary with Jaén.

HIGHLIGHTS OF THE ROUTE IN CÓRDOBA PROVINCE

Some of the best bits to be enjoyed on this section of the route include:

- The contrasting landscapes of the Sierra Súbbetica Natural Park
- The elegant town of Priego de Córdoba and its labyrinthine Barrio de la Villa
- Long views north towards the distant Sierra Morena
- High trails above the Iznájar reservoir, the largest in Andalucía

GETTING THERE/BACK

Bus: Rute has direct connections with Málaga, Córdoba, Granada and Cuevas de San Marcos while Priego de Córdoba has connections with Almedinilla, Granada, Alcalá la Real and Madrid.

The website, www.busbud.com, is a good starting point for both towns. See also www.alsa.es and www.autocares-carrera.es.

Taxi: numbers of local drivers/firms are listed in village information boxes.

GENERAL INFORMATION

Regional tourist office: www.turismodecordoba.org, tel 902 201 774.

STAGE 16A
Cuevas de San Marcos to Rute

Start	Plaza Federico García Lorca, Cuevas de S.Marcos
Distance	13.6km
Ascent	540m
Descent	340m
Time	3hr 40min
Highest point	681m
Refreshments	None en route

A short stage running on through the olive belt by way of farm tracks and quiet roads. There are beautiful views across the Iznájar reservoir during the walk's middle section.

Cuevas de San Marcos to Rute (13.6km/3hr 40min)

Exit the square in front of the church at its bottom, left corner down Calle Cervantes then bear right along Calle Molinos. Turn left along Calle Ramón y Cajal then at the next junction right along the **A-7376**. After 1.5km cross an **iron bridge** spanning the **Río Genil**. ◀

Beyond the bridge you enter Córdoba province.

El Puente de Luis Armiñan over the Río Genil

After 50 metres go right along a track that hugs the river's north bank. When you reach the hamlet of **Valdefresno**, take the first road right signed 'GR7 Rute 2hr 10min'. The road's surface becomes gravelled before, passing a sign 'Final

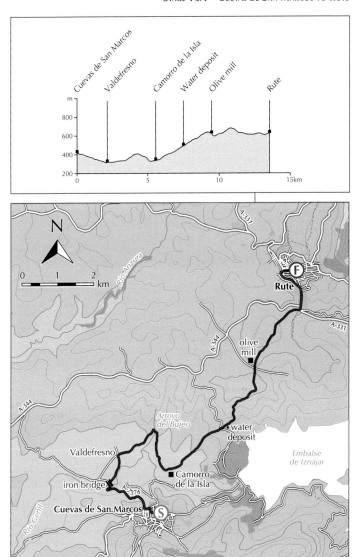

Looking out across the Iznájar reservoir

Carretera', it splits three ways. Maintain your course along the middle track, ignoring the track cutting up right.

The track climbs steeply through olives then descends, crosses the **Arroyo del Bujeo** then climbs to a junction. Here go right and continue down to a narrow lane. Turning left you cross a bridge before passing between a ruin and the farmhouse of **Camorro de la Isla**, which has a high chimney at its rear.

The road climbs steeply, passing beneath three sets of power lines. Beyond a white farmshed you reach a broad tarmac road. Head straight on then after 50 metres bear left along a second road, passing above a fenced **water deposit** with blue metal gates. The reservoir, **Embalse de Iznájar**, comes into view to the east. After a steady climb you reach a modern house at the top of a rise then descend to a cross-roads by an **olive mill** with a green hopper. Head straight on up a dirt track to the top of the next rise. ◄

Dropping down then passing a picnic area you reach the outskirts of **Rute** and a junction. Turn left and continue past Hotel María Luisa then Restaurante Venega. Turn right at a sign, 'Oficina de Turismo', to reach the leafy square of Plaza Nuestra Señora del Carmen.

Rute comes into sight while on clear days the Sierra Nevada is visible out east.

RUTE (ALTITUDE 624M, POPULATION 9857)

Accommodation, restaurant/bar/café, food shop, ATM, PO, pharmacy, TO, transport

For Andalucíans, Rute is synonymous with Christmas sweets, air-cured ham and anis. More than a dozen distilleries in the town produce the liqueur – *aguardiente* in Spanish – even though the custom of taking a shot at breakfast is fast disappearing. The Museo del Anís (tel 957 538 143) is housed within an old distillery and worth a visit. Rute also has a museum about ham production, La Casa-Museo del Jamón (tel 957 539 227). Olive growing, as you might guess, is cornerstone of the local economy.

Accommodation: Hotel El Mirador de Rute €/€€, www.miradorderute.com, tel 957 539 404. Large, modern hotel with restaurant, gardens and pool. El Rincón de Carmen €€, www.elrincondecarmen.com, tel 616 856 965. Friendly B&B 2km NE of Rute with pool and reservoir views.

Food: Bar Restaurante Venega, tel 957 539 279, is an inexpensive, central option.

Transport: Bus to/from Málaga, Córdoba, Granada and Cuevas de San Marcos. Taxi, tel 608 662 351

Town hall: www.rute.es, tel 957 532 929

Tourist office: www.turismodelasubbetica.es/rute, tel 957 532 929

PARQUE NATURAL DE LAS SIERRAS SUBBÉTICAS

At the southern edge of Córdoba province the Sierras Subbéticas Natural Park encompasses 32,000 hectares of the Baetic mountains. It was created in 1988 and since 2006 has been part of UNESCO's European Geoparks Network.

Rugged outcrops of limestone rising to over 1500m stand in stark contrast to forested hillsides of gall and holm oak and rolling groves of olives. The park reads like a geology lesson in limestone features with caves, sink holes, potholes, *navas* (flat areas between outcrops of rock) and dolines, all formed by the continuous action of water on the highly soluble rock.

Some 1200 plant species are found in the park, 30 of them endemic. It's most noted, however, for its birdlife and especially raptors: the Peregrine falcon is the symbol of the park, golden eagles nest here as does one of Spain's largest colonies of griffon vultures. Short-toed, booted and Bonelli's eagles along with eagle owls and black kites are also present. Mammal species include boar, ibex, foxes, wild cats, martens, badgers as well as the extremely rare, endangered Miller's water shrew.

STAGE 17A
Rute to Priego de Córdoba

Start	Plaza Nuestra Señora del Carmen, Rute
Distance	25.9km
Ascent	905m
Descent	875m
Time	7hr 30min
Highest point	979m
Refreshments	None on route
Notes	Waymarking is sparse and the path overgrown in sections making for a trickier stage than most. Best in long trousers. You could divide the stage by diverting 3km to Los Villares.

A beautiful day of walking along the northwestern flank of the Sierra de Rute and the Sierra de Alhucema as you enter the Parque Natural de Las Sierras Subbéticas.

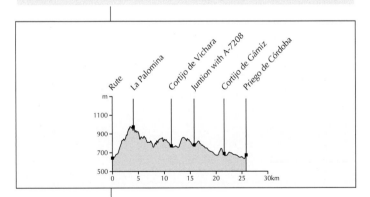

Rute to Priego de Córdoba (25.9km/7hr 30min)

Exit the square at its top, right-hand corner. Reaching the Iglesia de Santa Catalina, turn left and climb past the Museo del Jamón to reach El Paseo del Fresno. Exit this leafy square at its top left corner up a flight of steps, turn left then take the first right. Climbing past garages you reach a concrete road

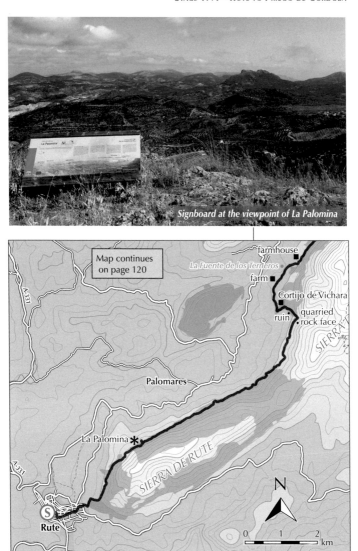

Signboard at the viewpoint of La Palomina

Map continues on page 120

and a sign, 'GR7 Priego de Córdoba'. From here climb a path parallel to a fence to your left. Follow the fence as it cuts right to reach a concrete track.

Maintain your course along the track which arcs left, hugging the lower edge of a pine forest. Ignore a way-marked path that shortly cuts down left. Where the track ends, go right up a narrow path. Passing an old *calera* (lime kiln) you reach a sign pointing left to a viewpoint at the rocky bluff of **La Palomina**. ◄

It's worth a 100 metre detour for the views north to the Sierra Alcaide, Pico Bermejo and La Tiñosa.

The path runs on, crossing a number of scree slopes, as you pass through stands of oak and pine. Waymarking for a local walk helps plot a course over a tricky section where trees lie across the path. The hamlet of **Palomares** comes into view, down to your left.

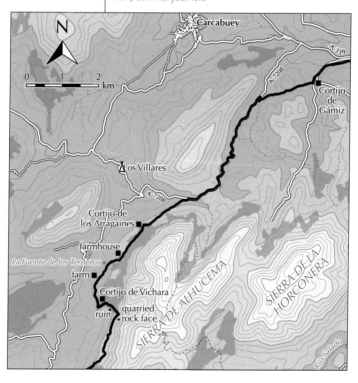

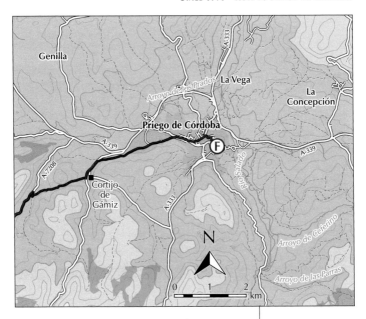

Angling up right the path runs above olive groves, way-marked with wooden posts pointing back to Priego. After crossing a steambed at the head of a gully it traverses more open terrain. Reaching another gully the path angles left then descends along a ridgetop where you can just make out faded GR waymarking on the rocks.

Bearing right the path adopts a more level course through low-growing oaks, running towards the base of a **rock face** that has been quarried in the past. Here you reach a boulder field where you should go left, descend for 40 metres across the rocks then bear hard back right. Crossing more open terrain the indistinct path reaches a flat meadow with a handful of ancient oaks. Sticking to its lower side you come to a track, which leads down past a **ruin** and a group of tumbledown corrals.

Passing a damaged signboard, 'La Ganadería en la Sierra', you reach **Cortijo de Vichara** where, passing left of a water deposit and the ruined farm, you come to a junction. Turn right and continue past another damaged signboard.

Cutting left for a few metres you reach a spring, La Fuente de los Terneros.

After 800 metres you pass a large **farm**. Continue straight ahead to arrive at a signboard for 'Las Vías Pecuarias' (Drovers' Paths) and a fork. ◄ Keep right along the main track.

Pass just to the right of a farmhouse then, reaching the second of two walnut trees, angle right for 20 metres then go left and continue on along a narrow path. When you reach an olive grove, bearing right to pass above a concrete hut. After 15 metres, angle right away from the olive grove to pick up the continuation of the footpath.

The path runs on through stands of broom and oak. Passing a sign for 'Sierra Horconera' you merge with a track which descends steeply to reach a clearer track. Here turn right. ◄ After climbing, the track levels before it ends in an olive grove by a marker post. Here angle down left then go right in 25 metres along an overgrown path. It soon merges with a track that leads down to the A-7208. Here go right. Or turn left along the A-7208 for 2.5km to **Los Villares** where there's a **campsite**.

Turning left would take you down to Cortijo de los Arraiganes.

LOS VILLARES (ALTITUDE 657M, POPULATION 67)

Accommodation, campsite, restaurant

Los Villares is a hamlet 3km northwest from the point where the GR7 meets with the CO-7208 and could be a midway stopover on Stage 17A. It has no infrastructure apart from the Posada and visitor centre listed below.

Accommodation: Posada La Niña Margarita €, www.casasdelasubbetica.com, tel 638 281 362. S/c houses, two dorms sleeping four and six and camping. (Tent+2ppl €15). With pool and restaurant.

Área Recreativa Los Villares: www.facebook.com/CV.LosVillaresAND, tel 957 000 929. A 60-hectare protected area with waymarked paths and an information centre about the Sierra Morena including a gallery dedicated to the Iberian Lynx.

Priego de Córdoba comes into view.

Follow the A-7208 for 4km. Just beyond the km2 post turn right along a track that descends, crosses a bridge then reaches a junction. Here go left. Passing a ruin, you reach a fork. Keep right and follow the track up and over a ridge. ◄

Descend between stone walls and continue along the track as it angles right then reaches a lane. Turn left, pass **Cortijo de Gámiz** and the lane merges with a wider road. Take the next track to the right, which climbs to Priego de

Córdoba where you should bear right along Avenida de España. After 900 metres go right at a sign for Conjunto Histórico-Artístico and head uphill to the Plaza del Ayuntamiento.

PRIEGO DE CÓRDOBA (ALTITUDE 655M, POPULATION: 22,585)

Accommodation, restaurant/bar/café, food shop, ATM, PO, pharmacy, TO, transport

A highlight of the GR7's northern variant, Priego is one of Córdoba province's most beautiful towns. Its old town centre, Barrio de la Villa, is an enchanting plexus of narrow streets girthed by the walkway of El Aldarve from where there are stunning views to the northeast.

Several grand, civic and religous monuments speak of the town's prosperity during Spain's Golden Age. Don't miss the baroque churches of La Asunción and La Aurora while the neoclassical Fuente del Rey – it has 139 spouts and a statue of Neptune and Amphitrite rising from the water – wouldn't look out of place at Versailles.

Accommodation: Within the pedestrianised Barrio de la Villa, La Posada Real €/€€, www.laposadareal.com, tel 957 541 910. Charming B&B close to great restaurant. Casa Baños de la Villa €€, www.casabanosdelavilla.com, tel 957 547 274. Pristine small hotel with full spa facilities. Also in centre, Hospedería San Francisco €€, www.hospederiasanfrancisco.com, tel 957 701 917. An enchanting place with rooms with views in a converted 16th century convent.

Food: Several options in town centre. Califato, tel 653 970 496, has al fresco dining on the square next to the castle. Asador La Muralla, tel 957 701 856, is also on the square and specialises in grilled meats. La Pianola Casa Pepe, tel 957 700 409, has a shady terrace and cosy inside dining with traditional cuisine.

Transport: Bus to/from Lucena, Cabra, Córdoba, Granada, Alcalá la Real and Montilla. Taxi, tel 651 748 734 or 610 678 641

Town hall: www.priegodecordoba.es, tel 957 708 400

Tourist office: www.turismodepriego.com, tel 957 700 625

STAGE 18A
Priego de Córdoba to Almedinilla

Start	Plaza de la Constitución, Priego de Córdoba
Distance	12.1km
Ascent	310m
Descent	315m
Time	3hr 10min
Highest point	768m
Refreshments	Bar in La Concepción (5.2km)

A stiff climb first thing then on through olive groves to Almedinilla where it's worth taking time out to visit its fascinating museum.

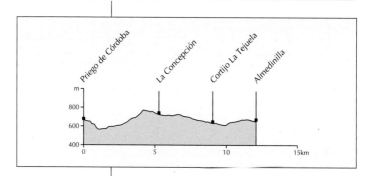

Priego de Córdoba to Almedinilla (12.1km/3hr 10min)
Exit the square along Calle Cava past a bank then bear left along Calle La Ribera following a sign, 'Conjunto Histórico Artístico'. Turn right at the end of the street then, passing a stone cross, bear left down Calle Dean Padilla, which becomes Calle Puerta Granada. Reaching the **A-339**, turn right then take the first left along a narrow road that leads to a fork by a breaker's yard. Keep left and follow a track up to another fork where you should keep right. Following the track steeply upwards, ignoring side turnings, you eventually reach a faded GR7 sign pointing right for La Concepcíon.

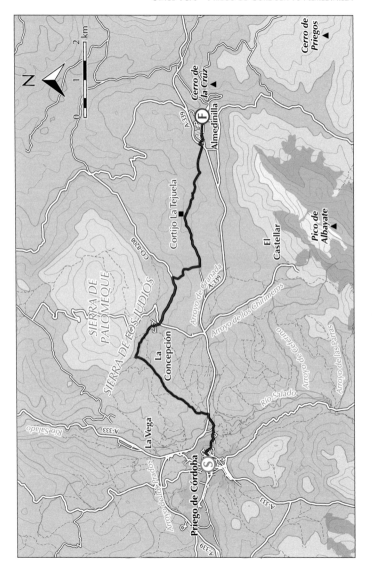

From here follow a stony track down to **La Concepción** where, bearing right and heading downhill, you pass a spring before reaching the La Plaza de la Iglesia. Continue past a bar to a roundabout then turn left following a sign, 'CO-8208 El Poleo/Las Higueras'. At the end of a crash barrier, 100 metres beyond a warning sign for bends, turn right down a track. ◄

Here the GR7 has been diverted due to the planting of a new olive grove.

The track bears left before reaching a junction with a narrow lane. Turn right and pass between houses to reach a second junction with a mirror. Here turn left, signed 'Las Paredejas Bajas'. Reaching **Cortijo La Tejuela** turn right along a dirt track which soon crosses a streambed over a concrete bridge. Follow the track as it climbs, then levels as you pass through more olive groves. It eventually loops right to reach a junction and a Stop sign. Head straight across the A-339 then bear left down into **Almedinilla** past Mesón Los Cabañas to reach Plaza la Era and the old threshing circle in front of Hospedería La Era.

ALMEDINILLA (ALTITUDE 655M, POPULATION 2409)

Accommodation, restaurant/bar/café, food shop, ATM, PO, pharmacy, TO, transport

Almedinilla is a quiet, pretty village at the heart of the olive belt. On the nearby Cerro de la Cruz, excavations revealed an Iberian settlement and necropolis while Roman remains were discovered close by in El Ruedo. The GR7 passes the village's fascinating Historical Museum as you leave Almedinilla (see tourist office website for details).

Accommodation: Hospedería La Era €€, www.hospederialaera.es, tel 645 231 710. Small inn and restaurant showcasing organic produce next to an ancient threshing floor. Casa La Nuez €€, www.casalanuez.com, tel 744 480 776. B&B rooms and yurt with evening meals a 5-minute drive from village. Owners can collect walkers from Almedinilla.

Food: Los Cabañas, tel 957 702 067, and La Bodega, tel 957 703 066, offer traditional Spanish fare.

Transport: Bus to/from Priego and Córdoba. Taxi, tel 669 723 559

Town hall: www.almedinilla.es, tel 957 703 085

Tourist office: www.almedinillaturismo.es, tel 957 703 317

Old olive presses in the Almedinilla museum

STAGE 19A
Almedinilla to Alcalá la Real

Start	Plaza de la Era, Almedinilla
Distance	25km
Ascent	965m
Descent	700m
Time	7hr
Highest point	1104m
Refreshments	In Pilas de la Fuente del Soto (10.4km)
Notes	Add 2.5km/40min if diverting to Pilas de la Fuente del Soto.

A mixture of paths, tracks and quiet lanes lead you on through the sea of olives, passing unusual karst formations close to Pilas de la Fuente del Soto. A challenging stage due to the height gain as the GR7 passes from the province of Córdoba into that of Jaén.

127

TREKKING THE GR7 IN ANDALUCÍA

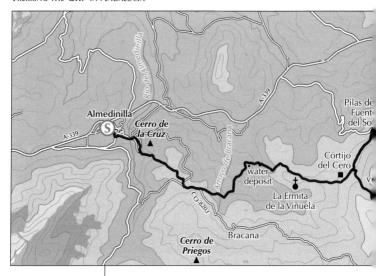

Almedinilla to Alcalá la Real (25km/7hr)

From the square head south then east along the Ronda de Andalucía. Following signs for Museo Histórico cross a bridge over the **Río de Almedinilla** then turn right along a paved road to reach the museum. ◄

The museum has exhibits about olive oil and the Roman and Iberian settlements discovered close to the village.

Here bear left, uphill, following a sign, 'Salto del Caballo'. Reaching a narrow road turn right then after 50 metres left at a wooden railing up a path that loops steeply up then adopts a course parallel to a gully, which is to your right. Where the path becomes less clear maintain your course along the edge of olive groves, passing left of a circular water deposit. The path improves then widens with a wall now running to your left. Reaching the ridgetop it merges with a wider track. ◄

Looking back you can see the archaeological site of Cerro de la Cruz.

Passing a farmhouse the track angles right then after 200 metres reaches a fork where, keeping left, you reach a minor road. Turn right then after 100 metres, at a junction with the **CO-8203**, go left, signed 'Bracana 1.5km'. After 400 metres at a fork bear left passing a 40km limit sign. Continue down a narrow lane, which soon crosses the **Arroyo de Bracana** then arcs left. Reaching the end of a wall beneath a **water deposit** with a tower turn right up a track. At the next fork, where the left turn would lead across a concreted ford, keep straight on.

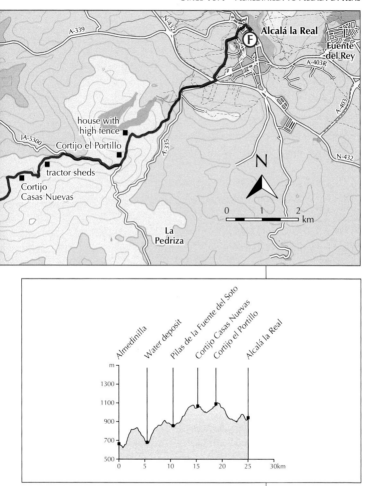

The track arcs left, still climbing. At the next fork, go right. Reaching a junction head straight on, looking for a white arrow on a tree. Reaching the top of a rise you pass left of a chapel, **La Ermita de la Viñuela**, then continue past a damaged GR7 sign, 'Las Pilas 35min'.

The castle and church in Alcalá la Real

Descend through olive groves as the track merges with a road where you should turn left and pass the hilltop farm of **Cortijo del Cerro**. Where the road bears right you reach another road cutting right. GR7 signs point both ways. ◀ Here turn right past a 10T limit sign along a tarmac road which climbs steeply through low-growing oaks with unusual rock formations over to your left. Passing a solitary **villa**, continue along the track that runs past an old *era* (threshing floor) with GR7 paint flashes. Crossing a rise the track runs downhill before adopting a northerly course as views open out to the northeast.

Continuing straight ahead you reach Pilas de la Fuente del Soto though there's little to see. The village has a spring and a bar with erratic opening times.

As the track loops left, turn right along a track signed 'GR7 Alcalá La Real 2hr 10min', passing right of a farm then the partially ruined **Cortijo Casas Nuevas**. Maintaining your course past a pylon you reach a second pylon and a clearer track.

Look for white arrows on this next tricky section.

◀ Angle right for 75 metres then cut left down an indistinct track that drops down then crosses a stream via a small, concrete bridge. Angling left, parallel to the stream, you reach a second point where tractors can cross. Here turn right then after 30 metres left and cross another stream. Bearing left and crossing another streambed you reach a clearer track that leads on past two tractor sheds before descending to the **JA-5300**.

Turn right and follow the road for 1.6 kilometres. Where it arcs right go left along a tarmac track signed 'GR7 Alcalá la Real 1hr 25min'. Passing right of **Cortijo el Portillo**, the track crosses a rise then reaches a fork as Alcalá La Real comes into view.

Keep left and continue climbing to a **house with a high fence**. Here turn right down a stony track. Continue past a farm with a pool following a line of pylons. Reaching a tarmac road follow it right for 20 metres then bear left along a dirt track parallel to the **A-335**, which you meet after 800 metres. Follow the A-335 over a bridge to a roundabout where you should exit left, signed 'Castillo de la Mota', then follow a road up past a cemetery. Passing west of the castle and church, continue past a white cross then descend Calle Real. Reaching house number 32, turn right then take the first left to reach the Plaza del Ayuntamiento.

ALCALÁ LA REAL (ALTITUDE 922M, POPULATION 21,758)

Accommodation, restaurant/bar/café, food shop, ATM, PO, pharmacy, TO, transport

Dominated by the crenellated walls of its Arab fortress or *alcazaba*, Alcalá occupied a key position on the frontier between Muslim and Christian Spain on one of the region's most important trade routes. It was reconquered by an army led by King Alfonso XI of Castille, hence the *Real* (royal) of its name.

Don't miss climbing La Mota and following the walkway that encircles the fortress. It's a particularly memorable excursion at sunset.

Accommodation: Atelier B&B €€, www.atelier88.es, tel 644 771 593. Cosy and friendly British-run B&B at the top of town just beneath La Mota. Hotel Torrepalma €€, www.hoteltorrepalma.com, tel 953 581 800. Comfortable 3-star option in town centre with restaurant. Hospedería Zacatín €/€€, www.hospederiazacatin.com, tel 679 899 739. Simple guest house and restaurant with home cooking. Pensión Río de Oro €, www.hostalriodeoro.com, tel 953 580 337. Inexpensive rooms above a tapas bar.

Food: Rincón de Pepe, tel 953 580 337, for al fresco dining on main square.

Transport: Bus to/from Jaén, Granada, Priego and Córdoba. Taxi, tel 617 265 185

Town hall/tourist info: www.alcalalareal.es, tel 953 580 000

JAÉN PROVINCE

El Torreón de Cuadros (Stage 24A)

If Jaén is Andalucía's least known province this is in large measure due to its inland position, far from the beaches and resorts of the Andalucían costas. Yet the province is home to four natural parks and to the UNESCO World Heritage sites of Úbeda and Baeza, two of Spain's most stunning Renaissance towns.

Entering the province close to Alcalá la Real the route adopts a north-easterly course following the course of the Sierra de Alta Coloma to Frailes. Running on to Carchelejo then Cambil it next passes through the wild landscapes of the Sierra de Mágina Natural Park. Beyond the park you drop back into the

OLIVES, OLIVES AND...MORE OLIVES

Jaén is the largest producer of olive oil in the world, responsible for almost half the oil produced in Spain and one-fifth of world production. It's been estimated that 68 million trees in the province cover an area of more than half a million hectares. The rugged beauty of its sierras, with pine and oak-clad hills, stands in sharp contrast to the olive monoculture even though other crops such as cotton, wheat and almonds are also in evidence together with a growing number of vineyards.

The GR7's northern variant dips in and out of the olive belt as it runs through the Subbaetic and Prebaetic mountains. Several peaks top 2000m, the highest of them being Pico Mágina (2167m) in the Sierra de Mágina Natural Park.

Looking back west on the approach to Torres (Stage 23A)

olive belt before reaching Quesada and beyond the town – a grand finale to the GR7's northern variant – the majestic Cazorla Natural Park with five stages of exhilarating mountain trail.

HIGHLIGHTS OF THE ROUTE IN JAÉN PROVINCE

Some of the many highlights of this section include:
- Beautiful and little-known hilltop towns and villages
- The grandiose mountains and wildlife of the Cazorla Natural Park
- Remote and spectacular trails through the Sierra de Mágina Natural Park

GETTING THERE/BACK

Bus: regular services link the villages on the nothern variant of the GR7, most operated by Alisna Graells (www.alsa.es). See individual village boxes for more information.

Taxi: numbers of local drivers/firms are listed in village information boxes.

GENERAL INFORMATION

Regional tourist office: www.jaenparaisointerior.es, tel 953 248 041.

STAGE 20A
Alcalá la Real to Frailes

Start	Plaza del Ayuntamiento, Alcalá la Real
Distance	10.2km
Ascent	310m
Descent	265m
Time	2hr 30min
Highest point	1012m
Refreshments	None on route

After a steep ascent out of Alcalá you pass through the outskirts of its straggling dormitory village, Santa Ana. The latter part of the walk is more beautiful with soaring vistas across farmland to the distant peaks of Sierra Nevada.

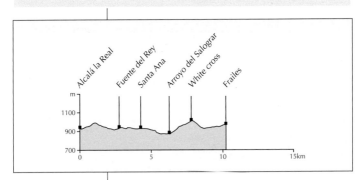

Alcalá la Real to Frailes (10.2km/2hr 30min)

Exit the square at its bottom left corner then turn left. Take the first right at a sign, 'Ruta del Califato', along Calle Utrilla. Follow the street as it climbs and leaves the town past a *mirador* (viewpoint) then maintain your course along a sandy track past a signboard, 'Rutas por la Sierra Sur de Jaén'.

Reaching a fork, bear left and continue parallel to a fence. Descending with a stone wall to your right you reach a crossroads at the edge of **Fuente del Rey**. Here, turn left following a red arrow. The track narrows to become a

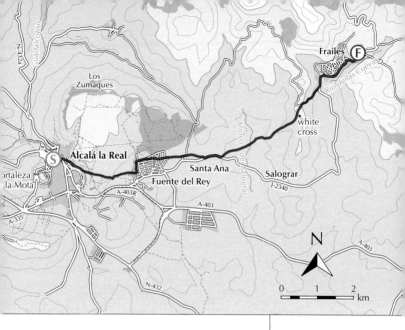

path then climbs to a junction. Carry on straight ahead up Calle Fuente Somera. Reaching the entrance to Club Fuente del Rey, turn right. Continue past fenced villas then head straight on at a crossroads along Camino de la Huerta.

The tarmac road becomes a dirt track that merges with a lane, which you follow for 100 metres. Where the road bears left maintain your course back onto a dirt track. At a fork keep right past a karting track to reach a tarmac lane. Here turn right. Reaching a roundabout just to the east of **Santa Ana**, turn left along the **J-2340**, signed 'Frailes'.

After 450 metres angle left along a dirt track which leads across open fields. Reaching a crossroads, head straight on. Bearing left past a 30km limit sign the track reaches a stone wall. Here turn right, cross the **Arroyo del Salagrar** then continue steeply up the old *cañada* (drovers' track). Passing a shrine with a **white cross** you reach the brow of the hill where **Frailes** comes into view. Descending, the track merges with a tarmac road which leads down to the J-2340. Turn left and follow the road through the village with the Río de las Cuevas to your right to a small square and the Fuente Mecedero (fountain).

Wayside memorial on the approach to Frailes

FRAILES (ALTITUDE 967M, POPULATION 1592)

Accommodation, restaurant/bar/café, food shop, ATM, PO, pharmacy, transport

If Roman and Arabic remains attest to earlier settlement Frailes is first mentioned in the 16th century when *frailes* (friars) from Alcalá la Real built a chapel close to its abundant spring waters. The chapel was later expanded and renamed La Iglesia de Santa Lucía.

Frailes lived a period of prosperity at the end of the 19th century when a small spa resort was established at the edge of the village.

The writer Michael Jacobs (1952–2014) lived here and wrote a book about the village, *The Factory of Light*.

Accommodation: Mesón Hostal La Posá €, tel 953 593 218. Cosy bar/restaurant with no-frills rooms. Hostal Ardales €, www.hostalardales.webcindario.com, tel 600 388 589. Five spick-and-span rooms in newly-built B&B at edge of village.

Food: Annapurna Gastrobar, tel 650 286 126, offers an unusual mix of Indian, Middle Eastern, Mexican and Spanish dishes.

Transport: Bus to/from Alcalá la Real and from there to Granada and Jaén. Taxi, tel 610 966 229

Town hall/tourist info: www.frailes.es, tel 953 593 002

STAGE 21A
Frailes to Carchelejo

Start	Fuente Mecedero beside the J-2340
Distance	35.2km
Ascent	1415m
Descent	1580m
Time	10hr
Highest point	1491m
Refreshments	None on route
Notes	You could wild camp close to Cortijo de Los Prados Bajos.

This is a wild, challenging and beautiful stage of the GR7. After a long ascent past deserted farms beneath the Pico de Paredón you follow the plunging course of the Barranco de Valdearazo before a spectacular path zigzags down and across the river. From there a stiff climb leads to the pass at La Peña del Palo before the descent to Carchelejo.

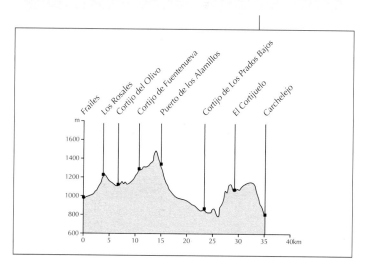

Frailes to Carchelejo (35.2km/10hr)

From Fuente Mecedoro, head east along the J-2340. Reaching a fork 300 metres past the km15 post, turn right at a sign, 'Hoya de Salobral', along a quiet lane with the Río de las Cuevas to your right. Passing a group of houses marked 'El Charro', the road climbs then passes through **Los Rosales**. Here it loops right then climbs to a junction where to the left is a small **shrine to the Virgin**. Here, leave the road at a sign, 'GR7 Carchelejo 8hr 30min'.

Continue down a broad track ignoring a left turn signed 'Cueva la Yedra'. After following the valley floor then bearing east the track climbs towards a ridge topped by wind turbines with the stream of **Puerta Alta** down to your right. Looping right then left it runs past **Cortijo del Olivo** where you should ignore a track left marked 'Cerezo Gordo'. Crossing a rise the track's tarmac surface gives way to dirt before you pass the ruins of **Cortijada de Cañadapadilla** then loop right and cross a streambed. At a 60km limit sign and junction keep left and continue up through stands of oak past a second ruin **Cortijo de Fuentenueva** as you pass beneath the steep face of the **Pico de Paredón** and the line of **turbines**.

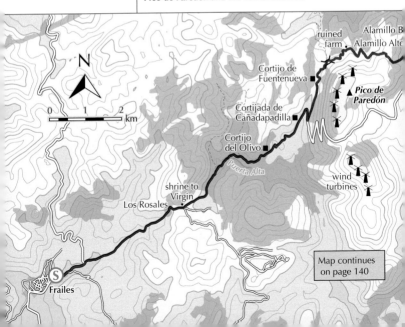

Map continues on page 140

Goats and their guardian on the approach to Cortijo Alamillo Alto

Reaching a **pass** (1307m) and a three-way spilt, leave the main track by angling right and climbing, still parallel to the flank of the Pico de Paredón. Passing through a wire gate you come to a **ruined farm** where you should go through a second gate. Angling left the track passes a spring with a bath-tub trough then angles back right.

Descending you lose sight of the turbines as you reach a point where the track arcs back left. Careful! Here maintain your course up an indistinct path for 100 metres to a GR7 marker post then bear left following faded GR paint flashes. The path zigzags up to a solitary oak with GR markings. Bear right and continue to the top of the rise (1491m) and a fence. Go through a wire gate then turn down right on a southeasterly course along a track, which descends through oaks to a gate made of a bed base.

50 metres beyond the gate, leave the track to its left down a narrow path that leads steeply down through the trees with a *barranco* (gorge) to your left before running towards a fence and track at **Puerto de los Alamillos** (1311m). Around 20 metres before the fence, go left to pick up a path that leads down to merge with the track leading up to the pass on a hairpin.

Bear left past the farms of **Alamillo Alto** then **Alamillo Bajo** and continue down the track along the spectacular

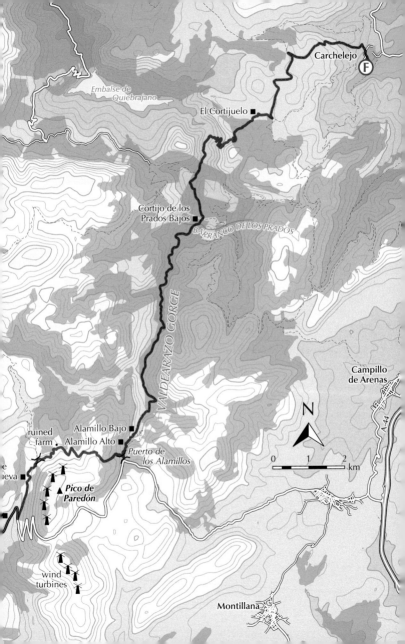

Barranco de Valdearazo. After 8km you'll reach a junction by a farm with solar pannels, **Cortijo de los Prados Bajos**. Here go straight ahead then after 30 metres cross a bridge over the **Barranco de los Prados**. Angle back left to rejoin the course of the Valdearazo Gorge.

At the next fork keep left and cross the river via a concrete bridge. Around 750 metres beyond the stream the track loops left. Here continue straight ahead past a sign, 'Refugio de Pesca', along a narrow path which, roped in parts, drops down to the Valdearazo which it crosses via a footbridge then climbs steeply in a series of loops. ▶

As you climb, the Embalse de Quiebrajano comes into view to the northwest.

Reaching the top of the rise (1141m), continue straight ahead following a sign, 'GR7 Carchelejo'. The path descends to flatter land and the farm of **El Cortijuelo**. Pass through a gate between corrugated pannels and bear right along a track to a junction with a tarmac road. Here, turn left at a sign, 'Carchelejo 1hr 30min'. Continue for 2.3 kilometres, passing a ruined farm, then leave the road to the right along a dirt track. Narrowing, the track descends through olive groves. Where it levels turn right at a marker post down a rocky path to reach the west side of **Carchelejo**. Angle right and continue down to the Plaza de la Constitucíon.

CARCHELEJO (ALTITUDE 804M, POPULATION 1441)

Accommodation, restaurant/bar/café, food shop, ATM, PO, pharmacy, transport

Carchelejo and the neighbouring village Cárchel together form the municipality of Cárcheles. The mainstay of the local economy is olive growing with groves stretching away from the village in all directions. Carchelejo is also known for its charcuterie: you pass the main factory as you leave the village on the GR7.

Accommodation: Mezquita de Mágina Rural Apartments €/€€, www.apartamentosmezquitademagina.wordpress.com, tel 679 228 003. S/c houses and apartments around a cobbled courtyard. Hotel-Restaurante Oasis €€, www.restaurantehoteleloasis.es, tel 953 302 083. The nearest hotel (6km), close to where the GR7 passes beneath the A-44. There are other s/c houses and apartments in the village. See: www.carcheles.es/turismo/casas-rurales.html.

Food: Mesón Zafra Manolo, tel 636 860 147 offers traditional tapas and meals.

Transport: Bus to/from Granada and Jaén. Taxi in Campillos de Arena (15km), tel 600 411 025

Town hall/tourist info: www.carcheles.es, tel 953 302 003

STAGE 22A
Carchelejo to Cambil

Start	Plaza de la Constitución, Carchelejo
Distance	13km
Ascent	520m
Descent	565m
Time	3hr 45min
Highest point	833m
Refreshments	None on route

A mixture of track and footpath leads through rocky, mineral-rich terrain, following the courses of the Barranco de la Parrilla and the Río de Cambil via olive groves and irrigated orchards.

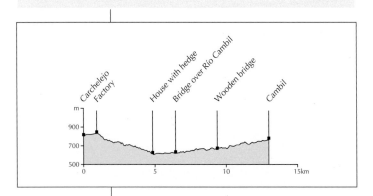

Carchelejo to Cambil (13km/3hr 45min)
Exit the square along Calle del Rosario then turn right along Calle San Marcos. Continue past the Guardia Civil HQ to the **JV-2227**. Turn left along the road past a **charcuterie factory** then turn right along a concrete track that descends to the valley floor of the **Barranco de la Parrilla**. The track runs along the southern side of the valley. ◄ Reaching a point where the track is closed by a chain, cut right up a path

To the north a solar farm is visible.

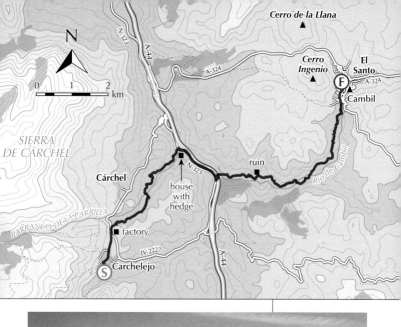

Looking northwest towards Cárchel

marked by a GR7 post. **Cárchel** comes into sight through a gap in the mountains to the northwest.

Contour round the valley side as the path crosses a streambed then reaches a fork. Take the lower, left branch.

The path descends, skirts the top of an olive grove then, at a marker post, bears left and descends to a track. Follow the track down then cross the Parrilla stream via a bridge.

At a fork, follow a sign, 'GR7 Cambil 2hr 25min', down right along a rougher track. Ignore two tracks cutting in on the right, and stick to the main track which runs closer to the river before petering out in an olive grove. Continue parallel to the river for 100 metres to pick up the track again which, climbing, becomes clearer. At the next fork, keep right then descend back towards the river passing a house with solar pannels then a **hedged house** with a pool to reach the **N-323**.

Turn right along the road, parallel to the **A-44** motorway. Passing the km61 post, just before an 80km limit sign, go left along a track that passes beneath the A-44 then bears left. Take the next turn right and cross a bridge over the **Río de Cambil**. Passing a ruin the track climbs to a fork by a second ruin. Keep right and continue on through olive groves, now close to the river, passing a chain blocking vehicule access.

The track runs above two riverside houses before climbing away from the valley floor. ◀ Crossing a bridge then passing through a breach in the hillside you reach a **ruin**. 10 metres beyond the ruin, turn left up an indistinct path to reach a marker post. Here turn right and make your way round the side of the valley. There's no obvious path but by sticking to the top of the olive groves and crossing two small gullies you'll soon pass right of a ruined farm.

> You now pass beneath a hillside with fantastically banded lodes of ochre and sienna.

Around 50 metres beyond the ruin, reaching a stand of poplars, bear slightly left to reach a track which climbs away from the river.

Passing beneath another ruin you reach a junction with a clearer track. Turn right, downhill, passing another ruin beside a large umbrella pine. Passing along the top of a field following a line of water pipes you reach the river. ◀ Continue along a water channel which you shortly cross via a wooden bridge. Sticking close to the river you reach a footbridge where you can cross to the opposite bank.

> The old bridge has been washed away.

From here follow a track up to a junction with a broader track. Turn left and continue along the west side of the valley passing left of a farm. Crossing a tributary of the Cambil, the track descends and crosses to the river's northwest bank. From here a broad track climbs past several smallholdings to **Cambil**. Continue past a builder's yard to reach the Plaza de la Constitución.

Mineral landscape above the Cambil river

CAMBIL (ALTITUDE 760M, POPULATION 2739)

Accommodation, restaurant/bar/café, food shop, ATM, PO, pharmacy, TO, transport

At the southwestern border of the Sierra de Mágina Natural Park, Cambil's streets of whitewashed houses wrap sinuously round two rocky outcrops, one topped by the ruins of a Moorish tower. Its most notable buildings are the 16th century Iglesia de Nuestra Señora de la Encarnación and the Antiguo Hospital, one of the province's finest examples of baroque architecture.

Accommodation: Hostal/Restaurante Los Castillos de Cambil €/€€, tel 649 144 066. Comfortable bedrooms above a popular restaurant. Hostal Alcaidia de Mágina €/€€, www.laalcaidia.es, 953 300 327. Modern hotel and restaurant beside the A-324. Houses and apartments can be be rented in the village: see listings on town hall website.

Food: Both hotel listings have good food. In the village, a couple of bars serve tapas.

Transport: Bus to/from Jaén. Taxi: in Campillos de Arenas (15km), tel 600 411 025

Town hall/tourist info: www.cambil-arbuniel.es, tel 953 300 427

STAGE 23A
Cambil to Torres

Start	Plaza de la Constitución, Cambil
Distance	27.7km
Ascent	1105m
Descent	980m
Time	8hr 30min
Highest point	Puerto de la Mata, 1659m
Refreshments	None on route

This stage is a wonderful if challenging day of track walking through the Sierra de Mágina past the ruins of the castle of Mata Bejíd before crossing the high pass of Puerto de la Mata (1659m).

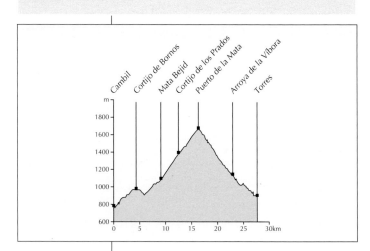

Cambil to Torres (27.7km/8hr 30min)
Exit the square past the village's ancient elm tree. Bear left at a roundabout then reaching the top of the village and the **A-324** go left and continue up a road signed 'Bornos/Bercho/

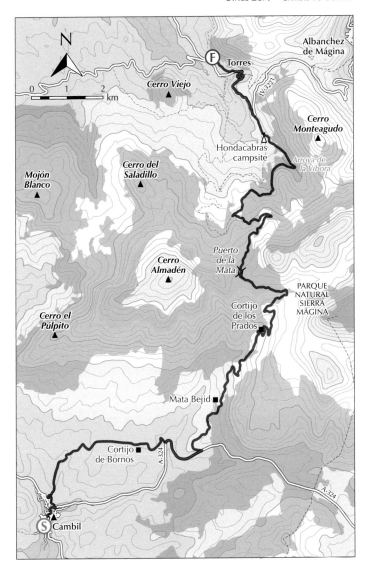

Nacimiento'. At the first fork keep left passing a sign, 'GR7 Torres 6hr 20min'.

The road climbs steeply. There are great views back to Cambil. A little over 1 kilometre from the village keep right at a fork, sticking to the main track. The track winds its way through rocky terrain. At the next fork, signed 'N-324 Almadén', keep right. The track adopts an easterly course through olive groves past a number of farm buildings. ◄

To the south, on clear days, the Sierra Nevada is visible.

When you reach an intersection of five tracks, carry on straight ahead following a sign, 'N-323(sic) Cambil'. The track runs past the fenced enclosure of **Cortijo de Bornos** before descending to the A-324. Here go left then after 1.4 kilometre turn left up a track signed 'Sendero Puerto de la Mata'. You now enter the **Parque Natural Sierra Mágina**.

PARQUE NATURAL SIERRA MÁGINA

Rising proud above the surrounding olive belt to more than 2000m, the Sierra de Mágina marks a natural boundary between the provinces of Granada and Jaén and in former times between Moorish and Christian Spain. Numerous medieval castles and watchtowers within the park's 19,900 hectares testify to its strategic importance in the medieval period.

The sierra's lower reaches are covered with pine forest and indigenous woodland of holm, gall oak and aceraceae interspersed with hawthorn, juniper, savin and turpentine while the more tortured terrain of its higher slopes is virtually bare of vegetation.

The inland position of the Sierra de Mágina means that it sees harsher winters and heavier snowfall than other parts of Andalucía, as it's subject to colder, continental weather systems that push in from the north. Warmer, moist fronts rolling in from the Atlantic are forced rapidly upwards within just a few kilometres by the barrier of its mountains giving rise to high precipitation along the park's western belt. The eastern reaches of the park receive far less rain and are characterised by semi-arid landscapes with much sparser vegetation. These differing climate zones have fostered myriad plant life with an estimated 1250 species found within the park.

The park is home to 18 species of raptor, which include peregrine falcons, griffon vultures, Bonelli's and golden eagles while imperial eagles have recently been reintroduced. Mammals present include foxes, badgers and deer with ibex and wild boar commonly sighted.

Further information: Centro de Visitantes Parque de Sierra de Mágina/ Mata-Bejid, Ctra. A-324 Cambil-Huelma km 15.5, www.facebook.com/ CV.MataBejidAND/, tel 682 692 652 – exhibitions about the park's geology, flora and fauna with a picnic area and a small network of waymarked paths.

Centro de Visitantes Parque Natural Sierra Mágina, tel 953 779 718 – housed within the castle of Jódar with exhibitions about the animals and plants found in the park as well as the history of Jódar.

Climb for 2 kilometres through olives then *dehesa* (woodland) to pass the ruined farm/fortress of **Mata Bejíd**. ▶

In front of the ruin is a beautiful, lofty era.

Climb through oak forest on the main track for 2.9 kilometres to reach the ruined farm of **Cortijo de los Prados**. ▶ At a junction 2.5 kilometres beyond Cortijo Los Prados, turn left following another sign, 'Sendero Puerto de la Mata'. The track continues climbing through stands of deciduous and evergreen oaks. The Sierra Nevada, along with the antennae-topped peak of the **Cerro Almadén**, are once more visible.

Divert left for 100 metres at a sign, 'Fuente', to reach a spring, though it's sometimes dry.

Passing a barrier you reach the pass of **Puerto de la Mata** (1659m). From here you descend through pine forest as **Torres** comes into view far below. When you reach a junction after 3.5 kilometres, keep right and follow the green-and-white way-marking. Crossing **Arroyo de la Víbora** the track arcs left, passes the **camping area of Hondacabras** (open only in summer) before reaching the **JV-3221**. Continue straight ahead. When you reach the village bear right at a roundabout, signed Centro Urbano, to reach the Plaza del Ayuntamiento.

Torres seen at sunset

TORRES (ALTITUDE 886M, POPULATION 1434)

Accommodation, campsite, restaurant/bar/café, food shop, ATM, PO, pharmacy, transport

Fanning out beneath the Cerro de la Vieja's southern slopes, close to the fertile banks of the river Torres and numerous springs, Torres' origins are inextricably linked to its abundant waters. While olive growing is the bedrock of the local economy there are also extensive cherry orchards close to the village as well as irrigated vegetable plots along the banks of its river. The remains of a castle built by knights of the Calatrava order are visible at the top of the village.

Accommodation: Casa Rural Arenaria €€, tel 678 468 588. Friendly hotel with excellent restaurant in village centre. Hotel Rural Puerto Mágina €€, www. puertomagina.com, tel 953 363 192. On a hillside 3km from Torres with restaurant, gardens and pleasant rooms.

Food: Arenaria is the number one choice.

Transport: Bus to/from Jaén and Mancha Real. Taxi, tel 637 821 498

Town hall: www.aytorres.es, tel 953 363 011

Tourist office: www.torresturismo.es, tel 953 363 011

STAGE 24A
Torres to Bedmar

Start	Plaza del Ayuntamiento, Torres
Distance	16.4km
Ascent	660m
Descent	900m
Time	4hr 45min
Highest point	1164m
Refreshments	In Albanchez

After a steep ascent to a high pass (1250m) a narrow path leads down to Albanchez de Mágina (also known as Albanchez de Úbeda), a quintessentially andaluz village beneath a castle-topped crag. From here follow quiet lanes and tracks round the lower reaches of the Sierra Mágina passing close to the Cuadros watchtower and sanctuary.

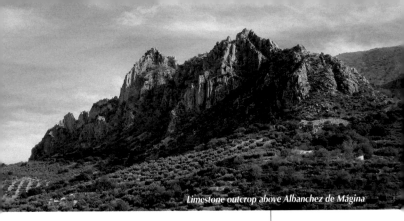
Limestone outcrop above Albanchez de Mágina

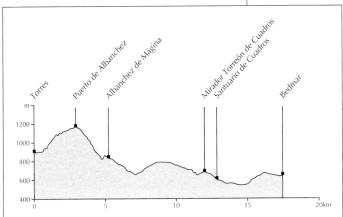

Torres to Albanchez de Mágina (5.4km/1hr 30min)

From the square, exit the village the way you entered. Reaching a roundabout maintain your course up the **JV-3221**. Cross a bridge then turn left up a dirt track signed 'Albanchez de Úbeda 1hr 20min'. Around 150 metres from the road, just past a manhole, cut left up a narrow path. At the next divide, keep right. The path merges with a concrete track then reaches a junction by a metal gate. Here, go left.

Pass to the right of a farm, and follow the track as it narrows to become a path that climbs steeply to a cherry grove. Here turn right along a track which, angling left, runs

151

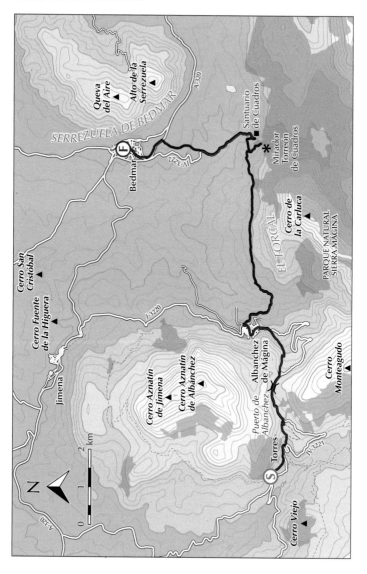

up to the JV-3221. Turn left and follow the road over the **Puerto de Albanchez** (marked 1250m but actually about 90m less). Around 10 metres before the km5 post turn left down a narrow path. ▶

Crossing a water channel the path zigzags steeply down, loose underfoot, to a tarmac road. Turn left then, reaching the JV-3221, left again. Continue past a *mirador* (viewpoint) then branch left at a sign, 'Centro Urbano', to reach the village's main square, La Plaza de la Constitución.

Out east the high ridgeline of the Cazorla Park is visible as well as Bedmar to the northeast.

ALBANCHEZ DE MÁGINA (ALTITUDE 830M, POPULATION 1027)

Accommodation, campsite, restaurant/bar/café, food shop, ATM, PO, pharmacy, tourist info, transport

One of the most spectacularly situated village's on the GR7 trail, Albanchez de Mágina's cluster of narrow, whitewashed streets embrace a rocky pinnacle at the base of the Aznaitín, topped by a crennelated watchtower. Don't miss climbing the 360 steps up to the tower, built by Christian settlers soon after the Reconquest, for one of the most memorable views in the province.

Accommodation: Lunares y Salinera €, www.casalunaresysalinera.com, tel 687 165 648. S/c house with a terrace with great views. Vivienda Rural La Seda €€, tel 671 184 894. Beautiful s/c house at bottom of village sleeping 6, minimum stay 2 nights. Hostal Casería San José de Hútar €€, tel 953 357 474 or 630 683 650. Seven beautiful rooms with views and a pool as well as an excellent restaurant 4km from Albanchez beside the road to Jimena. Camping El Cantonet, www.campingelcantonet.es, tel 608 670 406. 3km from Albanchez next to road to Jimena, pool, restaurant and two s/c apartments (Tent+2 ppl, €12).

Food: Atocha 3.0, tel 628 123 680, in village centre for tapas-style dining.

Transport: Bus to/from Jaén and Úbeda. Taxi in Jimena (8km), tel 689 817 097 or in Bedmar (8km), tel 648 100 911

Town hall: www.albanchezdemagina.es, tel 953 358 339

Albanchez de Mágina to Bedmar (11km/3h 15min)
Exit the square along Calle San Marcos. Reaching a junction turn left then at a Stop sign go right, signed 'Vivienda Rural'. Passing a spring, Fuente de la Seda, the road descends through groves of cherry, olive and almond with the rocky crags of **El Torcal** up ahead of you.

As the track levels, just past a small white building, turn right up a concrete track then bear sharply left after 25

The tower is a 550 metre diversion from this point; it's a great picnic spot.

Turning right for 100 metres leads to the Santuario de Cuadros and Hostal Rural de Cuadros, an enchanting place to overnight.

metres at a sign, 'GR7 Bedmar', and continue along a narrow lane through olive groves. Tarmac gives way to dirt surface: ignore smaller tracks cutting into the groves to your left and right. As you reach a crossroads by an old stone wall, head straight on. Olives give way to pines as the track runs towards the peaks of the **Serrezuela de Bedmar** and, further east, Golondrina. Descending steeply you reach a sign pointing right for **Mirador Torreón de Cuadros**. ◄

If not visiting the tower, carry on straight ahead. The track descends then arcs right to a car park. ◄

At the car park, turn left down the **JV-3222**. Continue past several houses then 300 metres past the km2 post, go right up a steep track. Reaching a fork keep right and climb past a water deposit to a picnic area. Head straight ahead then, reaching the A-320, turn left. Passing a sign, 'Bedmar', angle right and continue past Hotel El Paraiso de Mágina to the main square of **Bedmar**, La Plaza de la Constitución.

BEDMAR (ALTITUDE 645M, POPULATION 2700)

Accommodation, restaurant/bar/café, food shop, ATM, PO, pharmacy, tourist info, transport

Bedmar and its ruined castle

Dominated by the extensive ruins of the Arab hilltop fortress of Al-Manzar and the 15th century Christian castle Castillo Nuevo, Bedmar's narrow streets hug the eastern flank of the Serrezuela de Bedmar. Its beautiful 16th century Iglesia de la Asunción, with an unusual octagonal belfry built of wafer-brick, is worth a visit. The town is officially known as Bedmar Garcíez since being linked with its neighbouring village although for locals it remains just plain 'Bedmar'.

Accommodation: Hostal Rural de Cuadros €, www.hostalruraldecuadros.com, tel 685 259 041. Close to GR7 as you arrive in Bedmar, an exceptionally beautiful mountain retreat. El Paraíso de Magína €€, www.elparaisodemagina.com, tel 953 760 010. Brash, roadside hotel/restaurant at west side of village. There are also s/c village houses to let close to the village: El Cercadillo €€/€€€, www.cortijoelcercadillo.com, tel 615 547 361. S/c houses with pool next to GR7 just before it reaches the JV-3332. Casas Rural Río Cuadros €€, www.riocuadros.com, tel 616 966 224. Two casas rurales passed on the approach to Bedmar with third house in village.

Food: Bar Casa Seba, tel 645 877 053, next to the Plaza de España has great tapas and *raciónes*.

Transport: Bus to/from Jaén and Úbeda. Taxi, tel 648 100 911

Town hall: www.bedmargarciez.es, tel 953 760 002+

STAGE 25A
Bedmar to Jódar

Start	Plaza de la Constitución, Bedmar
Distance	9.2km
Ascent	550m
Descent	545m
Time	2hr 50min
Highest point	1127m
Refreshments	None on route

After a steep ascent from Bedmar a looping farm track leads down to Jódar through groves of olive and almonds.

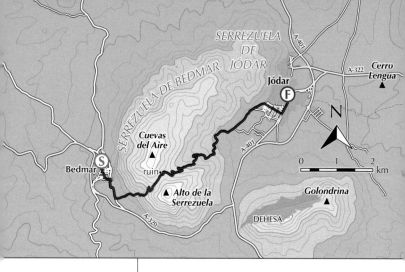

Bedmar to Jódar (9.2km/2hr 50min)

Leave the square along Calle Mercado then bear left up Calle Rambla. After the street narrows bear right along Calle Virgen de la Cabeza. Pass left of a group of warehouses following a row of street lamps. ◀ Reaching faint GR7 flashes on the kerb go left up a dirt track towards a gap in the **Serrezuela de Bedmar**, passing left of an almond grove. As the grove ends the track narrows and a path leads you close to the southern face of the gulch, passing right of two wrecked cars as you ascend. The path is marked with more VP posts. Angling right at a marker post, 'Jódar, 1hr 15min', the path loops on up then merges with a track which leads over the pass, passing right of a **ruin**.

You're on a vía pecuaria *(drovers' track) with green posts marked VP.*

Follow the track down to the outskirts of Jódar, backed by the Cerro Hernando. Passing a number of fenced smallholdings you reach a divide by the village water deposit. Keep left then at the next fork right and descend to the bottom of Calle Granada to traffic lights. Turning left you reach the Paseo Primero de Mayo and a bandstand.

Descending towards Jódar and Cerro Hernando

JÓDAR (ALTITUDE 649M, POPULATION 11,805)

Accommodation, restaurant/bar/café, food shop, ATM, PO, pharmacy, tourist info, transport

Backed by the Cerro de San Cristóbal and looking out across the valley of the Río Jandulilla, Jódar's narrow streets encircle a twin-towered castle which is now home to the Sierra de Mágina visitor centre. In Moorish times it was capital of a *cora* (administrative district) that included present day Jaén.

Once known for its esparto-woven products, olive production is now the mainstay of its economy.

Accommodation: Hotel Ciudad de Jódar €€, www.hotelciudaddejodar.com, tel 953 785 051. Modern hotel at edge of village with restaurant, pool and nicely appointed bedrooms (currently the only place to stay in Jódar).

Food: Restaurante Los Molinos, tel 953 785 914, is a busy village-centre restaurant with traditional Spanish cuisine.

Transport: Bus to/from Jaén and Úbeda. Taxi, tel 670 883 578

Town hall: www.jodar.es, tel 953 785 086

Tourist office: www.saudar.com, tel 953 78 40 12. Centro de Visitantes Parque Natural Sierra Mágina, tel 953 779 718. In the castle of Jódar with exhibitions about the animal and plantlife of the park.

STAGE 26A
Jódar to Quesada

Start	Bandstand on Paseo Primero de Mayo, Jódar
Distance	35.3km
Ascent	605m
Descent	580m
Time	9hr 45min
Highest point	677m
Refreshments	None on route

This stage starts with an initial long section of track then road walking leading through olive groves to the sleepy village of Hornos de Peal. The second half of the walk has more of interest as you pass beneath the Arab castle of Toya before a stiff climb leads you up to Quesada.

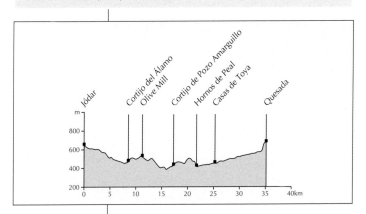

Jódar to Quesada (35.3km/9hr 45min)
From the bandstand in Jódar at the end of the Paseo Primero de Mayo drop down Calle Luis Carvajal to the village Centro de Salud. Here go right along Calle Sanabria to a roundabout on the **A-401**. Turn left then after 100 metres bear right at a sign, 'Camino Cortijo de Palomares', down a tarmac road. Reaching a crosssroads keep straight ahead along a dirt

track. Continue for 600 metres then, at the next fork and a fallen sign for 'GR7 Quesada 7hr 10min', branch left. Passing through a breach in the hillside spanned by a metal pipe you reach the **A-322** where you should turn right. ▸

The first ranges of the Cazorla mountains come into view out east.

Cross the Río Jandulilla and the road leads past **Cortijo del Álamo**. Reaching the km10 post, you'll cross a **railway track** then pass an **olive mill**, Almazara San José. At the next junction turn right at a sign, 'Larva 14km'. As you cross a rise the road leads down to flatter terrain as you cross the valley of the Río Guadiana Menor.

At the next junction continue along the A-322, signed 'Huesa and Quesada'. The road shortly crosses a bridge over the **Guadiana Menor**. Immediately beyond the bridge cut left along a track passing left of the hill of **Alto de la Colmena** then at the next junction turn left. The track bears round to the right and passes left of the **Cortijo de Pozo Armarguillo**. Climb towards **Cortijo de Mansuti**, which straddles a rise, to reach a fork. Branch left after 50 metres to pass right of a concrete hut marked with GR paint flashes. Crossing a rise Quesada comes into view out east.

Reaching the next fork, signed 'Quesada', go right and continue down into **Hornos de Peal**. Passing right of the church, now 21.7km from Jódar, you descend to a broad track. Turn right then pass beneath a row of palm trees to reach a fork. Keep right, heading uphill. Crossing a rise you come to another fork where you should continue straight ahead. The ruined **Castillo de Toya** comes into sight up ahead. Reaching a fork take the higher, right option which runs above the track you've just left before looping right then after 200 metres back left. At the next fork, keep left. ▸

The right fork leads up to the ruined castle, which is worth a 500m up/500m down diversion.

The track runs through a group of pines before passing right of the **Ermita de San Marcos**. Bear left and you'll reach the JA-7106 and a spring. Turn right and continue through the linear hamlet of **Casas de Toya**. At the end of the hamlet, just past a *consultorio* (doctor's surgery) turn left and cross a bridge over the River Toya then climb a farm track. Bearing right it merges with another track before reaching a fork. Keep right then cross a streambed via a concreted **ford**.

La Ermita de San Marcos

Continue along the track, roughly parallel to the river, now marked Río de Quesada on the IGN map. The track runs past numerous farms, many in ruins. Passing warehouses, now 6.8km from the ford, you reach the A-315. Cross the road and continue along a track. ◄ Around 450 metres after crossing a bridge over the Río de Quesada, you'll reach a fork. Keep right and at the next junction, right again. Reaching the first houses of **Quesada**, bear left and continue into the village centre to the La Plaza de la Constitución.

Quesada is visible up ahead, topped by its church tower.

QUESADA (ALTITUDE 677M, POPULATION 5303)

Accommodation, restaurant/bar/café, food shop, ATM, PO, pharmacy, tourist info, transport

With the distant peaks of the Sierras de Cazorla, Segura and Las Villas Natural Park as backdrop, Quesada straddles a low ridge from where there are views across the olive groves that stretch away to all points of the compass. Roman, Visisgothic and Arab artefacts and shards discovered on the site of the present village attest to the presence of its earlier inhabitants. 10km from the village, within the Cueva del Agua, a high waterfall is accessed via a spectacular walkway, the municiplality's most famous landmark.

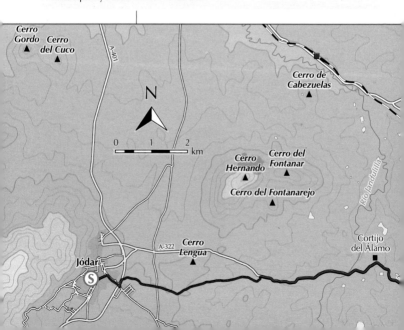

Accommodation: Hotel Sierra de Quesada €€, tel 615 623 909. Small twins and doubles above a restaurant with views. Sierraguadalquivir, www. sierraguadalquivir.com/casas.htm, tel 610 070 689. S/c houses and apartments in the village centre. Hotel Complejo Rural Cortijo El Marqués €€, www. jaenrural.com, tel 619 702 185. Beside the GR7 on the way to Cazorla shortly before the JV-7107.

Food: El Curioso, tel 657 504 775, has an attractive dining room and great food.

Transport: Bus to/from Cazorla, Úbeda and Baza. Taxi, tel 635 204 888

Town hall: www.quesada.es, tel 953 733 025

SIERRAS DE CAZORLA, SEGURA Y LAS VILLAS NATURAL PARK

The Parque Natural de las Sierras de Cazorla, Segura y Las Villas lies at the eastern edge of the province of Jaén. You enter the park midway between Quesada and Cazorla. This is Spain's largest protected area and covers 214,000 hectares of remarkably diverse terrain. There are vast extensions of pine forest, broad river valleys including that of the Río Guadalquivir, deep canyons, spectacular water-falls and rugged dolomitic peaks rising to over 2000m.

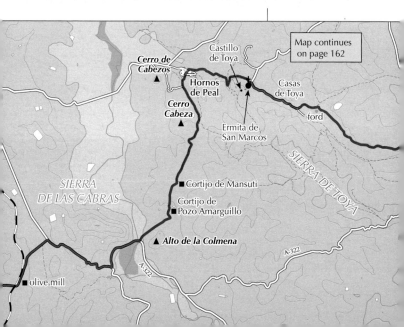

Map continues on page 162

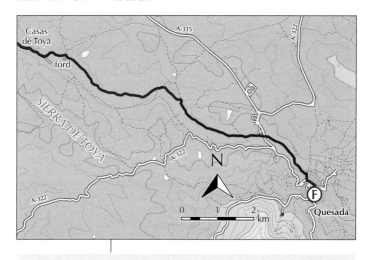

The abundance of game on the forested hillsides made the region a popular place to hunt for many centuries but by the 1950s the pickings were becoming so scarce the area was declared a national hunting reserve. The idea was simple: to increase the number of moving targets. Red deer and wild boar were reintroduced, mouflon brought from France and fallow deer from the mountains of Segovia. Numbers were monitored, hunting controlled and it soon paid rich dividends. The population of Spanish ibex (*Capra hispánica*) alone rose tenfold in two decades and Cazorla was back on the map as a place to pot game.

The subsequent declaration of the reserve as a natural park in 1986, after becoming a UNESCO biosphere three years earlier, together with much tighter controls on hunting helped make the region one of the best in Spain for the observation of wild animals. Add to this an impressive roll call of birds of prey, which includes several species of eagle, griffon and Egyptian vultures, goshawks and hobbies, along with the region's exceptional plant life – there are more than 2000 species with two dozen being endemic – and you begin to get the measure of the park's biodiversity.

Tourist information: www.cazorla.es, tel 953 710 102, as well as via www.sierrasdecazorlaseguraylasvillas.es.

There's a Punto de Información about the natural park beside the Plaza de Santa María within the ruined church, tel 953 710 102.

The Torre del Vinagre Visitor's Centre at the centre of the park has extensive information, tel 953 713 017. It's close to the end of Stage 29A.

STAGE 27A
Quesada to Cazorla

Start	Plaza de la Constitución, Quesada
Distance	18.1km
Ascent	845m
Descent	720m
Time	5hr 30min
Highest point	1198m
Refreshments	None on route

A long climb leads steeply up from Quesada to the western reaches of the Cazorla Natural Park. The latter part of the stage is far easier as you descend on mountain paths past the monastery of Montesión to Cazorla, one of Andalucía's most beautiful mountain villages.

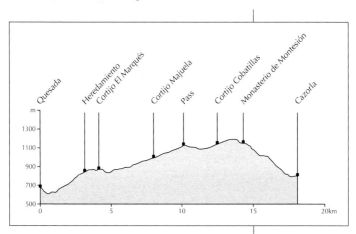

Quesada to Cazorla (18.1km/4hr 50min)
Exit the square passing left of a bank down La Cuesta de San Juan. Take the first right then descend Calle Los Espinillos to a sign, 'GR7 Cazorla 4hr 25min'. Here go right then zigzag down and cross the Río de Quesada. Following a concrete road, you reach a three-way split. Take the lower, left fork. At

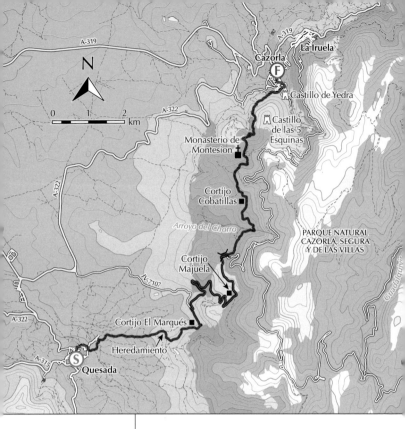

The landscape becomes wilder and more grandiose as you pass jagged outcrops of limestone.

the next divide keep left again along a tarmac road that soon adopts an easterly course, passing several houses. Reaching a fork by two cypress trees keep right on the main track, El Camino de la Torrecilla. Looping right you pass the houses of **Heredamiento** before the track arcs back left. Reaching a junction by a house with a black metal gate keep left and follow the track steeply on up. ◄

At the next fork above **Cortijo El Marqués** bear left. After looping hard left the track levels then climbs past a house to meet the **JV-7107**. Turn right, signed 'Cazorla 3hr 30min', and follow the looping road on up. After 2.4 kilometres you pass a house marked Casa María then, just beyond it, **Cortijo Majuela**.

The Monasterio de Montesión seen on the approach to Cazorla

Reaching the top of the pass and a signboard for 'Parque Natural Sierras de Cazorla, Segura y de las Villas', leave the JV-7107 to its left along a forestry track, ignoring a smaller track off left.

Bearing right the track descends through pine forest. Walk for 700 metres to come to a fork where a track cuts steeply down left. Here, keep right. In 600 metres the track crosses the **Arroyo del Chorro** where it arcs left before adopting a northerly course. Crossing more open terrain you pass high above **Cortijo Cobatillas**. At the next fork, some 800 metres past the farm and just past a huge cairn, turn right. You'll pass a GR7 post in 20 metres then come to a junction with a clearer track. Turn left following a sign, 'Cazorla 3.4km'. ▶

The monastery of Montesión comes into view.

Descending you pass two concrete huts, one white, the other yellow. Continue walking for 100 metres then branch left left and descend past the **Monasterio de Montesión** to rejoin the track. Here turn left and continue your descent, passing left of the hilltop **Castillo de 5 Esquinas**. Approaching Cazorla, you come to a junction. Turn right and continue down to the Plaza de Santa María. Exit the square past a traffic light then continue up to the Plaza de la Corredera, the neural centre of **Cazorla**.

CAZORLA (ALTITUDE 800M, POPULATION 7574)

Accommodation, restaurant/bar/café, food shop, ATM, PO, pharmacy, tourist info, transport

Cazorla and the Castillo de la Yedra

Gateway to the Cazorla Natural Park, at the point where Jaén's vast olive belt meets with the Baetic mountains, Cazorla numbers among Andalucía's most beautiful mountain towns. Its narrow streets converge on three squares: La Plaza de la Constitución, La Plaza de la Corredera – the neural heart of the town – and La Plaza de Santa María, backed by a ruined cathedral and the lofty Castillo de la Yedra. The village lies at 800m and due to its high, inland position is subject to colder winters than most parts of Andalucía and will often see heavy snowfall in winter.

Accommodation: Molino La Farraga €€, www.molinolafarraga.com, tel 653 492 198. Delightful B&B in millhouse with pool and botanical garden, five-minute walk from the Plaza de Santa María. Hotel Guadalquivir €€, www.hguadalquivir.com, tel 953 721 248. Just beneath the main square in a pedestrian street, quiet and welcoming. Cuidad de Cazorla €/€€, www.hotelciudaddecazorla.com, tel 953 825 272. Comfy 3-star option with cafeteria on main square. Albergue Inturjoven €, www.inturjoven.com, tel 600 163 715. A top notch youth hostel above the main square.

Food: Bistro Casa Alfonso, tel 953 721 463; Leandro, tel 953 720 632; and Lusco Taberna, tel 953 721 350, all offer top-notch dining. There are many less expensive choices, the most atmospheric being those in and around the leafy Plaza de Santa María.

Transport: Bus to/from Granada, Jaén and Úbeda. Taxi, tel 609 73 81 22 or 608 854 701

Town hall and tourist info: https://cazorla.es, tel 953 720 102

Tourist office: www.turismoencazorla.com, tel 953 969 191

STAGE 28A
Cazorla to Vadillo Castril

Start	Plaza de la Corrredera, Cazorla
Distance	16km
Ascent	950m
Descent	770m
Time	5hr 30min
Highest point	1380m
Refreshments	None on route

Forestry paths lead from Cazorla to a high pass before descending to the Guadalquivir Valley and Vadillo Castril, a forgotten enclave within the park with a fascinating past.

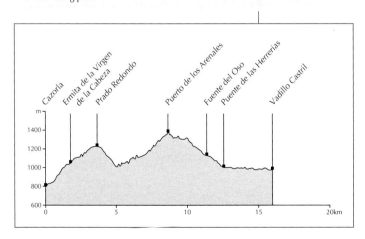

Cazorla to Vadillo Castril (16km/5hr 30min)

Exit the square up Calle del Carmen, signed 'Sendero GR7 por Herón'. Passing a youth hostel take the next right then follow signs to the top of Calle Herón to a sign, 'GR7 Vadillo 5hr 20min'. From here climb a steep path that crosses a water channel, bears left then loops up through pines to a road by a *mirador*. Cross the road and climb to the chapel of **La Ermita de la Virgen de la Cabeza**. Here bear right past a spring for 25 metres then turn right up a rocky path which, initially indistinct, arcs right then back left.

Breaking out of the pines then descending for a short distance the path climbs to the isolated farm of **Prado Redondo**. Pass just above the farm and bear left to pick up the path, which descends steeply before running towards the rocky outcrop of **La Mocha** (1157m). Here the path arcs right to reach a junction with a path running up from La Iruela. Turning up right you shortly pass a spring, El Fuente de Rechite.

Climbing with a *barranco* to its left the path passes beneath a barrel-roofed hut then arcs left and after 75 metres reaches a fork. ◀ Take the right fork and climb steeply to a junction. Here turn left and follow the zigzagging path up to

The lower, left fork is waymarked but for the GR247.

168

the pass of **Puerto de los Arenales**. From here there are vast views out east across the Guadalquivir Valley.

Bear right along the ridgetop for 75 metres then continue down a forestry path. ▶ Crossing a rock fall you reach a junction by a faded marker post. Take the left, lower fork which descends to a wider path. Keeping left you cross more open ground before entering trees once again. At the next junction, bearing right and passing close to a pylon, you reach the JF-7094.

The path is a masterpiece of sierra engineering.

Turning right here you pass above the **Fuente del Oso**. Walk a further 50 metres, then take a path down left, signed 'Sendero Fuente del Oso', which descends parallel to a fence, following it as it angles left. Reaching a fork, keep right and continue down to **Puente de las Herrerias**. Cross two bridges, the second spanning the **Río Guadalquivir**, to reach the JF-7092. Here turn left, parallel to the river. ▶ Ignore a GR sign that shortly points up right. Continue past the huge **Camping Puente de las Herrerias** then a spring, **La Fuente del Peroy**. The houses of **Vadillo Castril** are now visible through the trees to your left.

There are rock pools where you can swim.

If entering the village, just before a junction with the JF-7901, turn sharply left on a path that descends to a football pitch. Keep to the right of the Guadalquivir and cross it via a wooden bridge. Climb Calle Valdeazores then turn right to reach the Centro de Interpretación de la Cultura de la Madera.

VADILLO CASTRIL (ALTITUDE 981M, POPULATION 78)

Campsite, restaurant/bar/café, food shop

Vadillo Castril is a small government-built hamlet that grew up around the main sawmill of the natural park. Since its closure in 1988 the mill has been used as a training centre for forestry management.

Accommodation: Nowhere to stay in village. On the approach to Vadillo you pass Camping Puente las Herrerías €/€€, www.puentedelasherrerias.com, tel 953 727 090. A large campsite beside the Río Guadalquivir with restaurant, pool, log cabins, bungalows, a simple hostel and pitches for tents (Tent+2ppl, €18). Closed in winter.

Transport: Bus to/from Cazorla at junction El Empalme del Valle (3km from village).

Town hall/tourist info: see Cazorla.

STAGE 29A
Vadillo Castril to Coto Ríos

Start	Museum gates in Vadillo Castril
Distance	33.8km
Ascent	1180m
Descent	1485m
Time	9hr
Highest point	1443m
Refreshments	None on route

A long but easy stage to follow with gentle climbs and descents through some of the most impressive mountains of the Cazorla Park.

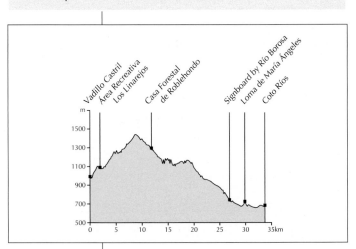

Vadillo Castril to Coto Ríos (33.8km/8hr 30min)

From Vadillo Castríl retrace your footsteps to the JF-7902. Reaching a junction where V Castril is signed left turn right along the JF-7901. After 35 metres angle left up a path that climbs to meet the road you left earlier. As you round the first hairpin turn left along a track signed 'Área Recreativa 1km'.

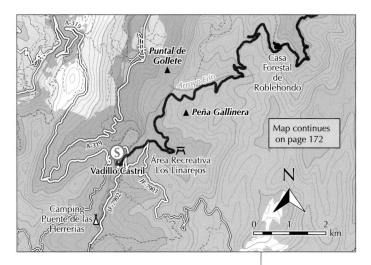

Follow the track down to the **Área Recreativa Los Linarejos** where it loops left, climbs, then passes a barrier. Continue on with the jagged outcrop of **Peña Gallinera** to your right. The track climbs gently before adopting a course close to the bed of **Arroyo Frío**. Leaving the stream it angles left over a tributary then arcs left a second time to cross to the Arroyo Frío's north bank. Looping upwards you pass two large cairns as you reach the highest point of the walk (1443m).

Views open out northwards as you descend through pine forest, passing a spring then, 3 kilometres beyond the pass, **Casa Forestal de Roblehondo**. Walk a further 250 metres to reach a junction. Turn right following a sign, 'Coto Ríos, 4hr 45min'. Continue along the track through stands of pine, oak and juniper crossing several bridges, passing by bands of buckled limestone backed by the rugged crest of the **Sierra de Guadahornillos**. Just under 15 kilometres past Casa Forestal de Roblehondo, the track descends past a barrier to reach the **Río Borosa** by a signboard describing the limestone fold above the river's opposite bank.

Turn left, cross the river then bear left and continue down a track along the river's right bank, passing the confluence of the Borosa and the **Arroyo de las Truchas**.

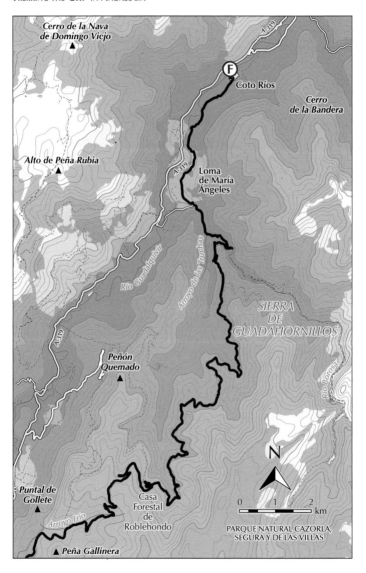

Cerro de la Nava de Domingo Vicjo

Coto Ríos

Cerro de la Bandera

Alto de Peña Rubia

A-319

Loma de María Ángeles

Arroyo de las Truchas

Río Guadalquivir

SIERRA DE GUADAHORNILLOS

Río Borosa

Peñón Quemado

A-319

N

Puntal de Gollete

Casa Forestal de Roblehondo

Arroyo Frío

0   1   2 km

PARQUE NATURAL CAZORLA, SEGURA Y DE LAS VILLAS

Peña Gallinera

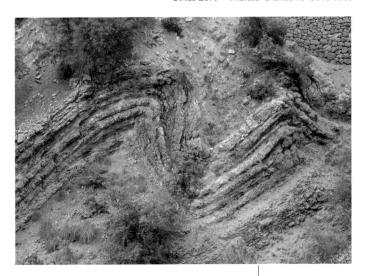

Limestone fold in the mountainside en route to Coto Ríos

Just beyond a barrier you reach the car park at the gorge's entrance. Carry on straight ahead following a sign, 'GR7 Coto Ríos 4.6km', shortly passing Restaurante Los Monteros. The quiet lane leads up past the spring of Fuente Puchardo then on through the hamlet of **Loma de María Ángela**.

Passing right of a football pitch you reach a sign, 'Coto Ríos 3.6km'. Here go through a metal gate and continue along a path looking for GR247 waymarking. Reaching the end of the supporting wall of a terrace, angle 45 degrees left to reach a track. Here bear left and head on through the pines with the **Río Guadalquivir** to your left. Passing through a gate the track's surface shortly turns to tarmac. Reaching **Coto Ríos**, head straight on into the village then take the second turning right to reach the village square.

COTO RÍOS (ALTITUDE 670M, POPULATION 305)

Accommodation, campsite, restaurant/bar/café, food shop, ATM, transport

A sleepy, grid-plan village built to house those who lost their homes when the Tranco de Beas reservoir was created. It receives many visitors thanks to two popular campsites close to some of the park's best hiking trails and river pools.

Rock pool on the Río Borosa

Accommodation: Apartamentos Los Villares €/€€, www.turismoencazorla. com/villares.php, tel 606 986 757. Three pleasant s/c apartments. Alojamientos Rurales Aguasblanquillas €€, www.apartamentoscazorla.es, tel 699 986 115. Two swish apartments in village centre sleeping 4–6. Hotel Mirasierra €€, www. mirasierrahotel.es, tel 953 713 044. Roadside hotel with pool and restaurant 2.5km from Coto Ríos next to road leading to Cazorla. Camping Chopera, www.campingchopera.es, tel 648 290 710. At entrance to village by the Río Guadalquivir with pool and shop. Open all year (Tent+2ppl, €16). Camping Llanos de Arance €/€€, www.llanosdearance.com, tel 953 713 139. Passed about 1.5km from Coto Ríos on stage 30A with pool and wooden cabins. Open all year (Tent+2ppl, €16–€19).

Food: Mesón El Rincón, tel 953 713 147, has traditional Andalusian cuisine with a terrace at west side of village.

Transport: Bus to/from Cazorla. Taxi, tel 609 017 747

Town hall/tourist info: www.santiagopontones.es, tel 953 433 737

STAGE 30A

Coto Ríos to Pontones

Start	The church of San Miguel Arcángel, Coto Ríos
Distance	30.3km
Ascent	1585m
Descent	930m
Time	8hr
Highest point	1733m
Refreshments	None on route

A long climb through some of the park's most dramatic limestone scenery past remote farms and deep gorges before descending through pine forest to Pontones.

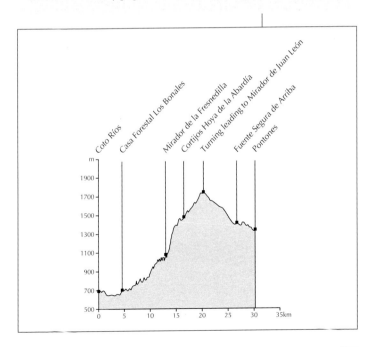

Coto Ríos to Pontones (30.3km/8hr)

Head east past the church's facade then turn right past a line of garages. Continue past a barrier along a track, which shortly angles left to run parallel to the **Río Guadalquivir**. Pass a cemetery then another barrier and descend to a tarmac road. Turn right and continue past the campsite of **Los Llanos de Arance**. The road becomes a gravel track which runs northeast, close to the river.

Approaching La Fresnedilla

Angling right then back left the track crosses the **Río Aguamulas** beyond which you pass a barrier and after 75 metres reach a fork. Turn right following a sign, 'Pontones 6hr 30min'. Ignore a track that shortly cuts down right. The track climbs past another barrier and, just beyond it, **Casa Forestal Los Bonales**. Follow the track on up, high above the gorge of the Aguamulas. ▶

You can clamber down to swim in beautiful rock pools.

Crossing a bridge over a tributary of the Aguamulas continue climbing, now between El Rastrillo to the north and Piedra del Mulón to the south. After walking 5 kilometres from Casa Forestal Los Bonales, the track loops tightly to and

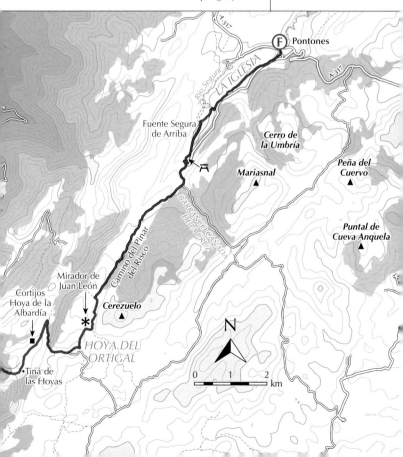

From here there are mesmerising views of the natural ampitheatre formed by the crest of Las Banderillas.

It's worth diverting a couple of hundred metres for the views of the northern reaches of the Cazorla park.

fro before reverting to an easterly course before ending at the **Mirador de La Fresnedilla**. ◄

From the *mirador* continue up a path, ignoring a turning that cuts right towards the ruined **Cortijo de la Fresnedilla**.

The waymarked path climbs steeply then crosses a streambed. Sticking close to the stream you reach a divide at 1332m. Here bear right and continue your ascent on a more gentle gradient with the **Arroyo del Hombre** down to your left. The path runs closer to the stream as it levels then, leaving the stream's gully, climbs again to a flatter area where you pass left of a ruined farm shed and a sign, '**Tiná de Las Hoyas**'.

The path crosses a meadow close to a streambed, marked with GR247 posts, then becomes clearer as it runs past the ruined **Cortijos Hoya de la Albardía**. Passing drinking troughs fashioned from tree trunks you reach a junction at a pass. Here branch right at a sign, 'Pontones 3hr 15min', now heading almost due south on a rough track which, passing a barrier, shortly climbs past more troughs.

Some 800 metres from the sign for Pontones the path arcs left, adopting an easterly course, before meeting a wider, driveable track. Keeping left and climbing on a NNE course, after 1.5 kilometres the track leads to the flat depression of the **Hoya del Ortigal** and a fork where the **Mirador de Juan León** is signed left. ◄

Cortijo de la Albardía

178

Keep right, now joining the track known locally as **Camino del Pinar del Risco**. Passing right of a low shed built against a rockface continue down through pine forest. Passing a barrier you reach a junction, now 4.6 kilometres from the Mirador de Juan León. Turn left along the **Barranco Cañada de la Cruz** and descend to a car park and **picnic area**. ▶

To your right is the source of the Río Segura.

Keep left and follow a narrow lane down past the hamlet of **Fuente Segura de Arriba** then maintain your course along a track, passing right of a farm shed. Angling up across bare rock you reach a cluster of houses at Fuente Segura de Abajo where you come to a junction. Turn right, cross a bridge over the **Río Segura** then follow the road over a rise. Where it arcs right, carry on straight ahead along a gravel track.

Just before reaching the road to **Pontones**, bear left at signboard about La Ganadería (livestock farming) between a fenced enclosure and a farm shed. A pretty path leads downwards with the bare flank of **La Iglesia** to its left. Crossing a streambed it climbs steeply to the tarmac road. Here turn left then take the next left 80 metres beyond two silos. Continue along Calle Perchel to the Plaza de la Constitución next to a spring, the church and the town hall.

PONTONES (ALTITUDE 1330M, POPULATION 1568)

Accommodation, restaurant/bar/café, food shop, PO, pharmacy, tourist info, transport

Pontones consists of two settlements, the higher hamlet of Pontones de Arriba and the lower village of Pontones de Abajo where food and accommodation are to be found. The Río Segura, whose source you pass as you arrive on the GR7, flows through the village centre. The village's elevation means that winters here can be very cold.

Accommodation: Ruta del Segura €€, www.facebook.com/restauranterutadelsegura, tel 953 438 287. Rustic-style hotel and restaurant 500m east of village. Refugio del Segura €€, www.refugiodelsegura.es, tel 953 438 107. Beautifully decorated apartments next to the Río Segura. La Posada del Perchel €, www.posadadelperchel.com, tel 651 971 498. An evolving mix of apartments, bedrooms and dorm' accommodation. No meals but close to restaurants.

Food: La Casa del Cordero, tel 953 123 565, offers inexpensive, home cooking.

Transport: To/from Puente Genave. Taxi, tel 630 758 356

Town hall/tourist info: www.santiagopontones.es, tel 953 433 737

STAGE 31A
Pontones to Santiago de la Espada

Start	Plaza de la Constitución, Pontones
Distance	13.4km
Ascent	450m
Descent	455m
Time	3hr 45min
Highest point	1639m
Refreshments	None on route
Notes	If walking the route in winter be aware that you could encounter snow on the higher sections.

One of the GR7's shorter stages but a beautiful walk nonetheless. After climbing across open farmland via tracks and narrow paths to a high pass the descent to Santiago follows the narrow valley of the Arroyo de Zurueta.

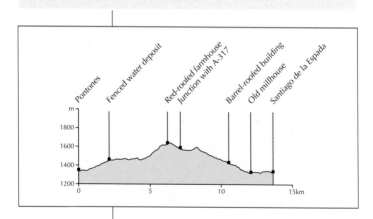

Pontones to Santiago de la Espada (13.4km/3hr 45min)
Exit the square along the west side of the church then turn left and cross a bridge over a stream. Turn right then left along Calle Endrinos, which runs out from Pontones to reach the **A-317** by a GR7 signboard. Turn right and follow

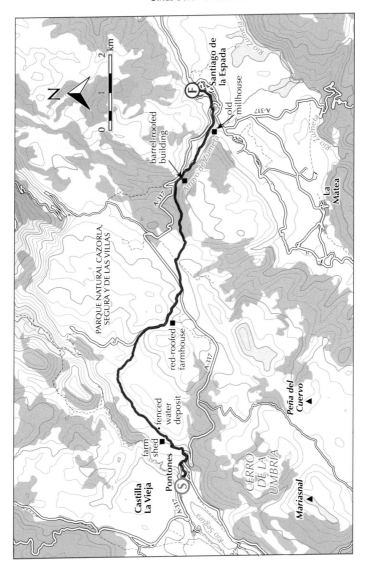

Leaving Pontones

Piles of stones or *majanos* are evidence that the land here was under cultivation in the past.

the road up to the point where it hairpins right. Here go left along a track signed 'GR7 Santiago de la Espada 3hr' (you're also on the GR247). The track loops right then left before passing right of a **farm shed**. ◄

Running past a **fenced water deposit** then a line of metal troughs the track bears left towards a farm building. Here maintain your course, following a sign, 'GR247 La Toba', along a narrow path. Marker posts guide you up along the edge of a stand of pine trees, close to a line of pylons. The path gradually swings east then southeast as you pass a second line of troughs.

A road comes into view up ahead as the path widens to become a track. Where it arcs left continue straight up a path which climbs to the road and a sign, 'GR7 Santiago de la Espada 1hr 45min'. Turn right and follow the road past a **red-roofed farmhouse** then over a rise and you'll reach the A-317.

Follow the road left for 140 metres then go right through a gap in a fence signed 'La Toba, 11.6km'. Posts mark the path's course across a meadow before it crosses a stone bridge. Sticking to the same course it climbs gently before passing through a gap in a fence. Around 100 metres beyond the gap angle up right past a marker post. The path arcs right to reach a track where a GR247 sign points left. You, however, should continue straight ahead along a path on a southeasterly course.

Reaching another track, again keep straight ahead. The path descends to the streambed of the **Arroyo de Zumeta**, which you follow down through pine forest, crossing from side to side. At one point the path angles away from the stream, shortly crossing two of its tributaries. The A-317 comes into sight to your left. Passing a **barrel-roofed building** you reach a fork where the left branch leads up to the A-317. Here keep right. Stepping stones shortly lead you back to the stream's right bank beyond which you pass a dam. After a little more than 1 kilometre the path loops left then crosses the Zumeta a final time via logs. Bear right and join a track that passes above an old millhouse then after 800 metres runs up to the outskirts of **Santiago de la Espada** and a roundabout. Here pass left of a petrol station then turn right along Avenida de Andalucía to reach the village centre and the Plaza de la Constitución.

SANTIAGO DE LA ESPADA (ALTITUDE 1,323M, POPULATION 1,492)

Accommodation, restaurant/bar/café, food shop, ATM, PO, pharmacy, tourist info, transport

The town takes its name from the Knights of the Order of Santiago who oversaw the repopulation of the village after the rendition of the Moors. Due to the municipality's mountainous, wooded terrain a mere three per cent of its land is cultivated, while forestry and the raising of livestock are the mainstays of the local economy.

Accommodation: Hotel San Francisco €€, tel 953 438 072. On the GR7 as you enter the village with restaurant below and no-frills rooms above. Pensión-Bar Avenida, tel 953 438 288. Also on GR7 as you arrive in village, more basic option with tapas in the bar below.

Food: Bar Papachin, tel 953 438 106, and Bar Los Barcos, tel 953 438 490, both prepare good tapas.

Transport: Bus to/from Puente de Genave. Taxi, tel 608 259 795

Town hall/tourist info: www.santiagopontones.es, tel 953 438 002

STAGE 32A
Santiago de la Espada to Puebla de Don Fadrique

Start	Plaza de la Constitución, Santiago de la Espada
Distance	34.3km
Ascent	755m
Descent	910m
Time	8hr 15min
Highest point	1600m
Refreshments	None on route
Notes	You might be tempted to skip the final stage of the northern variant of the GR7, a rather dull slog after the wild beauty of the previous days of walking.

After a pretty initial 5km the final stage of GR7's northern variant entails its longest stretch of road walking, following tarmac for almost 30km, allbeit by way of magnificent mountain terrain.

Santiago de la Espada to Puebla de Don Fadrique (34.3km/8hr 15min)

Exit the square to the southeast. Cross Plaza Canalejas then take the first right then next left. Continue along Calle San Antonio then Calle Hondo de Pecho to a junction at the south of the village. Carry on straight ahead following a sign, 'Cuevas del Engarbo 1hr', now descending a steep track. Immediately beyond a water deposit keep right at a fork and in 50 metres, at a second fork, keep right again.

Crossing the bed of **Arroyo de Zumeta** you reach a junction with a broader track. Turn left past a GR7 post then after 100 metres go right along a narrow track, which leads across the poplar-lined bed of Arroyo Bachiller before crossing a water channel. The track peters out as you climb towards a greenhouse, which you should pass 25 metres to its right. Maintain your course past a water deposit then, crossing a low rise, continue along a narrow path which zigzags down past the palisaded **Cuevas del Engarbo** before descending to the valley floor of the **Río Zumeta**.

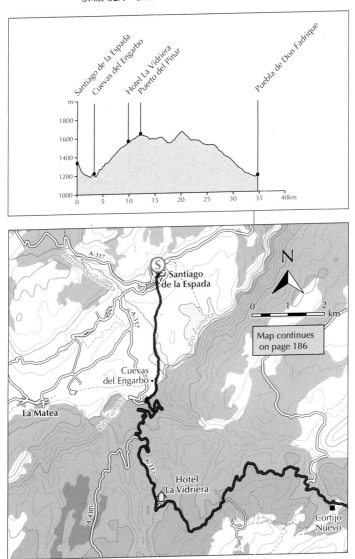

185

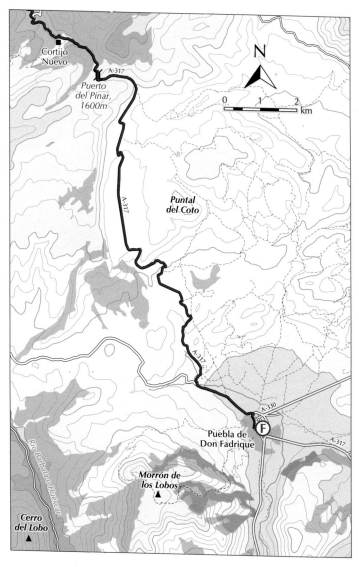

The path becomes less distinct but, keeping the river to your left you soon pass an enclosure with breeze block walls. Reaching a GR7 sign, 'Puebla de Don Fadrique 6hr', the path widens to becomes a track which shortly fords the river. You may need to take off your boots and wade across.

The track climbs to the **A-317**. Here turn left. ▸ After a long ascent through pine and low-growing oaks, passing **Hotel La Vidriera** (only open for special events) then the solitary farmsted **Cortijo Nuevo**, you reach the highest point of the walk at **Puerto del Pinar** (1600m), now 20km from Santiago de la Espada.

You'll be following the road without deviation for the next 30 kilometres.

From here, begin your descent of a little over 14 kilometres to **Don Fadrique**. Approaching the village you pass the cemetery. Take the fourth turning right beyond the cemetery, which winds up to Plaza Nueva. Head straight across the square then follow Calle Ramón y Cajal to reach La Plaza de la Constitución.

Puerto del Pinar, the highest point of Stage 32A

Views out east towards the Sierra de Enmedio

PUEBLA DE DON FADRIQUE (ALTITUDE: 1,168M, POPULATION 2292)

Accommodation, restaurant/bar/café, food shop, ATM, PO, pharmacy, tourist info, transport

At the eastern limit of Granada province, at the foot of the Sierra de Sagra and close to the provincial boundary with Albacete, Puebla de Don Fadrique is an attractive yet little-known village. It dubs itself La Puerta de Andalucía or 'Gateway to Andalucía'. The imposing Iglesia de Santa María de la Quinta Angustia dates from the 16th century and should not be missed.

Accommodation: Hotel Puerta de Andalucía €, www.puertadeandalucia. com, tel 958 721 340. Large, monolithic roadside hotel and restaurant with cheap and comfortable rooms. Apartamentos Don Fadrique €/€€, www. turismoruraldonfadrique.es, tel 958 721 116. Five s/c apartments with cosy restaurant. El Encanto Andaluz €€/€€€, www.encantoandaluz.es, tel 609 189 356. Beautifully decorated apartments, well worth the extra euros for a memorable final night on the GR7.

Food: Best eats in Apartamentos Don Fadrique (see above).

Transport: Bus to/from Huéscar and Granada. Taxi, tel 651 748 734 or 606 520 088

Town hall/tourist info: www.ayuntamiento.puebladedonfadrique.es, tel 958 721 011

THE SOUTHERN VARIANT

Stages 12B-34B: from Riogordo to
Puebla de Don Fadrique

Agave-lined path close to Tímar (Stage 23B)

STAGE 12B

Villanueva de Cauche to Riogordo

Start	The church, Villanueva de Cauche
Distance	23.8km
Ascent	580m
Descent	885m
Time	5hr 30min
Highest point	927m
Refreshments	None on route

A long 17km section of tarmac leads you on east, parallel to the southern flank of the Sierra de Camarolos. But there's little passing traffic, mesmerising views to the south and the final section of the walk is beautiful as you descend through olive and almond groves to Riogordo.

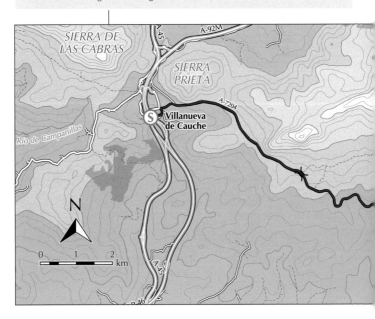

Villanueva de Cauche to Riogordo (23.8km/5hr 30min)

From the church in Villanueva de Cauche return to the junction with the **A-7204**. Here turn right and follow the road up and over a pass. From the top of the **pass** there are big vistas south to **Casabermeja** and east to the mountains above Nerja. Continue past a sign marking your entry to La Axarquía. Continue for 250 metres, then branch left at a sign, 'Alfarnate/Alfarnatejo', along the **A-4152**. The road leads past the houses of **Cerro del Águila** before passing above the circus school of **La Granja de Caperucita**. The road levels then descends. 700 metres past the km13 post turn right down a track at a GR7 post.

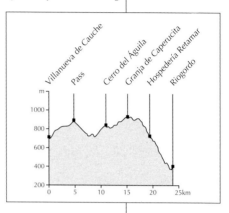

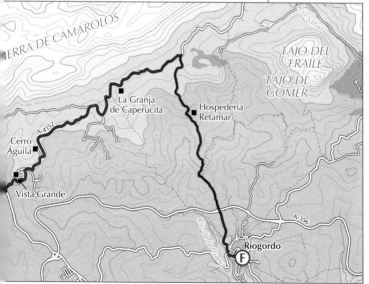

Looking back towards Villanueva de Cauche

Descending through almond groves you pass **Hospedería Retamar** beyond which you reach a junction where a GR7 sign points left to Ventas de Zafarraya. ◄ Continue straight on down. After crossing a bridge the track's surface turns to tarmac. Reaching **Riogordo**, follow signs for Ayuntamiento to the Plaza de la Constitución and town hall.

You'll return to this point on Stage 13B of the walk.

RIOGORDO (ALTITUDE 390M, POPULATION 2701)

Campsite, restaurant/bar/café, food shop, ATM, PO, pharmacy, tourist info, transport

In the early 19th century the village offered fierce resistance to the French forces during the Guerra de la Independencía when its priest excelled as captain of cavalry. Riogordo later gained a degree of notoriety thanks to the *bandoleros* (highway brigands) who worked the mountain passes leading through the mountains close to the village.

Accommodation: Restaurante La Era €, www.hostalmesonlaera.es, tel 665 947 352. Comfortable rooms and good food. Close to village: Finca Gordo €€/€€€, www.fincagordo.com, tel 711 004 176. Luxurious B&B 20min walk north of village with pool and meals on request. Owners can collect walkers from Riogordo. Hotel Balcón de los Montes €€, www.balcondelosmontes.es. Comfy small hotel in El Colmenar, 6km from Riogordo.

Food: Bar Molina, tel 630 963 216, is a friendly place for traditional tapas and *raciónes*, popular with local ex-pats.

Transport: Bus to/from Málaga and Colmenar. Taxi in Colmenar (6km), tel 625 836 089

Town hall/tourist info: www.riogordo.es, tel 952 732 154

STAGE 13B
Riogordo to Ventas de Zafarraya

Start	Plaza de la Constitución, Riogordo
Distance	28.6km
Ascent	1040m
Descent	520m
Time	7hr 30min
Highest point	943m
Refreshments	Bars in Pulgarín Alto and Guaro

After a steep ascent from Riogordo, the stage levels as you head east along the southern flanks of the Sierra de Enmedio and Sierra de Alhama via high mountain tracks. After a short climb from Guaro you reach the old railway line, now a *vía verde* (former railway line converted to walk/cycle path), which leads past a lofty *mirador* (viewpoint) to reach Ventas de Zafarraya.

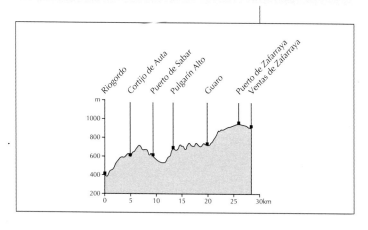

A signboard tells that
the farm is reputed to
have been home to a
rebel Moorish leader.

Riogordo to Guaro (20.2km/5hr 15min)

From Riogordo exit the square then bear right at signs for
Málaga then Casabermeja. Cross a bridge and follow a track
steeply up north to the junction you passed on stage 12B of
the walk. Here go right at signs, 'GR7 Ventas de Zafarraya
6hr' and 'Ruta de la Sierra'. You will now pick up GR249
waymarking. When you reach the partially ruined **Cortijo de
Auta** the track divides. ◄

Keep straight on, passing between two metal posts. After
crossing the farm's threshing floor the track fords a stream.
There's a footbridge 15m to the right if the stream is in spate.
After climbing it levels as you pass through more open terrain. At a junction with a broader track turn right following
GR249 waymarking. The track runs south past a signboard,
'Mirador Tajo de Gomer'. After 125m, at the next junction,
turn left. Continue past several houses to the top of a rise
and an electricity hut. Here go left. Cross another rise and
descend to the **Puerto de Sabar pass** (598m).

Turn left along the MA-7204. Descending, the road
crosses the Río Sabar then passes **Restaurante Gerardo**.
After 550 metres, reaching four tall pines and a bank of letter

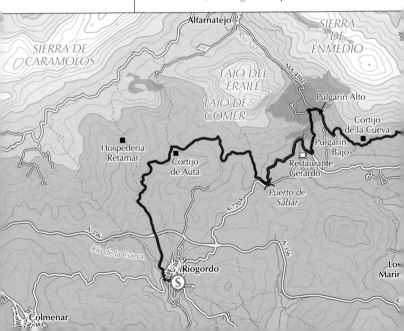

boxes, leave the MA-7204 to its left up a steep track. Climb through olive groves as the track runs up to a junction with a tarmac road.

Turn right then pass a spring to reach the MA-4102. Go right and continue through the hamlet of **Pulgarín Alto**. ▸ Where the road angles right go left along a track past the houses of **Pulgarín Bajo**. After 100 metres, at a fork, keep left then at the next fork left again. After 250 metres, at a third fork, turn right along a rough track that soon levels, running on east across the lower reaches of the **Sierra de Enmedio**. After 1km you reach **Cortijo de la Cueva**. Here angle left following a sign, 'Periana'.

Continue east along a rough track for 2.5 kilometres and pass **Cortijo de Zapata**, then descend to a junction with the **A-4103**. Head straight on. Pass the hamlet of **La Lagunilla** (there's a shaded spring to the right of the road) to reach **Guaro** (20.5km).

Cortijo Pulgarín is a good place to eat, now 14km into the walk.

Guaro to Ventas de Zafarraya (8.4km/2hr 15min)

Head straight through the village or cut left to see the point where the Río Guaro rises. Tarmac turns to dirt as the track

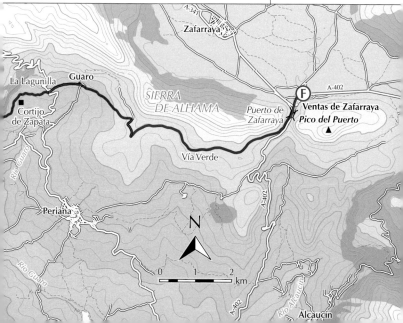

The beginnning of the disued railway track

climbs to a junction. Here go right, signed 'Periana 5.2km'. At the next junction turn left, ignoring GR249 waymarking.

You're now on the **railway line** that once connected Málaga and Ventas de Zafarraya, now a walking and cycling path or *vía verde*. See village description for further information.

Panoramic views open out to the Viñuela reservoir and the Mediterranean.

Follow the **vía verde** parallel to the southern side of the **Sierra de Alhama**. ◄ Cross a bridge then continue through two tunnels to reach the *mirador* at **Puerto de Zafarraya**. Here, just before a bridge, turn down left to the A-402. Continue along Calle Delicias past Aquí Te Quiero Ver then go right at the Caja Rural bank to reach the church and square at the centre of **Ventas de Zafarraya**.

VENTAS DE ZAFARRAYA (ALTITUDE 906M, POPULATION 1302)

Accommodation, restaurant/bar/café, food shop, ATM, PO, transport

The present-day settlement expanded along the edge of the cog railway line, which was built to transport produce from the cultivated plain east of the village down to Málaga. Completed in 1922 the railway ushered in an era of prosperity for local farmers while the trip up to the village became a popular excursion for wealthy Malagueños. The train made its final journey in 1960 before seeing new life as a *vía verde*. Many immigrant workers are employed picking and packing the vegetables that are grown close to the village.

Accommodation: Aquí Te Quiero € , tel 958 362 001. Next to GR7 as you head into town, basic and friendly restaurant with rooms. Casa Bartolo € , tel 958 362 012 is another basic hostel with restaurant. Mesón Al Andalus € , tel 958 362 139. Friendly restaurant with basic rooms in Pilas de Algaida, 2km from the village, passed on stage 14B.

Transport: Bus to/from Málaga Taxi in Periana (10km), tel 615 149 776

Town hall: www.ventasdezafarraya.es, tel 958 362 000

GRANADA PROVINCE

On the descent towards Trevélez (Stage 22B)

The long section of the GR7 that passes through Granada is unquestionably one of the highlights of the walk in Andalucía. Leaving the vast, cultivated plain at Ventas de Zafarraya the route runs east along the northern slopes of the Sierras de Tejeda, Almijara and Alhama before reaching the spa town of Alhama de Granada by way of its spectacular gorge.

From Alhama the next stages lead on via Arenas del Rey and Jayena before you pass through remote mountain terrain to reach the Lecrín Valley. Here the route threads its way past a number of pretty villages by way of irrigated terraces to Nigüelas where you reach the western reaches of the mighty Sierra Nevada.

Climbing over a high pass with vast views back to the west you enter the Sierra Nevada National Park as the GR7 loops down to the busy spa town of Lanjarón, gateway to a string of Spain's highest mountain villages, Las Alpujarras.

The seven days along the southern reaches of the Sierra Nevada are hard to beat. It's here that you're most aware of the imprint left by eight centuries of Moorish occupation: the Alpujarras' cubist jumble of flat-topped houses and the meticulously crafted terraces that surround them could be lifted straight from the Rif mountains of northern Africa. Here the GR7 dips in and out of steep-sided *barrancos* (gulleys/gorges), at times running beside *acequias* (water channels) which, like the miles upon miles of drystone walling, are true miracles of human endeavour. At this stage the

GR7's waymarking is often damaged or non-existent while at others you coincide with the GR240 ('La Ruta Sulayr') and a network of short distance (PR) footpaths.

It's not hard to see why Las Alpujarras are very much on the tourist trail, especially at their more easily accessed, western end. There's masses of accommodation on offer and prices are generally lower than elsewhere on the route. And for the whole of the stretch in Granada province you're in tapas country: each drink you order will be served with a different one and you may well find that if you have three drinks you'll have eaten to your fill.

Beyond Las Alpujarras a challenging day of walking leads up to the GR7's highest point, El Puerto de la Ragua (2041m), before you descend to the vast plain at the northern foot of the range. Passing a huge solar plant that has cut the original footpath (forcing you to divert round the plant's boundary fence – plans to remark the trail have not as yet materialised. Check for any updates on www.cicerone.co.uk) the route runs on into the wild, little known Sierra de Baza. You next traverse the semi-desert landscapes of Altiplano de Granada, home to Europe's largest collection of cave houses and some of Spain's earliest archaeological sites. A final section of remote mountain trail leads you to Puebla de Don Fadrique and the GR7's end point in Andalucía.

HIGHLIGHTS OF THE GR7 IN GRANADA PROVINCE

Some of the many highlights of this section include:

- The ancient, cultivated terraces of the Lecrín Valley
- Hiking in the foothills of mainland Spain's highest mountain
- The high, Berber-like villages of Las Alpujarras and their *acequias*
- Bathing in hot springs of Alhama de Granada and Baños de Zújar
- Crossing the pass at La Ragua, the highest point on the GR7
- The desert-like landscapes of the Hoyo de Baza and its *casas cuevas* (cave houses)

OTHER WALKS

The Sierra Nevada is a major walking destination and you could easily build in extra days to hike any number of trails.

The ascent of El Mulhacén, Spain's highest peak, is one of the park's most challenging day walks and is normally tackled from Capileira or Trevélez.

The Cicerone guide, *Walking and Trekking in the Sierra Nevada* by Richard Hartley, describes day walks and multiday treks in the park.

The Nevadensis bookshop you pass as you reach Pampaneira has a superb selection of walking guides and maps, including information about the GR240 (see below).

The Sierra de Baza is far less known as a walking destination although there is a small network of marked trails. See the boxed text for details of its tourist office.

GETTING THERE/BACK

By air: Granada has regular flights from Madrid with Iberia (www.iberia.com) and Air Nostrum (www.airnostrum.es).

By bus: Nearly all of the larger towns on the GR7 in the province like Alhama, Lanjarón, Baza and Cazorla have regular connections with Granada operated by the Alsina Graells company, which is often referred to simply as Alsa.

The villages of the Lecrín Valley have three buses daily to and from Granada while nearly all the villages of Las Alpujarras have two daily buses. Puebla de Don Fadrique, the GR7's endpoint, has two buses daily to Granada and four to Baza.

All services are operated by Alsa (www.alsa.es).

By taxi: Contact details for local drivers and companies are listed in the village information boxes.

TOURIST INFORMATION

Granada tourist office: Calle Cárcel Baja 3, 18001 Granada, www.turgranada.es, tel 958 247 146

Nevadensis bookshop in Pampaneira (www.nevadensis.com)

Looking back towards Trevélez (Stage 23B)

STAGE 14B
Ventas de Zafarraya to Alhama de Granada

Start	The mirador at El Boquete de Zafarraya
Distance	20.4km
Ascent	410m
Descent	440m
Time	5hr 45min
Highest point	1093m
Refreshments	At hotel Los Caños de la Alcaicería @9.7km

Leaving the plain northeast of Ventas de Zafarraya the stage gathers in tempo as you enter the Parque Natural de las Sierras de Tejeda, Almijara y Alhama via broad forestry tracks and ends on a high note as you pass along the sandstone gorge of the River Alhama.

Ventas de Zafarraya to Alhama de Granada (20.4km/5hr 45min)

From the *mirador* at **Puerto de Zafarraya** follow the narrow gauge rail line along the top of Ventas de Zafarraya. Passing through a rocky defile the track divides. Keep left then bear right past the old railway station then a sports pitch to reach the yard of the **Hortoventas fruit packers**. Passing right of its last warehouse continue along a track parallel to the A-402. Reaching the A-402, turn right and continue through the hamlet of **Pilas de Algaida**.

Around 200 metres beyond the sign marking the end of Pilas, leave the A-402 by angling right across a warehouse yard then continue along a track which climbs past another warehouse. Reaching a spring and water troughs bear right then cross a low rise to reach a junction. Go left, continue past breeze-block

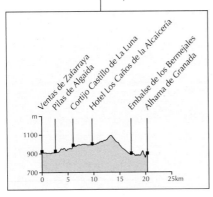

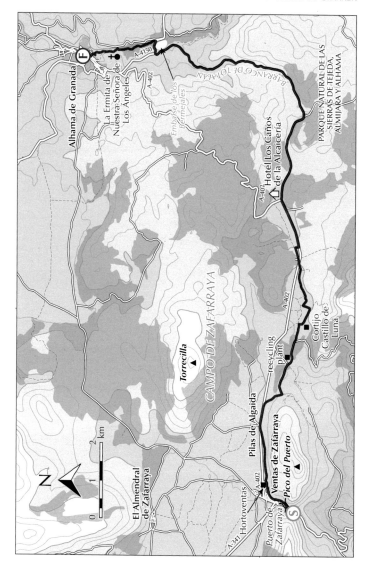

buildings and a covered water deposit then descend to a junction by more farm sheds. Head straight on following a sign, 'Zona de Acampada La Alcauca', passing right of a plastic **recycling plant**.

Upon reaching a fork and a second sign pointing right for 'La Alcauca', keep left and continue down a rutted track between fields of tomatoes and farm buildings. At a junction just beyond a white hut, two tracks cut up right towards **Cortijo Castillo de Luna**. Take the left track then, just before reaching the farm, angle left. Pass between the farm's buildings bearing slightly left and continue along a track to reach a concrete road. Here, turn left and descend for 200 metres then go right at a shed with a green metal roof.

Reaching a fork keep left and continue eastwards. After crossing a farmyard, passing just right of two small huts, you reach the A-402. Turn right and continue for 20 metres then angle left along a farm track. Maintain your course straight across a field to reach a better surfaced track where, turning right, you return to the A-402 where you should turn left. After 1.4 kilometres, reaching **Hotel Los Caños de la Alcaicería**, leave the A-402 passing right of the hotel then continue past a sign, 'Parque Natural de las Sierras de Tejeda, Almijara y Alhama'.

Continue along a broad track until, descending to a white building, you come to a fork and a sign pointing right for 'La Maroma'. Here keep left along another broad track which after 1.5 kilometres arcs gently left before adopting a northerly course. Stick to the main track along the **Barranco de Totalán** and you eventually pass left of a reservoir, the **Embalse de Los Bermejales**, to reach the **A-4150**. Turn right, cross the **Río Alhama** in front of the dam then turn left at a GR7 sign, 'Alhama 2km'. ▶

You'll be returning to this point at the beginning of stage 15B.

A broad track leads into the sandstone gorge of the Río Alhama. Cross a wooden bridge to the river's west bank to pass **La Ermita de Nuestra Señora de los Ángeles**. Continue for 225 metres past the chapel then turn right down a path which descends through poplars before passing left of a mill-house. Beyond the mill angle hard left for 75 metres then turn right up a narrow road that zigzags up to the village. Bear left past Artesanias Las Peñas and take the first right along Callejón Perez Garzón to reach La Plaza de la Constitución at the centre of **Alhama de Granada**.

ALHAMA DE GRANADA (ALTITUDE 890M, POPULATION 5980)

Accommodation, restaurant/bar/café, food shop, ATM, PO, pharmacy, tourist info, transport

One of Granada province's most beautiful towns, Alhama's historic quarter hugs the western side of a deep sandstone gorge. A couple of kilometres from the village is the Balneario (spa resort) de Alhama. The hot springs were first documented during the Roman period while the Moors embellished the baths in Almohad style in the 12th century. They're still frequented by Spaniards who come to take the waters within the spa and in thermal pools next to the river.

Accommodation: La Maroma Rooms and Views €€, https://alojamiento-rural-la-maroma-rooms-views-alhama-de-granada.negocio.site/, tel 665 448 758. Top spec rooms overlooking the gorge. Pensión San José €, www.sanjosealhama.net, tel 958 350 156. In village centre, small and basic rooms with restaurant downstairs. La Seguiriya €€, www.laseguiriya.com, tel 958 360 636. Six rustic-style rooms with terrace garden overlooking the gorge and good home cooking. Hotel Balneario €€/€€€, www.balnearioalhamadegranada.com, tel 958 350 011. 3km from Alhama beside the hot springs with full spa facilities.

Food: Characterful bars and restaurants in and around the main square. The cosy Bar El Tigre, tel 958 350 445, is one of the best.

Transport: Bus to/from Granada and Vélez Málaga. Taxi, tel 609 740 199

Town hall: Tel 958 350 161

Tourist office: www.alhamadegranada.info, tel 958 360 686

STAGE 15B
Alhama de Granada to Arenas del Rey

Start	Plaza de la Constitución, Alhama de Granada
Distance	22.3km
Ascent	550m
Descent	555m
Time	6hr
Highest point	1137m
Refreshments	None on route

After retracing your footsteps along the Alhama Gorge, a broad farm track leads you along the valley of the Río Alhama. After climbing to a high plateau from where there are stunning views south towards the coastal mountains you begin a long descent to Arenas del Rey.

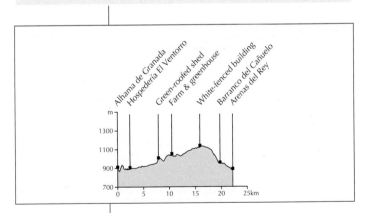

Alhama de Granada to Arenas del Rey (22.3km/6hr)
From the square retrace your footsteps back along the gorge of the Río Alhama to a faded GR7 sign marking 'Arenas del Rey 21km'. Here turn left along the **A-4150** past **Hospedería El Ventorro**. Just before the Km2 post turn right past a 60km limit sign along a track.

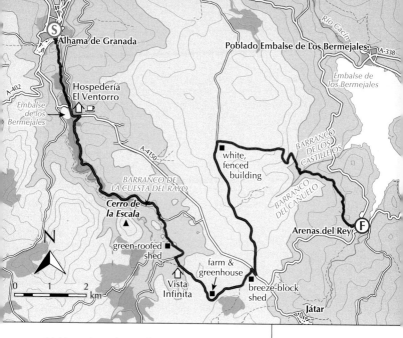

Sticking to the track, initially with the **Río Alhama** to your right, you eventually pass by a track cutting in right signed 'Fuente El Tanguillo, Fuente El Aragonés, Huerta Cuberos'. Ignore this. After 700 metres, after passing beneath a power line, turn right down a steep, shaley path which bears left, parallel to the bed of **Barranco de la Cuesta del Rayo**.

Continuing on its same course the path merges with a track. Follow the streambed for 200 metres to a fork by a black-and-white coto (hunting reserve) sign. Here, angle right out of the streambed up a steep track, passing a GR7 post. Climb steeply through holm oaks to cross the brow of a hill and reach a broader track. Turn left. Continue past a **green-roofed shed** to reach the top of the rise then a junction with a tarmac road. Here, go right. ▶

After 300 metres leave the road to the left. Look for faint red-and-white waymarking on a rock. Cross an open swathe of ground and bear right across a streambed then continue up a steep track through low-growing oaks. As the track levels it merges with a broader track at a marker post. Continue up the track for 75 metres then, at the point it cuts

To the south the highest peaks of the Sierras de Tejeda, Almijara and Alhama are now visible.

right towards the gate to **Vista Infinita** (see accommodation), maintain your course past a threshing circle.

Reaching a fence the track arcs right before looping round a **farm and greenhouse** where you should ignore a track leading off right. Passing a group of houses it merges with another track that leads past a **breeze-block shed** to the A-4150.

Turn right along the A-4150 following a faded sign, 'GR7 Arenas del Rey', then after 200 metres turn hard left along a dirt track. Crossing more denuded terrain the track runs along a high ridge through almond groves, its surface turning to tarmac before you pass left of a **fenced, white building**. Take the next track to the right. ◄

To your left a track flanked by rocks leads into an almond grove.

After crossing a vineyard the track descends on an easterly course before angling right and descending more steeply, eroded in sections. Looping left then right you come to a junction. Turn hard right down a rough dirt track, passing a GR7 post after 20 metres. At a second junction, again go right and follow the track down and across the **Barranco del Cañuelo**. The track's surface improves, now running high above the **Barranco de los Castillejos**. ◄

The Embalse de los Bermejales reservoir comes into view to the west.

Descend through scrubby, open terrain then groves of olives and almonds and a track comes in from the right to merge with yours, leading you into **Arenas del Rey**. Take the second street to the left to reach the village square, Plaza Alfonso XII.

Poplars in their autumnal colours

ARENAS DEL REY (ALTITUDE 875M, POPULATION 1178)

Campsite, restaurant/bar/café, food shop, ATM, transport

A sleepy grid-plan village, Arenas del Rey was totally destroyed by the great earthquake of Christmas Day 1884 when 135 of its population were killed. The previous settlement was awarded the title of villa (similar to 'municipality') by King Charles III, hence the 'del Rey' of its title.

Accommodation: None in village. Complejo Rural El Molinillo €€, www.complejoruralelmolinillo.es, tel 650 961 492. 2.5km SE of the village with s/c rustic style houses and restaurant overlooking the reservoir. Owners can collect walkers from Arenas. Vista Infinita, www.cortijovistainfinita.be, tel 676 312 707. A beautiful isolated B&B next to the GR7 with one house and four beautiful yurts passed on stage 15B after 9.3km. Camping Los Bermejales €, www.campinglosbermejales.com, tel 958 359 190. 7km north of village by the Los Bermejales reservoir with s/c bungalows. Open all year. (Tent+2ppl, €14.)

Food: Two simple tapas bars in village.

Transport: Bus to/from Granada. Taxi: in Jayena (11km), tel 696 288 829

Town hall/tourist info: www.arenasdelrey.org, tel 958 359 103

STAGE 16B
Arenas del Rey to Jayena

Start	Plaza Alfonso XII, Arenas del Rey
Distance	17.2km
Ascent	595m
Descent	630m
Time	6hr
Highest point	1081m
Refreshments	None on route

A beautiful day of track and road walking as you roller-coaster in and out of the valleys of the Río Añales and the Río Cacín before a steep descent leads down to Jayena.

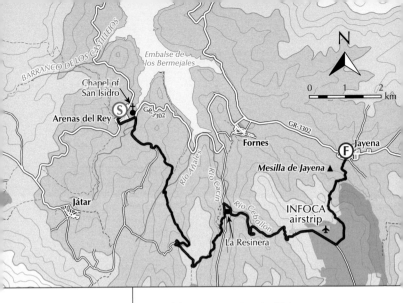

Arenas del Rey to Jayena (17.2km/6hr)

Exit the square along Calle Jaén then turn left along Calle Málaga. Reaching the **GR-3302** and a Stop sign, turn left. As you pass a signboard about the 1884 earthquake continue along the GR-3202 signed 'Fornes 10km'. Reaching the **Chapel of San Isidro**, 300 metres from the village, leave the GR-3202 to its right at a sign, 'Juan Ranas'.

Passing farm sheds the road climbs across a denuded hillside. Upon reaching a fork at the top of the rise, branch left and after 50 metres, at the next branch, keep right and follow the tarmac road down to the valley floor of the **Río Añales**. Ignore a first track cutting right and continue down to a point where the road arcs left. Here, go right following a line of pylons along the valley floor. Walk for 550 metres, then look for a white arrow on the road and turn left down a dirt track, which leads you across the Río Añales.

Beyond the river the track bears up right then passes through a fallen gate. Reaching a fork, keep right. The track climbs steadily through scrubby vegetation then stands of young pines. At the next fork, again keep right. Approaching the head of the valley the track arcs right, still climbing.

As you reach the top of the rise, the greenhouses along the Añales Valley come into view. Here, turn left up a steep

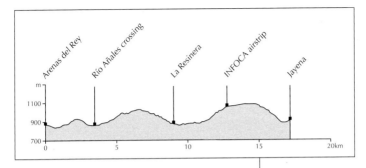

dirt track which climbs through low-growing pines. After crossing an abandoned almond grove, continue through a green metal gate to reach a broad fire break. Turn right then after 50 metres angle left across the fire break. Passing left of a *coto* (hunting reserve) sign, descend a short section of track that bears right to rejoin the fire break, which descends to a junction. Here, go left and follow the sandy track down to the valley floor of the **Río Cacín** where you meet a broad track. Turn left to come to the buildings of **La Resinera**.

Tapping pine resin near to La Resinera

The Sierras de Tejeda, Almijara and Alhama Natural Park's calcareous mountains and in particular its swathes of marble sand provide a perfect habitat for the cultivation of maritime pines (*Pinus pinaster*). **Resin** harvested from the trees was used to manufacture colophony (rosin) at the factory of La Resinera. Many people were employed and a settlement grew up around the factory, which was large enough to have its own school and chapel. The factory closed in 1975 and was subsequently transformed into a visitor centre and park offices.

209

*Descending
towards Jayena*

The sign details how
resin was extracted
from the pine trees.

After 150 metres turn right into the car park. Pass right
of an Information Centre (limited opening times) and continue along a road signed 'Aerodromo 3.6km', which runs
past the botanical garden of La Resinera then runs down to
a junction. Here, turn left at a sign, 'Pista de Aterrizaje'. The
track descends to the river, which you cross via a wooden
footbridge, then climbs with a cliff to its right and the **Río
Cebollón** down to its left.

Passing an old *calera* (lime kiln) the track fords the
river then loops left then right before reaching a fork by a
signboard. ◄ Branch left then after 50 metres continue
straight ahead, ignoring a track cutting left marked 'Mesa de
Fornes'. The track climbs then bears right, crosses a tributary
of the Río Cebollón, then angles back left to reach a fork.
Here, branch right off the main track along the boundary
fence of the **INFOCA (fire service) airstrip** for 500 metres
then turn right along a fire break. After 750 metres go left
along another fire break for 250 metres and look for a GR7
post to the left. Here, turn left along a narrow track which
winds through pine and oak. The track runs up to merge with
another fire break on a ridgetop running towards the flat-
topped peak of **Mesilla de Jayena**.

Follow the fire break's right-hand edge then after 150
metres branch right down a rocky path. The path widens to
become a track. Reaching a fork, keep right then descend to

the valley floor where, bearing left, you merge with a wider track which leads over the Río Grande then up to **Jayena**. Here, climb a flight of steps then cut right beneath an arch to La Plaza de la Constitución.

JAYENA (ALTITUDE 907M, POPULATION 1104)

Accommodation, campsite, restaurant/bar/café, food shop, ATM, PO, pharmacy, tourist info, transport

In the valley floor of the Río Grande between the Cerro de Piedra Sellada and the reservoir of Los Bermejales, Jayena takes its name from the Moorish settlement of Chayyana. Like nearby Arenas del Rey much of the village was destroyed by the 1884 earthquake but was quickly rebuilt thanks to the support of King Alfonso XII who helped raise the necessary funding.

Accommodation: Hospedería Rural La Almijara €, tel 958 364 157. Four basic rooms and two apartments above a popular bar/restaurant next to main drag through village. El Bacal Camping. Municipal site on the hillside of La Resinera, 5km from Jayena and close to the GR7. Contact Jayena town hall at least 10 days in advance for the necessary permit. You could also take a taxi to/from Complejo Rural El Molinillo (see Arenas del Rey village info).

Food: La Almijara (see above) is the best choice.

Transport: Bus to/from Granada. Tax, tel 696 288 829

Town hall: www.jayena.es, tel 958 364 07

STAGE 17B
Jayena to Albuñuelas

Start	Plaza de la Constitución, Jayena
Distance	31km
Ascent	765m
Descent	945m
Time	8hr 30min
Highest point	1327m
Refreshments	At Mesón Los Prados (15.6km)
Notes	The path leading down the Barranco del Cañuelo is quite overgrown so have long trousers in your pack.

A challenging stage of the GR7 leads you through magnificent mountain territory by way of the plunging *barrancos* (gorges) of a little-known corner of the Sierras de Tejeda, Almijara and Alhama.

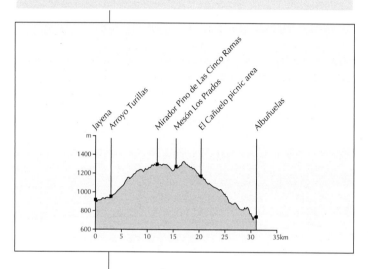

Jayena to Albuñuelas (31km/8hr 30min)
Exit the square at its bottom left corner past a statue of Christ. Descend a flight of steps, turn left then take the first steet right, which leads down and over a bridge. The road climbs with the valley of the **Río Grande** to your right before it arcs right and crosses the **Arroyo Turillas**. Beyond the stream head straight on past a 'Parque Natural' sign up a dirt track. ◄

You're now on an old drover's path, El Camino de la Cuerda de los Moros.

Reaching a fork keep left, sticking to the main track which arcs left as Jayena comes back into sight. Angling back right it resumes its former course. At a fork keep right, still climbing. Levelling, the track runs on along a high ridge, still in pine forest, to a point where a track cuts off right: ignore this. When you reach a fire break turn right and where the break angles left maintain your course. The track begins to descend, looping hard right as you pass through an area where pine resin is harvested. Descending, you pass a green barrier then come to a junction. Go left.

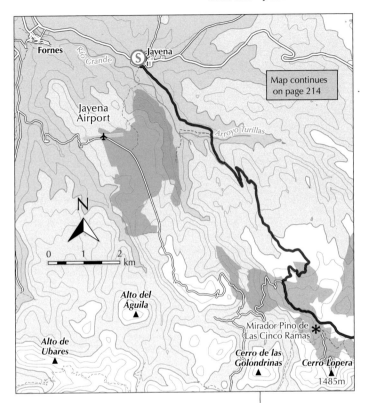

Climbing gently the track levels as views open out to the south across the Barranco de las Pulgas, which is down to your right. The track runs on to reach **El Mirador Pino de las Cinco Ramas** from where there are views south to the Sierra Chaparral. ▸

Beyond the viewpoint, at the first junction, keep left to cross a high, open plateau. Descending gently you pass the fenced farm sheds of **Cortijo de los Prados**. Continue down through stands of oak dotted with pine as the track passes beneath the farm school of **Huerto Alegre**.

Exit the gates of Cortijo de los Prados then turn right after 250 metres to reach restaurant **Mesón Los Prados** and

The eponymous 'Pine of the 5 trunks' died in 2017. It was purported to have been more than 200 years old.

Looking south from the viewing point of El Pino de las Cinco Ramas

the **A-4050**. Turn left along the road then 100 metres past an abandoned building leave the road to its right and follow a stony track up through pines. Cross a streambed to reach a broader track. Here go right and follow the track down through pine forest. After the track describes a loop it angles back east; at this point look for a GR7 post left of the track and a white arrow on a drainage culvert.

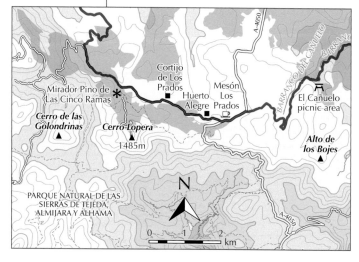

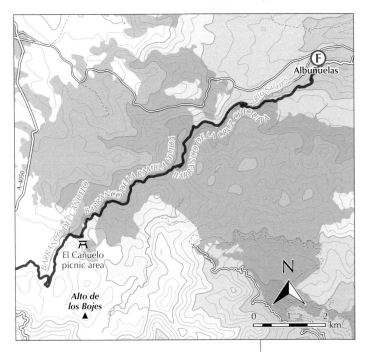

Here, cut left down a narrow path which merges with a forestry track that leads down to reach a marker post. Here angle left across a streambed and continue down the left bank of the **Barranco del Cañuelo**. Crossing an opening in the trees the path crosses the streambed as the *barranco* narrows down. Dropping into the streambed after 50 metres the path resumes its course along the right bank, passing a spring then widening to become a track. At a fork, take the lower track which descends to the picnic area of **El Cañuelo** where you meet the track you left earlier.

Turn left along the main track which adopts a course following the **Barranco de La Rambla Huida**, crossing it a number of times before passing through a breach in the hillside as you pass into the next valley to the east, **El Barranco de la Cruz Chiquita**. Reaching the valley floor the track arcs right then descends to a junction. Turn hard left and follow the track gently downhill. Looping right it crosses the Barranco de La Rambla Huida, a tributary of the Chiquita. Climbing gently high above the **Río Salares** you pass a fenced forestry building then descend to a track cutting hard off to the right.

Here turn right, follow the track down and across the river beyond which it angles left then climbs. Reaching a fork keep left and head on towards **Albuñuelas**, which is visible up ahead. Passing above a house, just as the track arcs right, turn left down a path which descends steeply to the **Río Salares**, which you cross via a small bridge. From here climb a path up to the village where you pass a GR7 sign. Reaching another sign marked Goleta turn right, left, then right again down Calle Estacíon to reach La Plaza del Ayuntamiento.

ALBUÑUELAS (ALTITUDE 728M, POPULATION 830)

Accommodation, restaurant/bar/café, food shop, PO, ATM, pharmacy, transport

A linear village at the head of the beautiful Lecrín Valley composed of three clusters of houses: El Barrio Alto, El Barrio Medio and Fernán Nuñez. More than 100 villagers lost their lives and most houses were destroyed when the 1884 earthquake struck.

Groves of citrus and other subtropical fruits flourish in the valley, which enjoys a microclimate several degrees warmer than the valleys of the nearby Sierra Nevada.

Grapes were grown here during the Roman period while the Moors settled the Barrio Alto area and built the Torre del Tío Bayo.

Accommodation: El Cortijo del Pino €€/€€€, www.elcortijodelpinolecrin.com, tel 958 776 257. An art-filled farmhouse B&B on a high bluff overlooking the village with five beautiful bedrooms. Casa Rural El Mirador de la Habana €/€€, tel 654 601 825. S/c house with valley views but minimum two-night stay.

Food: Mesón Tres Lindes, tel 958 776 279, offers home cooking with a terrace for al fresco dining.

Transport: Bus to/from Granada via Dúrcal. Taxi in Dúrcal (15km), tel 677 411 095

Town hall: www.albuñuelas.es, tel 958 776 031

Tourist info: www.turismovalledelecrin.com

STAGE 18B

Albuñuelas to Nigüelas

Start	Plaza del Ayuntamiento, Albuñuelas
Distance	14.9km
Ascent	680m
Descent	480m
Time	4h 30min
Highest point	931m
Refreshments	Bars and shops in Salares, Restábal and Murchas

After following quiet tracks through the cultivated terraces of the villages of the Lecrín Valley a steep path leads over the Cuestas del Almendral to Nigüelas and the western reaches of the Sierra Nevada.

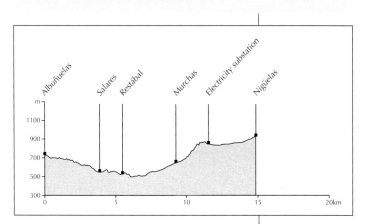

Albuñuelas to Restábal (5.5km/1h 30min)

From the square head east along Calle Estacíon, continue through Plaza de Gracia then cut right down Calle Bajo. Reaching a car park, go left and continue along a concreted track. ▶ Reaching the Barrio Bajo (lower village) of Albuñuelas, continue along Calle Ramal. At a stone with GR markings, turn right. The road bears right then left. Continue up Calle Zoraba then right along Calle Mojón, which angles

The track has frequent GR marking.

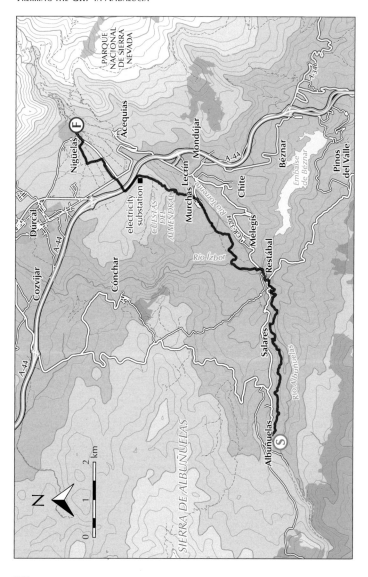

right at waymarking on the ground. Continue past a GR7 sign along a concrete track that runs down the valley of the **Río Albuñuelas** through terraced groves of citrus, olive and almond. The villages at the eastern end of the Lecrín Valley come into view.

Angling right the track descends steeply. At a spring go left and climb a track to the southern side of **Salares**. Continue along a track skirting the lower village. Just past a car park turn right, cross a low bridge then follow the track steeply upwards. Reaching the second of two water deposits, turn left. Descending to a GR7 marker and, to your right, a blue arrow on a wall, turn left. After crossing a streambed, the track loops left and enters **Restábal** along Calle San Cristobal.

RESTÁBAL (ALTITUDE 538M, POPULATION 493)

Accommodation, campsite, restaurant/bar/café, food shop, pharmacy, transport

A quiet village surrounded by irrigated terraces of citrus and olives forming part of the larger municipality of El Valle. On the hill that dominates the village are the remains of an Arab fortress with a fine *aljibe* (water deposit).

Accommodation: Mesón Despensa del Valle €, tel 958 793 531. Restaurant with rooms and s/c apartments in an orange grove with pool and valley views.

Food: Bar Jovi, under same management as Despensa del Valle, for tapas–style meals.

Transport: To/from Granada. Taxi in Dúrcal (12km), tel 677 411 095

Town hall: www.elvalle.es, tel 958 793 181

Restábal to Nigüelas (9.4km/3hr)

Reaching the **GR-3204**, turn left. At a fork carry on straight ahead, signed 'Granada'. After 125 metres go left down a cobbled path, angle right across the GR-3204 then descend a second path to reach the road once more. Turn right, cross a bridge over the **Río Izhor** then turn left along a concrete track at a faded GR7 sign. The track climbs between groves of citrus. Just past a breeze-block wall, angle left along a narrow path which widens to become a track and descends to the Río Búho.

Continue along the river bank then follow the track as it bears right then climbs to a fork. Keep left, still climbing, then at the next fork go left again. At a third fork, taking another left, you reach a junction. Here turn right and continue on towards **Melegís**, which is visible up ahead. Just before a bridge across the **Río Torrente** turn left along a track to a white hut with a green door. Here go left and continue up a concrete section of track, heading towards windmills on a high ridge.

As you climb, another track merges with yours. Just before reaching **Murchas** you reach a fork. Keep right and continue through the village, passing right of the church of San Juan Evangelista. Reaching the end of Calle Isabel II and bearing left you come to signs for 'Nigüelas 5.5km' and 'Cementerio'.

Continue up a steep tarmac road, which shortly angles right by a palm tree, still climbing. Looping past a water deposit, you reach a 5.5T sign. Here go right, cross a water channel then climb a steep track towards wind turbines on the ridge of **Cuestas del Almendral**.

The track climbs across scrubby terrain. At a point where it arcs right cut left up an eroded path. ◀ Reaching a fork keep right and continue up to a broad track. Here turn right. Running down through almond groves, **Nigüelas** comes into view beyond the **A-44** motorway.

> The villages you passed earlier in the walk come into sight back west.

Another track shortly merges with yours. Continue past an electricity substation, parallel to the A-44. Angling right and crossing a bridge over the motorway the track meets the **GR-9067**. Cross the road and continue along a narrow track through almond groves. Reaching a junction turn left then at the next junction, where to your left is a water tank, go right. Passing a spring you reach a junction. Turn right then take the next turn left. Follow the road into the village past El Secreto del Olivo then climb a flight of steps to reach La Plaza de la Iglesia.

NIGÜELAS (ALTITUDE 933M, POPULATION 1150)

Accommodation, restaurant/bar/café, food shop, pharmacy, transport

An enchanting small village at the foot of the Cerro del Zahor where the GR7 enters the Sierra Nevada National Park, Nigüelas is the highest village in the Lecrín Valley. Its ancient olive mill, reputedly among the oldest in Spain, is home to an agricultural museum (open weekends 11am–2pm and 6pm–9pm).

Accommodation: There are two superb options in the village. La Huerta del Cura €€, www.lahuertadelcura.com, tel 647 484 969. One room and two apartments to one side of a quiet garden with pool with excellent home-cooked

La Plaza de la Iglesia in Nigüelas

suppers. El Secreto del Olivo €€, www.elsecretodelolivo.com, tel 673 346 700. Converted 18th century village house with nine beautiful bedrooms round a pebbled patio. Evening meals with prior arrangement. There are also a couple of s/c casas rurales in the village (see town hall website).

Food: Accommodation listings both have excellent food. La Tasca, tel 677 411 095, offers international cuisine and has a terrace with valley views.

Transport: Bus to/from Granada. Taxi in Durcal (5km), tel 677 411 095

Town hall/tourist info: www.niguelas.org, tel 958 777 607

PARQUE NACIONAL DE LA SIERRA NEVADA

Dominated by El Mulhacén (3479m), the highest peak in mainland Spain, and with more than 20 others rising to over 3000m, the Sierra Nevada National Park is Europe's second highest mountain range. As its name implies the park sees heavy snowfall in winters and is home to Europe's most southerly ski resort. After being classified a UNESCO biosphere then a Parque Natural, the area was given the additional kudos of Parque Nacional status in 1999 while more recently it was awarded

Green List status by the International Union for Conservation of Nature. It's Spain's largest national park and embraces more than 850,000 hectares of reserve.

The park's elevation coupled with its proximity to the Mediterranean has given rise to exceptionally diverse plant life. There are more than 2000 species of plants, shrubs and trees, of which more than 60 are endemic. The GR7's course along the sierra's southern flank runs mostly between 1000m and 2000m by way of mixed forests of pine, deciduous oak, juniper, broom, chestnut and maple.

Ibex are a common sight on the sierra's higher slopes while other species present include weasel, boar, fox, badger, beech marten and genet. The park's raptor population includes golden and Bonelli's eagles, peregrine falcons, kestrels and griffon vultures. It also has an astonishing roll call of butterflies and beetles.

Further information: www.juntadeandalucia.es and www.turgranada.es

The excellent Nevadensis bookshop in Pampaneira (www.nevadensis.com), which you pass early on the Sierra Nevada traverse, has a superb collection of guides and maps of the area.

STAGE 19B
Nigüelas to Lanjarón

Start	Plaza de la Iglesia, Nigüelas
Distance	18.8km
Ascent	745m
Descent	1020m
Time	5hr 15min
Highest point	1287m
Refreshments	None on route

A fine day of walking via the ancient drovers' path of La Cañada Real de Sierra Nevada as you skirt the western flank of the Sierra Nevada to reach Lanjarón, gateway to Las Alpujarras.

Nigüelas to Lanjarón (18.8km/5hr 15min)
Exit the square to the northeast passing right of a chemist. After 100 metres, you pass a sign, 'GR7 Acequias 2km', then descend and cross the **Río Torrente**. Turn immediately

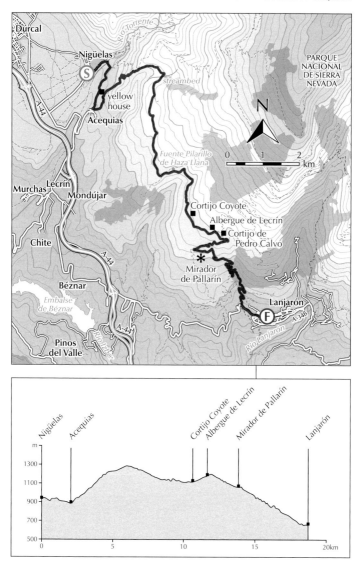

right then after 40 metres left up a concrete track. Take the first track right signed 'Acequias'. Descending past a mill, El Molino del Sevillano, you come to **Acequias**. When you reach house number 4 and La Plaza de la Constitución, turn left up a steep track passing a sign, 'Lanjarón 17km'.

At a fork by a water deposit keep left following a stone wall. Passing above a **yellow house** to your left, follow the track round to the right then after 20 metres go left up a path into pine forest. Reaching a forestry track on a hairpin bend, maintain your course, still climbing, ignoring a smaller track cutting right. At the next fork keep right following markings on a rock for Lanjarón and faded GR7 flashes. The track climbs through almond groves then loops right and crosses a **streambed**. Cypress trees line one edge of the track as you pass through more pines. ◄

From here there are long views out west towards the Lecrín Valley.

After 20 minutes you reach another fork where you should go right. The track runs through a huge almond grove before reaching a crossroads. Heading straight on, following a sign, 'Sendero Sulayr', you shortly pass a spring, **Fuente Pilarillo de Haza Llana**. The track rollercoasters round the mountainside before crossing a river bed, shored up with

Descending towards Lanjarón

wire-meshed rocks, then runs on past farms and houses to both sides of the track. Passing **Cortijo Coyote**, a small farm building immediately to your left, the track climbs before passing right of the **Albergue de Lecrín**. Around 125 metres past the *albergue* (hostel), reaching a junction, go right following a sign, 'Lanjarón 7km'.

After levelling the track descends. ▶ Beyond a stone building signed **Cortijo de Pedro Calvo** the track loops down, passing the **Mirador de Pallarín**. Ignore minor tracks cutting left or right. Running right of a deep *barranco*, the track descends through almond groves, concreted in sections. Entering a stand of cypress and acacia you pass a waterfall at the mouth of the Barranco de las Acacias. Continue down past fenced smallholdings to reach the **A-348**. Turn left, head straight across a roundabout along Avenida de la Alpujarra then Avenida de Andalucía to La Plaza de la Constitución.

Lanjarón comes into sight backed by the imposing massif of the Sierra de Contraviesa.

LANJARÓN (ALTITUDE 655M, POPULATION 3485)

Accommodation, restaurant/bar/café, food shop, PO, ATM, pharmacy, tourist info, transport

Standing gateway to the villages of Las Alpujarras and the southern slopes of the Sierra Nevada, Lanjarón is a busy spa town that sees plenty of to and fro action.

Spaniards still come to take the ferruginous waters at its spa, which retains a touch of belle époque splendour while mineral water from the town is exported throughout Spain. Several hotels, restaurants, bars and craft shops cater to its constant stream of visitors.

Accommodation: Hotel Central €, www.hotelcentral-lanjaron.es, tel 958 770 108. Dated, inexpensive and welcoming hotel in town centre. Hotel Alcadima €€, www.alcadima.com, tel 671 517 257. Swish family-run hotel with views, pool and restaurant. Hotel Miramar €€, tel 958 770 161. Central and comfortable option passed in town centre on GR7. OYO Hotel España €, tel 958 771 386. Inexpensive, central hotel with pool where the poet Lorca would stay.

Transport: Bus to/from Granada and Trevélez. Taxi, tel 659 849 768

Town hall/tourist info: www.lanjaron.es, tel 958 770 002

STAGE 20B
Lanjarón to Soportújar

Start	Plaza de la Constitución, Lanjarón
Distance	12.7km
Ascent	945m
Descent	650m
Time	4hr 10min
Highest point	1118m
Refreshments	In Cáñar (8.6km)

A steep climb out of Lanjarón leads to to Soportújar via a spectacular path that loops round deep *barrancos* with panoramic views south to the Sierra de Contraviesa.

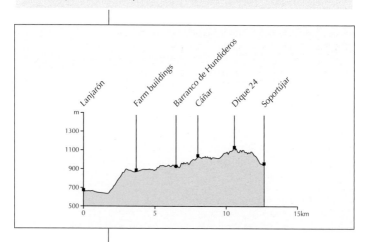

Lanjarón to Cáñar (8km/2hr 40min)

From the square, head east along Calle Señor de la Expiración which merges with the **A-348**. Follow the road past a petrol station then cross the **Río Lanjarón**. Around 250 metres beyond the bridge go left at a sign, 'Cáñar 7km', up a cobbled path that climbs to a tarmac road. Here, go left towards a black gate then turn right up a narrow path. When

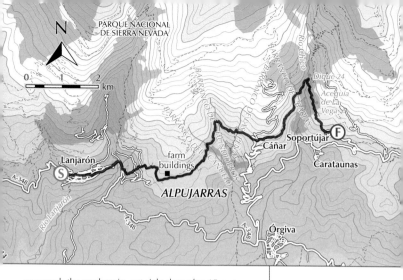

you reach the road again, cut right then after 15 metres, go left up a concreted track. Pass gates leading to a house to the right, then turn right back onto a cobbled path.

When you come to a tarmac road, turn left then bear right in 60 metres to rejoin the footpath that climbs past a water deposit then meets with the track once again. Cut left for 30 metres then angle right to rejoin the path. Merge with the track and continue climbing to a junction by a breeze-block wall. Here, keep right. Climb gently to pass left of a house with a putting green. At a green gate bear left up a path that crosses an *acequia* (water channel) then runs up to a concreted track. Turn down right to shortly pass a farm. ▶

Traversing more open terrain, now angling round to the south, you come to a junction. Go left following a sign, 'Caballo Blanco'. The track leads across a flat area through a grove of centenarian olives then passes right of **farm buildings** and a group of eucalyptus. 270 metres beyond the farm ignore a path off right signed 'GR142 Órgiva'; instead continue for 20 metres to a fork where a sign, 'Caballo Blanco', points left. Bear right along a track that runs across a denuded hillside. Descending, ignore a track that cuts in to the right. Cáñar is now visible up ahead. At the point where the track begins to climb, turn off left at a sign, 'Cáñar'. The path becomes less distinct but fading paint flashes help you follow the path through scrubby undergrowth.

The coast and the Mediterranean come into view to the south.

227

At a fenced water deposit bear left; then go left again at the next fork. The path, narrow and loose in parts, gradually arcs to the north. Cross the bed of **Barranco del Cañuelo** and carry on as the path climbs steeply to an olive grove beneath a ruined farm where it divides. Keep right, parallel to a stone wall.

The path improves, running high above the *barranco*. Descending steeply over loose shale you cross a wooden bridge over **Barranco de Hundideros**, beyond which the path zigzags up before levelling and running on towards Cáñar. Dipping into and out of **Barranco de las Peñas** the path crosses a stream via a wooden bridge then an *acequia*. Reaching a divide by a concrete bunker keep left to merge with a road that leads to a crossroads. Head straight over, pass beneath a *tinao* (roof or room spanning street in Las Alpujarras) then take the second street up left to reach the church and *ayuntamiento* (town hall).

CÁÑAR (ALTITUDE 1029M, POPULATION 343)

Accommodation, restaurant/bar/café, food shop

On a high ridge between two deep *barrancos*, Cáñar was originally a Moorish *alquería* (mountain farm), which was destroyed and abandoned at the time of the Morisco uprisings then repopulated with Christians from northern Spain. From its lofty vantage point the Mediterranean and Rif mountains in Morocco are often visible.

A spring in Cañar

Accommodation: Casa Rural Cáñar Fernando €/€€, tel 696 894 799. Pretty, rustic-style village house sleeping six but also let to couples.

Food: Bar Piki, tel 958 785 306, and Mesón Los Ángeles, tel 636 271 743, offer typical regional dishes along with tapas.

Transport: No bus connection. Taxi in Órgiva (10km), tel 665 251 862

Town hall: www.cañar.es, tel 958 785 301

LAS ALPUJARRAS

Las Alpujarras, often referred to as simply La Alpujarra, are a series of high villages that cling to the southern flank of the Sierra Nevada, facing out to the Sierra de Contraviesa and Gádor. The area surrounding the villages is encompassed within the Parque Nacional de La Sierra Nevada (see Stage 18B).

The life-giver of the region is the meltwater that runs off the high sierra for nearly the whole of the year and which has cut a series of deep valleys or *barrancos* radiating out from the central sierra. Since the arrival of the Moors, a number of meticulously crafted *acequias* have brought this same water to carefully-tended terraces, which cling to the steep slopes surrounding the villages: they are miracles of human endeavour. To see these plots of richly cultivated land in an otherwise harsh, often barren landscape, with watered groves of citrus, walnuts, almond and olives, feels like coming across an oasis in the desert.

The Moors were loathe to leave Las Alpujarras and lingered on for almost a century after the fall of Granada and the flat-roofed houses of these cubist-looking villages still speak of their North African, Berber origins.

The area sees many visitors, many of them walkers who come to explore an extensive network of waymarked paths, which include the GR7 and the newly-created GR240 (Ruta Sulayr).

Cáñar to Soportújar (4.7km/1hr 30min)

Pass the church and town hall, at the first fork keep right then descend to a second fork by house number 25. Bear left and continue down to a spring and a signboard for 'GR7 Trama Alpujareño'. Here, bear left at a sign, 'Camino del Dique 24', up a concrete track with a wooden railing to your right.

At a fork in front of the cemetery, keep right. As you pass a *mirador*, maintain your course along a path that adopts a course high above the *barranco*, passing marker posts pointing back towards **Cáñar**. The path gradually bears round to the northeast then climbs. Looping across the **Barranco de Barjas** the path angles left then right. Climbing steeply once again you pass behind the dam of **Dique 24** that spans the **Río Chico**. At the end of the dam go right down a flight of steps then follow the looping path up and over the **Acequia de la Vega**.

Climbing through cypress and pine trees the path runs close to an *acequia* before passing above a group of ruined buildings. Cross back over the *acequia* as the path merges with a track that runs down towards **Soportújar**. Reaching a fork with No Entry signs to each side, keep left and drop down through the village to the church and La Plaza de la Iglesia.

SOPORTÚJAR (ALTITUDE 944M, POPULATION 266)

Accommodation, restaurant/bar/café, ATM, food shop, pharmacy

A Moorish village grew up in the 9th century around an *alquería*, which was destroyed at the time of the Morisco rebellion. The Christians resettled the village and it grew to some 800 inhabitants. Between 1950 and 1980 its population shrank to one-third of that number following the rural exodus away from the sierra.

Nowadays the village celebrates a supposed connection with witchcraft although the origin of its *brujos* and *brujas* (witches) had nothing to do with sorcery but was rather just slang for the names of its male and female inhabitants.

Accommodation: El Horno de la Bruja €, tel 655 042 105. Two s/c apartments belonging to the friendly owner of the neighbouring Bar El Correillo with traditional alpujarreño fare. La Huerta €, tel 625 811 929. Two s/c rustic-style apartments sleeping up to four.

Food: Bar Romero, tel 958 787 540, is a cosy restaurant with witch-themed décor.

Transport: Bus to/from Granada and Trevélez. Taxi in Órgiva (7km), tel 665 251 862

Town hall/tourist info: www.soportujar.es, tel 958 787 531

STAGE 21B
Soportújar to Pitres

Start	Plaza de la Iglesia, Soportújar
Distance	12.6km
Ascent	1020m
Descent	720m
Time	3hr 45min
Highest point	1537m
Refreshments	In Pampaneira and Bubión
Notes	In 2019 the path was very overgrown between Soportújar and Bubión.

A beautiful if somewhat overgrown initial stage leads across the plunging Barranco de Poqueira. Beyond Bubión you climb to a high divide before descending to Pitres and the cluster of villages that make up La Taha.

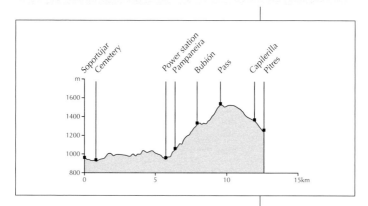

Soportújar to Pampaneira (6.5km/2hr)

Exit the Plaza de la Iglesia in Pampaneira past Taberna Romero. Cross a bridge and continue past a sculpture of a witch's head.

The witch sculpture at the outskirts of Soportújar

Reaching a sharp bend to the right go left up a concrete track at a sign, 'Puente Encantado'. Reaching the wall of a cemetery maintain your course. At the end of the wall bear right down a concrete track then after 20 metres go left along a dirt track which climbs, angles right then narrows to become a path.

The path crosses an *acequia* then climbs to a concrete track. Here turn right. After 450 metres turn left at a marker post along a dirt track. After another 300 metres bear right at another marker post along a narrow path which crosses a streambed, passes between ruins then past restored farm buildings. After descending it runs closer to the **A-4132**, which is now down to your right.

231

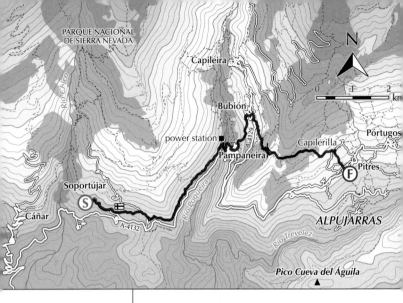

Passing behind a fenced olive grove the path angles up left to meet with a dirt track. Turn right then bear immediately left up a tarmac section of track. Passing left of a black metal gate continue along an overgrown path, passing above a house. The path crosses a streambed then passes above a second building with a solitary cypress tree.

Around 60 metres beyond the building, at a fork, keep right. The path runs downhill with steep drops to the right. Crossing a streambed it swings right, descends steeply then crosses a second streambed before it reaches a dirt track. Cross directly over this track. Passing behind a ruined stone hut the path merges with a track which you should follow up to the right, passing between a water deposit and a farmhouse. Reaching a junction by a black gate bear right, downhill.

25 metres beyond a metal pylon, where the track loops right, turn left up a narrow path that shortly passes a ruin. Pampaneira comes into sight. Crossing a streambed the path descends with a high wall to its left. Reaching a track that leads in to a gate, maintain your course, passing just right of the gate. ◄

The path is very overgrown at this stage.

When you reach a fork, take the higher option. After a few metres the path drops downhill then levels, running close to a water channel. Becoming less distinct it crosses an

232

open swathe of hillside before crossing another streambed. Descending more steeply, now cobbled in sections, the path meets the A-4132. Follow the road across the bridge spanning the **Río Poqueira** next to a **power station**.

130 metres beyond the bridge, just before a 'Road narrows' sign, go left up a path. Cross a track as the path climbs to meet the A-4132 on a tight bend. Maintain your course up into **Pampaneira**. At a junction go right then turn left along Calle Verónica to reach the church and the Plaza de la Libertad.

PAMPANEIRA (ALTITUDE 1062M, POPULATION 321)

Accommodation, restaurant/bar/café, food shop, ATM, PO, pharmacy, tourist info, transport

An obligatory port of call as you enter the high Alpujarras, Pampaneira's cluster of whitewashed, flat-roofed houses cling to the eastern flank of the plunging Barranco de Poqueira with long views south towards the Sierra de Contraviesa.

The pedestrianised streets around its charming main square are lined with bars, restaurants and craft shops. The village is at its best on weekdays; at weekends things can get a tad too busy.

Accommodation: Hostal Pampaneira €/€€, www.hostalpampaneira.com, tel 958 763 002. At lower end of the village, rooms with valley views and the recommended Casa Alfonso restaurant below. Hotel Rural Estrella de las Nieves €€, www.estrelladelasnieves.com, tel 671 420 833. Stunning views, beautiful and inexpensive rooms, with garden and pool.

Food: El Lagar, tel 673 636 394, is in a quiet street with great steaks as well as veggie options. The cosy Mesón Rural Alberto, tel 958 763 003, specialises in meats roasted in a wood-fired oven.

Transport: Bus to/from Granada and Trevélez. Taxi in Pitres (8km), tel 659 111 745, or in Órgiva (15km), tel 650 618 317 or 665 251 862

Town hall: www.pampaneira.es, tel 958 763 001

Tourist info: Nevadensis Bookshop (www.nevadensis.com). Excellent outdoor activity centre and shop with one of the best collections of maps and guides in Andalucía.

Pampaneira to Bubión (1.3km/25min)
Cross the square and climb a narrow street with a central water channel. Pass Fuente Cerillo and continue up Calle Príncipe taking the higher option at any fork. Reaching a

sign, 'Bubión 1km', bear left then, at a fork next to the last village house, left again. Climbing steeply you come to the outskirts of **Bubión** at the village washhouse where, bearing right, you reach the square and the church.

BUBIÓN (ALTITUDE 1033M, POPULATION 302)

Accommodation, restaurant/bar/café, food shop, ATM, PO, pharmacy, tourist info, transport

At the edge of the deep Poqueira gorge with a high church tower rising above its narrow streets of whitewashed houses, Bubión is one of the Alpujarra's most beautiful villages and has a far less touristy vibe than nearby Pampaneira. On clear days there are views north to the high peaks of the Sierra Nevada, snow-clad for much of the year, while to the south the Mediterranean is often visible.

Accommodation: Hostal las Terrazas €, www.terrazasalpujarra.com, tel 958 763 034. At the lower edge of the village, rustic-style rooms and s/c apartments with views over the Poqueira gorge. Hotel Villa de Bubión €€, www.villasdeandalucia.com/bubion, tel 958 763 973. One and two bedroomed s/c rustic-style houses with pool and gardens just above the village. Los Tinaos €/€€, tel 660 515 333. S/c apartments with valley views and a cosy bar showcasing local wine and hams.

Food: Lo Nuestro, tel 958 763 339, prepares excellent risottos and imaginative salads while El Teide, tel 958 763 037, is the old-timer where the food is always good.

Transport: Bus to/from Granada and Trevélez. Taxi in Pitres (8km), tel 659 111 745

Town hall/tourist info: www.bubion.es, tel 958 763 370

Bubión to Pitres (4.8km/1hr 20min)

Exit the square towards the east to reach the **A-4129**. Here turn right, downhill, then cut left up Calle Ermita at a GR7 sign, 'Capilerilla 3.5km'. Reverting to dirt the track passes beneath a horse ranch. Follow the track to a point where it loops hard left. 20 metres beyond the bend angle right along a narrow path.

The path zigzags steeply up before crossing a rocky **pass**, the highest point of the stage at 1537m. Around 80 metres beyond the divide head straight across a broad track. The path angles left, running on through a mixed stand of fir, pine and oak before passing right of a group of concrete

plinths. Reaching a five-way junction maintain your course then at the next fork take the lower, right option.

After descending for 400 metres turn right, following a white arrow, down a dirt track. After 25 metres bear left down a path that soon merges with the track. After 20 metres turn left again and continue down the path, which soon rejoins the track. Descending through terraces you reach **Capilerilla** at a bench next to a huge poplar. Here bear left, pass beneath three *tinãos* then go right at a sign, 'Pitres 0.5km', down a path lined by lamp posts. Passing the old wash house, maintain your course to reach the church and La Plaza de la Iglesia in **Pitres**.

Looking back towards Bubión

PITRES (ALTITUDE 1248M, POPULATION 494)

Accommodation, campsite, restaurant/bar/café, food shop, ATM, PO, pharmacy, tourist info, transport

Pitres is the largest of the seven villages that make up La Tahá, a region which in Moorish times was an independent administrative district or 'Ta'. The village has a relaxed, friendly feel with life centred around its square and high-towered church, which saw extensive renovation after being damaged during the Civil War.

Accommodation: El Balcón de Pitres €€, www.balcondepitres.com, tel 958 766 111. S/c cabins, houses and bungalows and campsite a 10min walk northwest from village with restaurant, pool, shop and laundry service (tent+2ppl, €15). Hotel San Roque €/€€, www.hotel-san-roque-pitres.granada-vive.com, tel 958 857 528. Pleasant hotel with restaurant.

Town hall: www.lataha.es, tel 958 766 061

Transport: Bus to/from Granada and Trevélez. Taxi, tel 659 111 745

STAGE 22B
Pitres to Trevélez

Start	Plaza de la Iglesia, Pitres
Distance	17.4km
Ascent	1105m
Descent	815m
Time	5hr 40min
Highest point	1733m
Refreshments	In Pórtugos and Busquístar

After following narrow paths and tracks linking three of the villages of La Taha, the path climbs through oak woodlands high above the *barranco* of the Río Trevélez before descending to Trevélez.

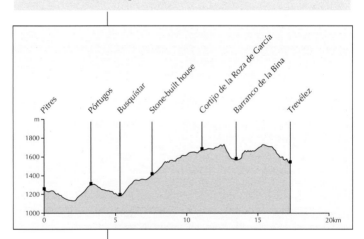

Pitres to Pórtugos (3.5km/1hr)

Exit the square to the right of a bank to reach the A-4132. Turn left and continue past Hotel San Roque for 75 metres then turn right at a sign, 'GR7 Atalbeitar 1.5km'. Reaching a fork, ignore a sign pointing left for Agua Agria. Keep right, descending, then cross the ferruginous **Río Bermejo** via stepping stones.

Reaching a fork after 50 metres, bear right then descend to a tarmac road which you should follow through the east side of the hamlet of **Atalbeitar** passing the old washhouse then a sign, 'GR7 Pórtugos 2km'.

The track climbs, crosses a bridge over the **Barranco de Castaños**, then angling left runs up to a three-way junction. Keep left along the main track then at the next fork branch right. Where the track loops sharply right maintain your course up a narrow path. Reaching a high wall turn right to reach the **A-4132**. ▶ Turn left, take the next right then continue up to the town hall and main square of **Pórtugos**.

Turn right along the A-4132 to reach Fuente Agria.

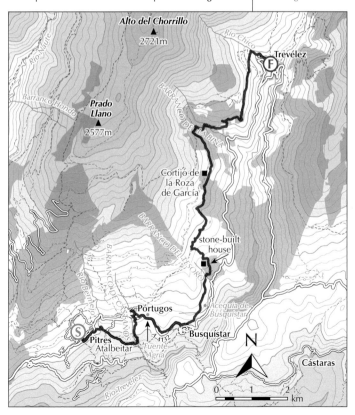

237

PÓRTUGOS (ALTITUDE 1308M, POPULATION 389)

Accommodation, restaurant/bar/café, food shop, ATM, PO, pharmacy, tourist info, transport

Surrounded by steep terraces watered by *acequias* and with streets of flat-roofed houses spanned by numerous *tinãos*, Pórtugos still bears the imprint of its Moorish past.

At the outskirts of the village the waters of its ferruginous Fuente Agria emerge from a rocky cleft. They are purported to cure a host of ailments and attract thousands of visitors every year.

Accommodation: La Placeta Guesthouse €€, www.alojamientorurallaplaceta.es, tel 696 859 615. Four beautifully decorated s/c apartments in village centre with garden and pool. Hostal Mirador de Pórtugos €, tel 958 766 014. Pleasant rooms in village centre with lively restaurant serving Alpujarran cuisine. Hostal Nuevo Malagueño €€, tel 958 766 098. Rather dated hotel with restaurant on the main drag through village.

Transport: Bus to/from Granada and Trevélez. Taxi: in Pitres (2.5km), tel 659 111 745

Town hall: www.portugos.es, tel 958 766 001

Pórtugos to Busquístar (1.9km/40min)

Highly mineral in taste, the limonite spring is said to cure ailments of the kidney and liver.

From the square retrace your steps past Jamones Diego Martín then go left at a sign, 'Pórtugos-Busquístar', down a concrete track which angles left to join the A-4132. Follow the road east past **Fuente Agria** and a chapel. ◄

Continue past the km23 post for 50 metres then turn left up a concrete track. Reaching a wall, bear right and continue along a path parallel to the A-4132. At a junction turn left and cross an *acequia*. At the next fork keep right and descend past a breeze-block building to meet the A-4132 once again. Follow the road east to the outskirts of **Busquístar**.

BUSQUÍSTAR (ALTITUDE 1162M, POPULATION 279)

Restaurant/bar/café, food shop, transport

At the southern end of the Trevélez Valley, looking south to the Sierra de Mecina, the sleepy village of Busquístar lies at the heart of Las Alpujarras yet sees few visitors.

On a hilltop close to the village the remains of a mosque are still visible. It was believed that Moorish treasure lay buried there but extensive excavations failed to unearth any spoils.

Accommodation: No hotels or hostels in village but good options in Pórtugos (2.5km) and Pitres (4.5km).

Food: Bar Paco, tel 958 857 504, at top of village close to where the GR7 leaves the village offers home cooking and a friendly welcome.

Transport: Bus to/from Granada and Trevélez. Taxi in Pitres (4.5km), tel 659 111 745

Town hall: www.busquistar.es, tel 958 766 031

Busquístar to Trevélez (12km/4hr)

Continue along the A-4132 above Busquístar to a fork. Here turn up left following a sign, 'GR7 Trevélez 10.5km'. Reaching a fork keep left and continue up between the cemetery and a football pitch. The track narrows to become a path. Reaching a fork go right then after 50 metres, at the next fork, bear left then cross the Acequia de Busquístar via a small bridge. The path climbs northwards through low-growing oaks. ▶

Descending, you cross the bed of **Barranco del Tesoro** then climb to merge with a track where you should maintain your course. Passing through stands of walnut the track runs past a fenced, **stone-built house** to a fork where you should go left. The track narrows and climbs steeply to a flat area. Here, go right at a GR7 post up a narrow path that climbs through oaks. Levelling it adopts a northerly course, crossing four streambeds.

Passing through more open terrain the path enters a stand of young pines where you cross a *barranco* where rocks have been wired up to form a dyke. After another steep ascent the path runs above a plantation of pines then descends and crosses another *barranco*. Reaching more open terrain you pass beneath **Cortijo de la Roza de García**. Beyond the farm the path crosses a track then a streambed before it climbs to merge with a forestry track.

Turning right you shortly pass a sign, 'Trevélez 4.8km'. 650 metres beyond this sign go right down a narrow path. ▶ It descends steeply through oak forest before crossing the **Barranco de la Bina** via a bridge made of tree trunks.

Views open out to the eastern Alpujarra.

Ignore Ruta Sulayr waymarking pointing along the track unless you wish to shorten the walk.

At this point the GR7 has been re-routed after being damaged by landslides.

Follow the stream down for 25 metres then angle left up the steep bank of the gully. ◄

Levelling, the path leads through a gate, descends then climbs to a flat area. After crossing an *era* (threshing floor), pass behind a ruined farm then climb once again.

GR waymarking reappears. At a concrete bollard angle left, still climbing. Continue past a large cairn to twin marker posts where the path arcs hard right then levels.

Head on through pines then go through a gate and cross a streambed. Emerging from the trees the path bears left then climbs to a forestry track. Here turn up left, pass through another gate then after 30 metres bear right along a path that cuts through a jagged outcrop of rocks.

Passing through another gate, Trevélez comes into view as the path merges with a broad track. Here go right, continue for 800 metres then, just past a ramshackle enclosure, turn right down a cobbled path which shortly crosses the track you just left. Passing over an *acequia* it descends then crosses the **Río Chico** in front of a dyke. Descend through the Barrio Alto of **Trevélez** then turn down left at a white bench to reach the Plaza Barrio Medio. ◄

If you're staying at La Fragua, turn left to reach the hotel and its restaurant.

TREVÉLEZ (ALTITUDE 1539M, POPULATION 742)

Accommodation, campsite, restaurant/bar/café, food shop, ATM, PO, pharmacy, tourist info, transport

Clinging steeply to one side of the Sierra Nevada's deepest *barranco*, Trevélez is mainland Spain's highest village with a difference in height of 150m between its barrio alto and barrio bajo and is known throughout Spain for its air-cured hams, which hang in every bar and restaurant.

Several hiking trails lead out from the village including a challenging route via Siete Lagunas to the summit of El Mulhacén. You'll meet many other walkers, especially if you book in at La Fragua (listed below and highly recommended) whose friendly owners have hiked trails the world over.

Accommodation: Hotel La Fragua I and La Fragua II €/€€, www.hotellafragua. com, tel 958 858 512. Twin hotels at the higher end of the barrio medio with a cosy restaurant overlooking the village. La Fragua II has larger rooms, a garden and a pool. Bar-Hostel Mulhacén €€, tel 958 858 587. In the lower village with traditional Alpujarran cooking. Hotel Rural Pepe Álvarez €, www. hotelpepealvarez.es, tel 958 858 503. Rooms with balconies to one side of road through the lower village. Camping Trevélez €, www.campingtrevelez.com, tel 958 858 735. Campsite with cabins 1km from the village next to the A-4132. Open all year (tent+2ppl, €16).

Food: Bars and restaurants line the road leading through the Barrio Bajo though the best place to eat is at Restaurante La Fragua in the barrio medio.

Transport: Bus to/from Granada. Taxi, tel 609 911 657

Town hall/tourist info: www.trevelez.es, tel 958 858 501

Arriving in Trevélez

STAGE 23B
Trevélez to Cádiar

Start	Plaza Barrio Medio, Trevélez
Distance	20.5km
Ascent	625m
Descent	1245m
Time	5hr 50min
Highest point	1761m
Refreshments	In Juviles (10km)

After a steep climb from Trevélez the route takes on a gentler tempo as you pass through pine forest before descending through stands of oak and cultivated terraces to Juviles. After skirting a deep *barranco* on the approach to Tímar you reach the Guadalfeo Valley, which leads on to Cádiar.

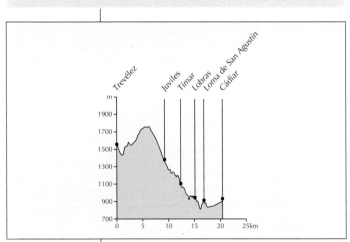

Trevélez to Juviles (10km/2hr 30min)
From the Plaza Barrio Medio in Trevélez exit towards La Fragua then turn right down Calle Cuesta. Continue down Calle Ladera to the **A-4132**. Turn left, cross the **Río Trevélez**

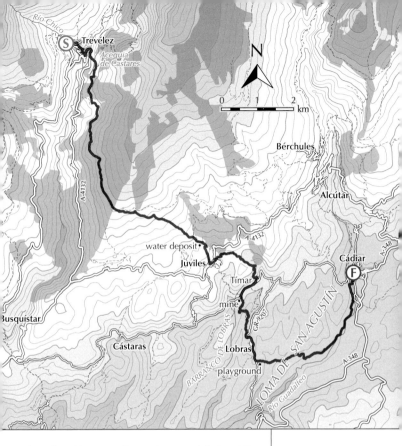

then after 100 metres take a path to your left signed 'Ruta Sulayr'. Crossing the **Acequia de Castares**, follow the path as it climbs through oak and pine then levels, descends then crosses a stream via a wooden bridge. Pass through a gate to cross a second stream. ▶

There are views back towards Trevélez and up to El Mulhacén.

The path widens to become a track before you reach a junction. Bear right. After 1 kilometre of level walking ignore a sign pointing left for Ruta Sulayr. The track climbs again then levels as you exit the pine forest at a crossroads.

Head straight on for 200 metres then turn right along a narrow path that runs across open, scrubby terrain. Cross two *barrancos* as it descends then crosses a track. At the point where it meets the track again, concreted at this point, follow it right then after 100 metres angle right to rejoin the path. Descending you meet the track a third time. Carry on straight ahead. Pass inspection huts and go through a gate then continue your descent passing left of a **water deposit**.

Descending towards **Juviles** you reach a dirt track. Turn right then after 25 metres cut left down an overgrown path. Descend past a cherry orchard and almond groves as the path merges with a track by a group of transmitter posts. Here angle left then back right down a concrete road passing a spring then a wash house to reach the A-4132 opposite a pharmacy.

JUVILES (ALTITUDE 1265M, POPULATION 142)

Accommodation, restaurant/bar/café, food shop, pharmacy, tourist info, transport

Like nearby Trevélez, Juviles is known for its air-cured hams. In Moorish times it was at the centre of a region where silk was produced but nowadays stands of chestnut have replaced the mulberry groves. The extensive ruins of an *alcázar* (fortress) on a nearby hilltop are reputed to date back to the 8th century.

Accommodation: Bar-Pensión Tino €, www.juviles.net/tino, tel 958 769 174. Tiny bar with home cooking, basic rooms and rooftop terrace in quiet backstreet. Apartamentos de Juviles €/€€, tel 650 877 319. S/c apartments with fireplaces and terraces. Minimum stay two nights.

Transport: Bus to/from Granada. Taxi in Cádiar (9km), tel 620 756 951

Town hall/tourist info: www.juviles.net, tel 958 769 032

Juviles to Tímar (2.5km/40min)
Turn left along the **A-4132**. Passing the second of two buildings marked Jamones Juviles, turn right down Calle Escuela then after 60 metres left along a track signed 'Fuente Agria'. At a fork keep left, signed 'Tímar/Alcútar'. After crossing a streambed follow the track up through groves of olive and almond to a junction. Ignoring a sign left for Alcútar maintain your course. Crossing an *acequia* the track narrows as it runs high above the **Barranco de Lobras/Los Molinos**. Passing through a rocky divide the path loops hard right before zigzagging downwards. Pass beneath twin water deposits and continue along a concrete road, which bears right to reach the main square of **Tímar**, the church and a spring.

Tímar to Lobras (2.6km/40min)

Head southwest from the square past a GR7 sign, 'Lobras 2km', then the last village houses. Pass beneath the cemetery to reach a group of ruined buidings, a former mercury mine.

> There were once two **mercury mines** and distillation plants in Tímar. They were in operation in the early years of the 20th century until the mountain's vermilion-coloured lodes of cinnabar (mercury sulfide, HgS) were exhausted.

Here turn left off the road at a sign, 'Era', along a dirt track which descends through olives, figs and almonds. Reaching a fork at the end of a concreted section, turn right. The track narrows to become a path with faded GR waymarking. Reaching the next junction again keep right. ▶

The path is overgown at this stage.

Crossing a ridge, now lined by towering agave, the path runs up to a denuded, shaley divide. Here turn left down a loose path. Crossing a streambed bear slightly left then climb up a looping, indistinct path. After 150 metres you meet a path next to the Acequia de los Castaños. Here turn right. After running close to the water channel the path merges with a track which leads to the **GR-9207**. Follow the road into **Lobras** past the old wash house, with a wooden railing, to your left.

Looking back up towards Tímar

Lobras to Cádiar (5.4km/2hr)

Follow the GR-9207 south from the village. Reaching a **children's playground** after 300 metres turn left along a dirt track at a sign, 'Cádiar 5km'. After descending for 125 metres and reaching a fork, keep right then drop down a steep section of track. Reaching the valley floor you pass a ruined mill then reach a crossroads where Lobras is signed left and Cádiar right on the GR142. Ignore these signs and head straight on and cross the streambed. Continue along its right bank along an indistinct track, maintaining your course.

The track narrows to become a path (ignore a track cutting up right), which climbs steeply out of the *barranco*. Reaching the top of the rise of *Loma de San Agustín* and a track, head straight on. The path crosses a streambed as you descend into the valley of the **Río Guadalfeo** (aka Río Cádiar). Cross an *acequia*; the path hugs its right side. Reaching water deposits, it broadens to become a track. Head straight on to a junction with a broader track. ◄

If staying at La Alquería de Morayma, turn right here.

Here bear left, parallel to the river. Eventually the track angles left then right and crosses the river. Turn left and continue along a road along the river's east bank. Reaching a football ground, turn right past a spring then climb past the Molino de Enmedio to reach the church and the Plaza de la Iglesia of **Cádiar**.

CÁDIAR (ALTITUDE 920M, POPULATION 1469)

Accommodation, restaurant/bar/café, food shop, ATM, pharmacy, transport

Hugging the east bank of the River Guadalfeo, at the edge of the broad valley separating the Sierra Nevada and the Sierra de Contraviesa, Cádiar has a more workaday feel about it than most villages of Las Alpujarras with a mix of traditional and modern architecture. The village is surrounded by groves of olives, citrus and subtropical fruits, which thrive thanks to its sheltered position and rich alluvial soils.

Accommodation: Hostal El Cadi €, tel 958 850 961. Basic hostel above a bar close to the church. Ruta de la Alpujarra €, tel 958 768 059. S/c apartments in modern block next to main road through village with restaurant beneath. La Alquería de Morayma €€, www.alqueriamorayma.com, tel 958 343 221. A beautiful group of houses, rooms and apartments built in the style of an Alpujarran hamlet among organic fruit groves, 2.5km from Cádiar (or a 1km diversion off the GR7 as you reach the Guadalfeo Valley, see walking notes). With superb food and wines it's one of the region's loveliest hideaways.

Food: La Alquería de Morayma has the area's best restaurant (see above).

Transport: Bus to/from Granada, Ugíjar and Almería. Taxi, tel 620 756 951

Town hall: www.cadiar.es, tel 958 768 031

STAGE 24B
Cádiar to Yegen

Start	Plaza de la Iglesia, Cádiar
Distance	17.1km
Ascent	1025m
Descent	910m
Time	5hr 10min
Highest point	1457m
Refreshments	In Narila, Bérchules and Mecina Bombarón

A steep climb early in the day to Bérchules then over a high pass above Mecina Bombarón from where a spectacular path leads on to Yegen through the more arid landscapes of the eastern Alpujarras.

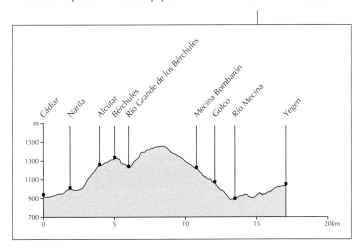

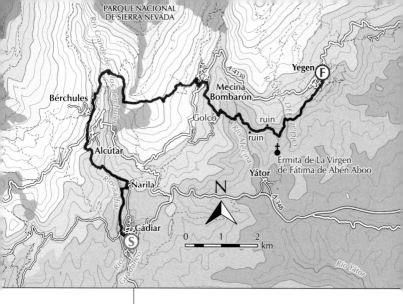

Cádiar to Narila (1.7km/30min)

Leave the square along Calle Mercado, passing right of the municipal market. The street angles right then left before descending to a sign, 'GR7 Narila 1.5km'. Cross a small square with a fountain and palm tree and pick up a walled path, which merges with a track running along the east bank of the **Río Cádiar/Guadalfeo**. Passing through fruit groves and stands of poplar you come to a sign, 'Sendero del Mar al Cielo'. Turn right here and climb up to **Narila**, which you enter along Calle 4 Esquinas.

Narila to Bérchules (3.2km/1hr)

Bear left at a sign saying 'Cádiar, 1.5km', pass beneath the church then leave the village along Calle de Pajares passing a sign, 'Alcútar 2km'. A concrete track leads back down through olive groves towards the Río Cádiar/Guadalfeo. Reaching a junction where Agua Fria is signed right, turn left. The track shortly crosses the Río Cádiar/Guadalfeo via a wooden bridge then bears right. Climbing through irrigated terraces it narrows to become a path, which zigzags up before crossing a track. When you reach another track in front of a dressed stone wall, turn right then turn left in 50 metres to rejoin the path, which soon merges with a concrete track.

Turn left at a junction by a telegraph pole to come to a spring next to the old wash house of **Alcútar**. Ignore a metal sign marking the GR7 right; bear left and climb to the square in front of the church. Pass beneath the church and a spring then angle left to join the **A-4130**, which you follow for 500 metres to **Bérchules**. Ignore a left turn to Hotel Los Bérchules and continue past Fuente de las Carmelas then the church.

BÉRCHULES (ALTITUDE 1320M, POPULATION 719)

Accommodation, restaurant/bar/café, food shop, ATM, PO, pharmacy, transport

One of the eastern Alpujarra's prettiest villages, Bérchules lies high above the Guadalfeo river (aka Río Grande de los Bérchules) which rises just a few kilometres to its north. The village is known for its August New Year's Eve party, which began in 1994 after the village was left without electricity on 31 December. Thousands of visitors now come to celebrate the new year in midsummer.

Accommodation: El Paraje €€, www.elparaje.com, tel 626 186 035. Beautiful, isolated B&B on a high bluff above village with pool and home cooking. Worth a 700m diversion off the GR7 as you pass Alcútar. El Mirador de Bérchules €€, www.miradordeberchules.net, tel 958 769 090. S/c rustic-style apartments set around a garden with pool. Hotel Los Bérchules €€, www.hotelberchules.com, tel 660 685 695. Close to GR7 as you arrive at bottom of village with valley-facing rooms, restaurant and pool. Apartamentos El Vergel de Bérchules €€, www.apartamentos-elvergeldeberchules.com, tel 659 756 885. S/c apartments at heart of village with panoramic views.

Transport: Bus to/from Granada via Lanjarón and to/from Almería. Taxi, tel 606 352 955

Town hall/tourist info: www.berchules.es, tel 958 769 001

Bérchules to Mecina Bombarón (6km/2hr)

Keep left at a fork along Calle Real then Calle Agua to reach a sign, 'GR7 Mecina Bombarón'. Here, turn right down a path that widens to become a track. Reaching the first, three-way divide by an ancient chestnut tree (left leads to a gate, right steeply down to the right) carry on straight ahead along a path that leads down into the *barranco*.

After crossing a wooden bridge over a streambed you then cross the **Río Grande de los Bérchules** over a second bridge. Bear right and climb steeply, passing north of a rocky outcrop. The path, indistinct at times, adopts a course parallel to a stone wall. Levelling, it passes a ruin then angles up to a metal gate beyond which you reach a forestry track. Turn right. Climbing gently this track soon merges with a second track before crossing a ridgeline (1457m). From here you're treated to a sweeping panorama of the eastern Alpujarra and the Sierra de Gádor. Follow the track, which is signposted at all junctions, down to **Mecina Bombarón**. ◀

The official GR7 path cuts right down a path about half-way down. In 2021 the path was impassable, invaded by briars.

Reaching the village the track becomes concreted. Descending Calle de la Sierra you arrive at Plaza Vieja and a spring. Leave the square via Calle Plaza Vieja. Continue down Calle Carreterilla, Calle 8 de Marzo then Calle San José to reach the A-4130.

MECINA BOMBARÓN (ALTITUDE 1213M, POPULATION 660)

Accommodation, restaurant/bar/café, food shop, ATM, PO, pharmacy, transport

A quintessentially *alpujarreño* village with an organic grouping of whitewashed houses surrounded by steep terraces and backed by a forest of chestnut trees, Mecina Bombarón lies on the main communication route along the southern side of the Sierra Nevada. The Moorish rebel leader Aben Aboo who led the ill-fated Morisco uprising was from the *taha* (district) of which Mecina formed a part.

Accommodation: There are several s/c apartments in the village: Altas Vistas €€, www.altasvistas.es, tel 958 851 370. Five apartments overlooking garden with pool. Min stay two nights. Casas Rurales Macabes €€, www.alojamientoslosmacabes.com, tel 696 472 678. Nine well equipped apartments sharing two pools. El Benarum €€, www.benarum.com, tel 958 851 149. S/c houses/apartments with shared spa facilities.

Food: Bar Joaquín, tel 638 190 390, offers traditional Alpujarran fare with a rustic dining room and a terrace-with-views.

Transport: Bus to/from Granada and Ugíjar. Taxi in Bérchules (8km), tel 606 352 955

Town hall: www.alpujarradelasierra.es, tel 958 851 001

Tourist info: www.mecinabombaron.com

Mecina Bombarón to Yegen (6.2km/1hr 40min)

Turn right along the A-4130 then left at Taberna El Portón down Calle Iglesia Vieja following a sign for Los Macabes. Pass the Colegio Público and continue down a concrete track passing beneath a high stone wall. Reaching a junction, branch right along a dirt track, lined by incongruous lamp posts, that descends to **Golco**. After reaching a junction with a concrete road and turning left, you shortly pass a sign, 'GR7 Montenegro 2.5km'.

Follow the road southeast from Golco to a picnic area by a spring and trough. Here the road becomes a dirt track. Follow the track for 400 metres. Passing a solitary pine tree, cut left along an overgrown path that soon passes right of an old *era*. Winding down past towering agaves it meets the track you left earlier. Turn left then, reaching the entrance to a group of cottages, go right along a path that descends then crosses the **Río Mecina** via a concrete bridge.

Beyond the river bear right through a stand of poplars then climb across a shaley outcrop as you enter more barren, mineral landscapes. The path crosses two dry streambeds then climbs and passes above a **ruin**. The Sierra de Gádor comes into view out to the east. Passing beneath another **ruin**, the path becomes cobbled in sections. GR7 waymarking reappears before the path angles sharply left. Reaching the next fork take the lower option beyond which the path runs above an olive grove before running up to a track. Here, turn left. ▶

The track climbs, bears sharply right, crosses the bed of the **Rambla del Judío** then runs on up towards **Yegen**. Passing beneath the cemetery it merges with a concrete track. Continue along Calle van Hansen, cross Plaza de la Ermita then climb to La Plaza de la Iglesia and the church.

Turning right would take you to the Ermita de la Virgen Fátima de Abén Aboo.

Approaching Yegen

YEGEN (ALTITUDE 1037M, POPULATION 438)

Accommodation, restaurant/bar/café, food shop, ATM, PO, pharmacy, transport

English writer Gerald Brenan lived in Yegen in the 1920s and immortalised the village in *South from Granada* (1957). Brenan's book gives a fascinating insight into life in a remote Alpujarran village at a time when the region was only accessible on foot or horseback (the very reason he chose to settle there). Lyton Strachey, Dora Carrington and Virginia Woolf were among Brenan's illustrious visitors.

Accommodation: El Tinao €, via www.booking.com, tel 958 851 212. Rustic-style, inexpensive rooms-with-views and a great restaurant run by a friendly Irish woman. Pensión La Fuente €, tel 958 851 067. Close to the village square with charming, rustic-style rooms, s/c apartments and a tiny restaurant. El Rincón de Yegen €€, www.elrincondeyegen.com, tel 958 851 270. Attractive small hotel and restaurant beside the main road through the village. La Almuñia de la Alpujarra €€, www.laalmuniadelaalpujarra.com, tel 958 851 072. Superb apartments with restaurant and big views.

Food: Café Bar Muñoz, tel 958 851 006, has a garden and serves good tapas and *raciónes*.

Transport: Bus to/from Granada and Ugíjar. Taxi in Válor (6km), tel 659 892 060

Town hall/tourist info: www.alpujarradelasierra.es, tel 958 851 001

STAGE 25B
Yegen to Laroles

Start	Plaza de la Iglesia, Yegen
Distance	17.9km
Ascent	660m
Descent	675m
Time	5hr 15min
Highest point	1254m
Refreshments	In Válor, Nechite and Mairena

One of the southern variant's most beautiful stages passes through four villages of the eastern Alpujarras. Highlights include mineral springs, traversing the deep *barranco* of the Río de Laroles and magnificent views on the higher section of the route.

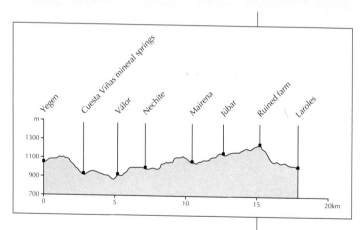

Yegen to Válor (5.2km/1hr 20min)

From the church, climb past the Fuente de los Tres Caños to the A-4130. Follow the road northeast then cross a bridge over the **Barranco de las Eras**. Around 30 metres past the km39 post turn left at a sign, 'Parque Natural'. 60 metres from the road go right down a dirt track heading towards Válor, which is visible up ahead. Dropping back to the

The water is purported to have curing properties and takes its name from the vineyards that were once planted here.

A-4130 head straight across the road down a path, ignoring a track that angles right.

Reaching a track turn left. Descending past a ruin then a newly-built house you reach the bottom of the barranco where you pass the **Cuesta Viñas mineral springs**. ◀

Just past the springs turn left up a tarmac road, which soon adopts an easterly course. Where it hairpins left, continue along a dirt track. Passing a water deposit you reach a junction next to a cement inspection hut. Here, go left.

The track passes another water deposit then descends to a broader track. Turn left again. Passing the gates of Villa Tobel you come to a concrete track. Here turn right and at the next fork left then descend and cross the Puente de la Tableta over the **Río de Válor**. ◀ Follow the road up into **Válor** passing above the municipal pool. Continue up to the A-4130 where you should turn right.

The Arab bridge has recently been restored.

VÁLOR (ALTITUDE 902M, POPULATION 672)

Accommodation, restaurant/bar/café, food shop, pharmacy, transport

Famous for its annual fiesta of Moros and Cristianos in which the events of the 16th century Morisco uprising are reenacted, Válor also is remembered for events during the Civil War when Republican militias retook the village from Franco's rebel forces. They held it for the Left until the end of the war when bloody recriminations took place.

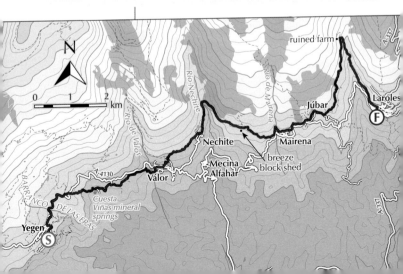

Accommodation: Hostal Las Perdices €, www.hlasperdices.com, tel 699 498 047. Simple but charming hostel, some rooms with south-facing balconies, with use of a neighbouring pool. Balcón de Válor €€, www.balcondevalor.com, tel 958 851 821. Nine s/c apartments sleeping 2–8 guests overlooking a garden and pool.

Food: Restaurante Aben Humaya, tel 958 851 810, offers superb, traditional cuisine.

Transport: Bus to/from Granada and Ugíjar. Taxi, tel 659 892 060

Town hall/tourist info: www.nevada.es, tel 958 760 007

Válor to Nechite (2km/40min)

Continue along the **A-4130** past a pharmacy. Just before Restaurante El Puente turn left at a sign, 'Sendero de los Castaños'. Sticking to the concreted road, which angles right then back left, you reach a sign saying 'GR7 Nechite 1.5km'. Here, turn right along a path that zigzags steeply up then merges with a concrete track. After climbing the track levels, descends past a water deposit before reaching a fork at a no entry sign. Branch left and head on towards Nechite along a path that runs close to an *acequia*, passing beneath centenarian chestnut trees.

Passing an electricity substation you reach a road at the outskirts of Nechite where, a few metres to the left, the road forks. Take the lower fork and descend next to a railing. Reaching the first houses of **Nechite**, turn right then after 25 metres, at a sign for 'Fuente del Rojo', go left. Passing beneath a ruin you reach a sign, 'GR7 Mairena 4km'.

Nechite to Mairena (4.1km/1hr 15min)

The path adopts a northerly course as it climbs gently across terraced hillsides above the *barranco* of the **Río Nechite**. Widening to become a track, flanked by a section of a drystone wall, it merges with a more distinct track. Bearing right the track descends to reach the northern reaches of the *barranco*, passing high above a millhouse. The track narrows to become a path, which descends then crosses the Río Nechite via stepping stones.

Beyond the river the path loops steeply up then, levelling, runs through a wooded swathe of hillside before crossing

Approaching Mairena

Vast views begin to open out once more to the south and east.

a smaller *barranco*, a tributary of the Río Nechite. Climbing on a southeasterly course you pass behind a **breeze-block shed** where the path widens then merges with another track. ◄ Maintain your course, now descending towards Mairena. Reaching a fork, keep left. After 200 metres you pass above a greenhouse with a netted roof. Continue along the track to a junction with a concrete track that runs some 30 metres above the A-4130. Turn left and follow the track as it loops across the *barranco* of the **Río de Mairena** then climbs to **Mairena**. Continue along Calle Ermita to the church.

MAIRENA (ALTITUDE 1083M, POPULATION 274)

Accommodation, restaurant/bar/café, transport

With soaring views across the Ugíjar Valley to the Sierra de Gádor from its high *mirador*, Mairena dubs itself 'El Balcón de Las Alpujarras'. It's one of the Alpujarras' prettiest villages with half a dozen streets of white-washed houses centred on the wafer-bricked church of Santo Cristo de la Luz.

Accommodation: Casa Viña y Rosales €€, www.alpujarras.alojamiento.raya. org, tel 958 760 177. Attractive B&B rooms in a 300-year-old village house with evening meals on prior request. Las Chimeneas €€, www.laschimeneas.com, tel 958 760 089. B&B with beautiful rooms, some with valley views, in converted village houses. Its adjacent restaurant serves acclaimed 'Moro' style food using organic ingredients, many sourced from the owners' farm.

Food: Restaurant at Las Chimeneas is open to non-residents.

Transport: Bus to/from Granada and Ugíjar. Taxi in Laroles (5km), tel 666 649 040

Town hall/tourist info: www.nevada.es, tel 958 760 007

Mairena to Júbar (1.4km/20min)

From the church, head east along Calle Iglesia to reach the A-4130. Turn left then left again past a sign, 'GR7 Júbar 1km'. After 35 metres the road arcs right. Here, turn left up a narrow path which is cobbled in sections. Reaching a track, descend for 20 metres then angle left and continue along the path which, merging with a track, drops back down to the A-4130. Here turn left then go left again in 25 metres at a sign, 'Júbar 0.5km'. Where the road angles hard right, turn left up a streambed then after a few metres angle right and climb a steep, rough path. Reaching a broad track, angle right to pick up the path once more, which shortly crosses directly over another track. ▶

The path is overgown but passable.

    Reaching **Júbar**, continue past a spring and picnic tables. Passing the old wash house and a second spring you reach a third spring. Here, turn left along Calle Real towards the village church.

Júbar to Laroles (5.2km/1hr 40min)

Just before the church, turn left up a concrete track at a GR7 sign, 'Laroles 4.5km'. The track reverts to dirt, running northeast through almond groves. ▶ As the track begins to descend you reach a fork. Here branch right, rejoining the main track after just 70 metres, which now adopts a northerly course. At the next fork keep left along the main track which descends, crosses a stream then climbs once again. Passing beneath a ruined farm, the track turns to concrete. Here turn right down a narrow path. After 75 metres the path passes right of a stone hut, bears right then descends and crosses a track. Running on towards Laroles, the path descends then runs along the river's west flank before crossing it via stepping stones beside a beautiful waterfall and rockpool.

Laroles comes into view through the trees.

Waymarking en route to Laroles

Beyond the river the path runs on towards Laroles. Climbing through almond groves you pass wooden railings where there are steep drops to your right as the A-4130 comes into sight. Crossing a dirt track the path climbs again, looser underfoot, before merging with a track where you pass beneath a high, drystone wall then right of an old mill. 70 metres beyond the mill, cut right towards a second mill. Angling left, continue down an indistinct path, which descends to merge with the track you left earlier that leads down to the A-4130. Bear left along the road to reach **Laroles**. Go right at fork just before a pedestrian crossing and drop down to the church and La Plaza de la Iglesia.

LAROLES (ALTITUDE 1015M, POPULATION 636)

Accommodation, campsite, restaurant/bar/café, food shop, ATM, PO, pharmacy, tourist info, transport

Flanked by irrigated terraces and groves of ancient chestnut trees, with panoramic views out to the Sierra de Gádor, Laroles is the easternmost village of Las Alpujarras and capital of the municipality of Nevada. In the village centre a statue of the Immaculate Virgin stands vigil over the spring of Fuente Cantarina, attracting many visitors who believe in her miraculous powers.

Accommodation: Alpujarras Camping €/€€, www.campingalpujarras.es, tel 958 760 231. Beautiful campsite with wood cabins and tipi-like tents 500m above Laroles with pool and restaurant (Tent+2ppl, €16). Closed all November. Hotel Real de Laroles-Nevada €€, tel 693 927 454. Friendly hotel in village centre with comfortable rooms above a restaurant. Balcón de la Alpujarra €€, tel 958 760 217. Simple apartments on road leaving village, some with views. Its sister restaurant, Fuente Mauricio, also has great views but receives mixed reviews.

Food: Restaurante Montesinos, tel 657 990 293, is the best place to eat in Laroles with friendly service and traditional Spanish cuisine.

Transport: Bus to/from Granada and Ugíjar Taxi, tel 666 649 040

Town hall/tourist info: www.nevada.es, tel 958 760 007

STAGE 26B
Laroles to Puerto de la Ragua via Bayárcal

Start	Plaza de la Iglesia, Laroles
Distance	16.2km
Ascent	1395m
Descent	375m
Time	6hr
Highest point	2041m
Refreshments	In Bayárcal
Notes	Beyond Bayárcal, a section of the path has been redirected along the road. Other sections are overgrown so best walked with long trousers. Check weather report if hiking the route in winter: conditions change rapidly at La Ragua, which is subject to high winds and heavy snowfall.

A demanding stage leading up the *barranco* of the Río Bayárcal to Puerto de la Ragua, the highest point on the GR7 at 2041m. Steel yourself for a total ascent of almost 1400m.

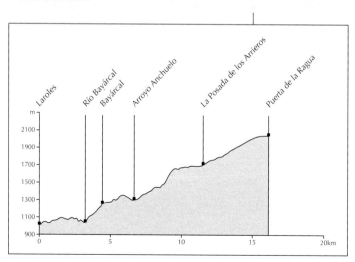

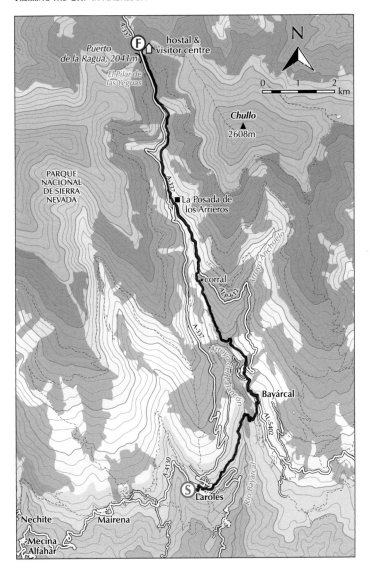

Laroles to Bayárcal (4.6km/1hr 30min)

Exit the square along Calle Rosario then climb to the top of the village. Turn right along the **A-4130** to reach a junction with the **A-337**. Turn right again towards Cherín. Walk 100 metres past a petrol station, then go left along a track signed 'Bayárcal 4.5km'. Reaching a fork take the lower, right option.

After approximately 2 kilometres, just before a pylon, turn right down a path at a damaged GR7 sign. The path descends into the *barranco* of the **Río Bayárcal** to reach a divide. Here, look for waymarking on a rock to your right, go right and continue down between stone walls. ▶

The path is indistinct in sections and overgrown.

Reaching the valley floor, carry on straight ahead and cross the Río Bayárcal via boulders. Climb to reach a clearer path, branch right then continue up to a junction where you should go left. Passing above a water deposit the track loops right and passes Laroles' waste treatment plant. Where it next arcs left, turn right up a footpath that shortly rejoins the track. At the next bend to the right leave the track to its left along a path marked with green-and-white flashes.

Leaving Laroles

Passing a ruin, you come to a junction. Keep right then left at the next fork. Continue past a spring then climb Calle Fuente Jiménez to a junction. Turning left you come to the church and La Plaza Mayor of **Bayárcal**.

BAYÁRCAL (ALTITUDE 1262M, POPULATION 284)

Restaurant/bar/café, food shop, ATM, pharmacy, transport

At the western edge of the province of Almería, high above the Barranco del Río Laroles, Bayárcal is a little-known yet pretty village with narrow streets radiating out from its high church tower. It's the only village in Almería province on the GR7 that runs back into Granada province a few kilometres to its north.

Accommodation: None in village, nearest places to stay are in Laroles.

Food: Restaurante El Nuño, tel 950 512 846, is the only place to eat in the village with simple, traditional fare.

Transport: Bus to/from Ameria. Taxi in Laroles (7km), tel 666 649 040

Town hall: www.bayarcal.es, tel 950 512 848

Bayárcal to Puerto de la Ragua (11.6km/4hr 30min)

Leave the square along Calle Granada, which becomes the **AL-5402** as you leave the village. Passing the km20 marker, turn right up a path signed 'GR140 Puerto de la Ragua'. Reaching a track, turn left to return to the AL-5402. Turn right along the road then, where the road hairpins right, continue along a track signed 'GR7 Puerto de la Ragua 4hr'.

Reaching a divide in front of a farm gate, angle left and follow a path downhill. Passing between stone ruins the path bears right then crosses a *barranco*. Angling back left it climbs through stands of oak. The path is quite overgrown on this section. At a fork by a GR7 post take the left, lower path then at the next bifurcation, and another GR7 post, turn up right. The path climbs, loose in parts, then descends towards the **Arroyo del Palancón**. Emerging from trees it runs towards an old **corral** then, angling right, zigzags indistinctly upwards. ◀

The original waymarking has faded but there are cairns.

Climbing to a flatter area to reach a GR post, maintain your course, still climbing steeply. The path improves as it passes right of an *era*. ◀ Some 20 metres before reaching the road, bear left. The path narrows, running parallel to the road, before descending to a sign for 'Punto de Informacion

The ALP-612 shortly comes into view.

Looking north towards Puerto de la Ragua from an old threshing floor

de la Ragua, 6.7km, GR7'. Ignore this sign. The path is impassable about 1km further on, beyond the point where it forks close to a bridge over the Palancón. Access about 500 metres beyond the fork is also blocked. Instead, angle right up a path signed 'Barranco del Riachuelo, 1.5km' to reach the **ALP-612**.

Turn left and follow the road for 1.65 kilometres to the point where it arcs left. Here turn right and pass left of the gates to **La Posada de los Arrieros**. Passing above the abandoned hotel continue along a path that runs up the west side of the Arroyo del Palancón. ▶

The path again is overgrown in parts.

At one point, ropes help you up over the rocks. Continuing up the stream's left bank the path enters a stand of pines then crosses to the right bank before passing an overgrown *era* then a ruined stone hut. Entering another group of pines you cross the stream once again, some 100 metres from the A-337, which is visible to your left.

Looping to and fro across the stream, the path runs on in a northerly direction. Crossing more rocky, open terrain it runs closer to the A-337, waymarked with paint flashes on the pines. The spring of **El Pilar de las Yeguas** comes into sight, some 75 metres to your left, beside the road. Passing a picnic area after 350 metres, you reach the Information Centre and the Albergue at **Puerto de la Ragua**.

PUERTO DE LA RAGUA (ALTITUDE 2041M)

The highest point on the GR7, Puerto de la Ragua is more than twice the height of England's highest peak. The pass sees heavy snow in winter and is a hub for cross-country skiing for up to five months a year. A network of waymarked footpaths leads out from the pass, which for centuries served as the principal route through the Sierra Nevada between Las Alpujarras and the Guadix-Baza plain.

Accommodation: The government-run hostal at the top of the pass, Albergue Puerto de la Ragua, is currently closed but may reopen. Check updates to this book on www.cicerone.co.uk.

Transport: No public transport. Nearest taxi in Laroles, tel 666 649 040

Tourist information: www.puertodelaragua.com

STAGE 27B
Puerto de la Ragua to La Calahorra

Start	Car park by Albergue, Puerto de la Ragua
Distance	11.6km
Ascent	65m
Descent	910m
Time	3hr 20min
Highest point	2041m
Refreshments	In Ferreira

An easy day of walking, nearly all downhill, as you leave the northern flank of the Sierra Nevada to reach the plain stretching north from La Calahorra towards the Sierra de Baza.

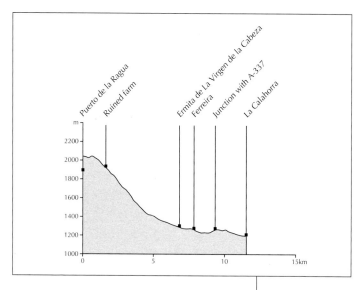

Puerto de la Ragua to Ferreira (7.8km/2hr 15min)

From the car park, cross the **A-337** by the km25 post. Bear right, cross a bridge made of railway sleepers then continue along a track parallel to the A-337. Angling left you reach a junction. Turn right, cross another track, then bear left uphill in 50 metres. At the next junction, turn right. The track levels, passes right of a pylon then arcs left. Here, leave the track to its right down a path waymarked with paint flashes on the trees. After crossing the **Barranco del Robo**, the path descends to the A-337.

Cross the road and continue down a path which shortly passes right of a **slate-roofed building** then runs up to a **ruined farm** where it angles right then left, now parallel to a stone wall. Descending through pines the path merges with a fire break. Continue along the left side of the break for 300 metres then turn left at cairns down a path, which descends to a track. ▶

Turn right along the track towards a farm then take a track to the left in 50 metres. After a few metres the track arcs right. Here, maintain your course down a path that zigzags down to the streambed of the **Arroyo Chico**. After hugging

The huge Andasol solar plant is visible to the north as well as the distant Sierra de Baza, the next range you'll traverse.

265

the stream's right bank the path loops from bank to bank. Ignore a path which at one point angles up right.

Passing a green gate the path bears right to reach a track. Turn left then reaching a fork take the left, lower option. Continue on past a track that shortly cuts left to cross the Arroyo Chico. Reaching a crossroads, continue straight ahead.

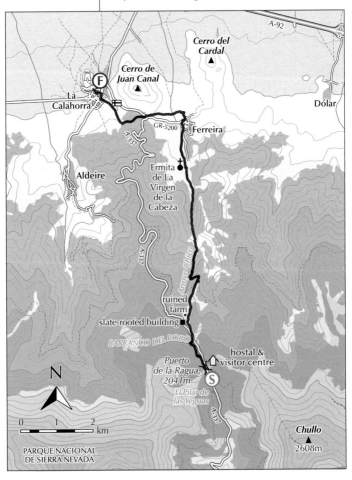

Soon you merge with another track where, heading straight on, you pass beneath a long, low ruin. Passing a house with a galvanised chimney pipe you come to another fork. Keep right. Walk 150 metres, then leave the track to its right along a path which runs beside a water channel. After another 150 metres, the path arcs left then descends to a track. Turning right you pass the chapel of **La Virgen de la Cabeza** where the dirt surface becomes tarmac. Passing a ferruginous spring (hence the name of **Ferreira**) head into the village to the church and La Plaza de la Constitución.

FERREIRA (ALTITUDE 1270M, POPULATION 299)

Restaurant/bar/café, food shop

Ferreira takes its name from the lodes of iron ore that were once mined in the area. One of the highest villages on the northern flank of the Sierra Nevada it sees long, cold winters while low rainfall means that much of the municipality's land, often subject to drought, lies barren. Within its Moorish fortress is a museum dedicated to Islamic architecture, El Centro de Interpretación de la Arquitectura Árabe (www.turismomarquesadodelzenete.com).

Accommodation: Nearest accommodation in La Calahorra (3.5km).

Food: El Hogar de Ferreira, tel 620 981 728. Inexpensive home cooking and local produce for sale.

Transport: Nearest taxi in Guadix (27km).

Town hall: Tel 958 677 217

Tourist info: see La Calahorra.

Ferreira to La Calahorra (3.8km/1hr 5min)

Exit the square down Calle Iglesia. Reaching a junction, turn right then after 75 metres, just beyond a bus stop, turn left at a sign, 'E4/GR7', and descend past the village cemetery. ▶ Reaching a water deposit the road bears right. At the end of the deposit, at a junction, turn left.

From here to La Calahorra the trail is marked with yellow Camino Mozárabe flashes.

Running level through almond groves, the track crosses two dry river beds before narrowing and climbing to the **GR-5200** just before it meets the A-337. Maintain your course, crossing both roads, and continue along a track that runs along the edge of a pine forest. At a fork, keep right. The track merges with a broader one that leads past the **cemetery** to the main road through **La Calahorra**. Turn right then left at a bank. Angling left then right past Hostal Rosabel, you reach the village square, La Plaza del Ayuntamiento.

LA CALAHORRA (ALTITUDE 1197M, POPULATION 661)

Accommodation, restaurant/bar/café, food shop, ATM, pharmacy, transport

Approaching La Calahorra at dusk

La Calahorra's stern and rather forboding castle is visible for miles distant, sitting proud above the village on a denuded hilltop. It was built in the early 1600s in Renaissance style by the Marqués de Zenete who was inspired by buildings he'd seen on his travels through Italy (open for visits on Wednesdays).

Leaving aside the *castillo*, the village has a rather down-at-heel feel to it, even if the church of Nuestra Señora de la Asunción speaks of a more prosperous past when La Calahorra lay on the trade route leading up to La Ragua.

Accommodation: Hostal and Restaurante Rosabel €, www.hostalrosabel. com, tel 958 677 540. Close to main square with inexpensive rooms and a restaurant offering top notch Spanish/fusion cuisine. Hostal Labella €, www. hostallabella.com, tel 958 677 000. Roadside hotel with attractive rooms and a beamed restaurant with home-cooked food. Hospedería del Zenete €€, www. hospederiadelzenete.com, tel 958 677 192. Glitzy 4-star hotel at edge of the town with restaurant, gym and sauna.

Food: Rosabel, tel 958 677 540, should be your number one choice.

Transport: Taxi in Guadix (24km), tel 699 593 532

Town hall/tourist info: www.lacalahorra.es, tel 958 677 040

STAGE 28B

La Calahorra to Narváez via Charches

Start	Plaza del Ayuntamiento, La Calahorra
Distance	54.6km
Ascent	1600m
Descent	1430m
Time	14hr
Highest point	2037m
Refreshments	In Charches
Notes	You can spilt the stage by wild camping or taking a taxi to Guadix (16km) or back to La Calahorra from Charches. It's no longer possible to stay at Cortijo de Narváez. From Narváez it's a 25min/€30 ride to Baza.

The longest GR7 stage entails wild camping or diverting to a nearby hotel from Charches. After making your way round a huge solar plant you cross the vast plain to the north of Calahorra, beyond which you enter the wilder landscapes of the Sierra de Baza.

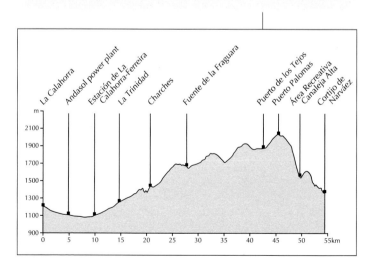

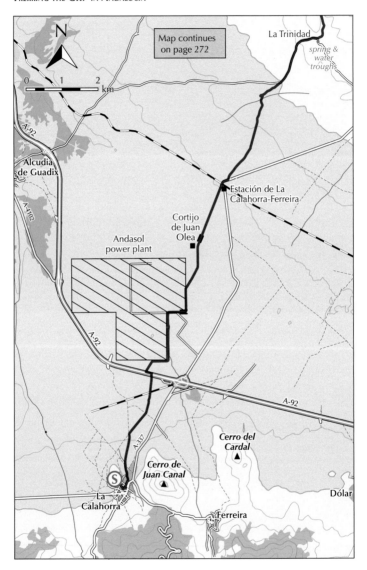

La Trinidad

spring & water troughs

Map continues on page 272

N

0   1   2 km

A-92

Alcudia de Guadix

A-4102

Estación de La Calahorra-Ferreira

Andasol power plant

Cortijo de Juan Olea

A-92

A-92

A-337

Cerro del Cardal ▲

Cerro de Juan Canal ▲

Dólar

La Calahorra

Ferreira

La Calahorra to Charches (21.1km/5hr 30min)

Exit the square along Calle Los Canos. Passing Hostal Rosabel, turn left and exit the village following signs for Castillo. Reaching a fork, keep right along a dirt track, passing right of a farm with twin silos at its eastern side. You will shortly cross an irrigation channel.

Around 700 metres beyond the farm, reaching a crossroads by a pylon, go right. At the next junction head straight ahead then cross an **abandoned railway line**. Carry on for 700 metres then follow a tunnel beneath the **A-92**, then turn left up a tarmac road. After 150 metres take the first track to the right. This leads to the boundary fence of the vast **Andasol solar plant**. ▸

The fenced plant has cut the original GR7 route.

This is Europe's first parabolic trough **solar plant** and is the largest plant of its kind in the world, capable of generating up to 50MW of power. The curved reflectors focus heat on a central pipe, heating its water in order to produce steam. This in turn drives the turbines that generate electricity.

The Andasol solar plant

Turn right and continue parallel to the fence for 450 metres, then follow it as it angles left. After 900 metres, crossing a metal bridge with blue rails, you reach a security hut. Turn right and continue along a tarmac road which, reverting to track, reaches the eastern side of the plant. Cross a **bridge** with yellow railings then turn left, still parallel to the fence. Continue for 600 metres, then angle right, away from the fence, along a track with a dry water channel to your left.

Pass **Cortijo de Juan Olea** and cross a **bridge** over a dry *rambla* (causeway of river, often dry). The track runs past a metal-roofed farm shed then, turning to concrete, comes to a junction. ◄ Bear left, cross the **railway line** then follow the road as it arcs right to reach a red-brick ruin with bird boxes on its inner walls.

To your right are the buildings of the abandoned Estación de la Calahorra-Ferreira.

Here, turn left along a track that runs across the plain. Stick to the main track, ignoring turnings off right. Around 2.5 kilometres from the old station the track descends into a river bed. Follow it left for 75 metres then cut right up a track that merges with a road as you arrive at the boundary of the Sierra de Baza Natural Park. Follow this road on through the tumble-down hamlet of **La Trinidad**.

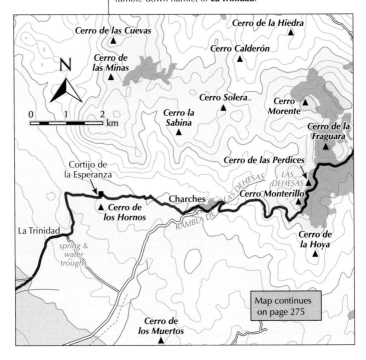

Map continues on page 275

The plain of La Vega beyond La Calahorra

PARQUE NATURAL DE LA SIERRA DE BAZA

Subject to cold weather sytems pushing in from the north as well as milder weather fronts rolling in from the Mediterranean and Atlantic, the Sierra de Baza has been classified as an *isla bioclimática* (bioclimatic island) and given natural park status due to the unusual diversity of its habitats. The natural park encompasses 53,000 hectares of the Subbaetic range, which rises abruptly ahead of you to more than 2200m as you traverse the Guadix-Baza plain on the GR7. The park attracts few visitors even though it encompasses a hauntingly beautiful tract of Andalucía.

On the sierra's lower slopes, cultivated groves of olives and fields of cereal give way to forests of maple, holm and gall oak interspersed with plantations of stone, Aleppo and Corsican pine. These run up to higher, indigenous stands of Scots and European black pines. Above the tree line cushion broom, low-growing juniper and gorse are among the more common plants. In total 1500 species have been identified in the natural park's calcerous terrain.

Mammals found in the park include red deer, foxes, rabbits and hares along with ibex, which were reintroduced in the 1980s, while badger, wildcats, marten, wild boar and roe deer are all present. With its varied biotopes, the natural park is home to more than 100 bird species. Raptors include griffon vultures, golden, short-toed and booted eagles, kestrels, peregrine falcons and eagle owls while red partridge, hoopoe, golden orioles, woodpeckers and turtle doves are common sightings in the valleys and woodlands of the lower reaches of the park.

Further information: Centro de Visitantes de Narváez – contact via Baza tourist office, www.turismobaza.es, tel 958 861 325. Reached at the end of Stage 28B, the centre has comprehensive information about the flora, fauna and geology of the park as well as its hiking trails. In 2021 its hostel accommodation remained closed though it may reopen. Check updates for this guide at www.cicerone.co.uk/995.

Reaching a spring and water troughs to the right of the road, turn left along a dirt track. Bearing left it adopts a northerly course for 1.25 kilometres. 100 metres beyond a pylon turn right along another dirt track. After 150 metres, bear right along a narrow track that follows the course of a streambed. Soon you'll see **Cortijo de la Esperanza** up to your left where the track angles up to a junction close to the farm. Turn right, descend, cross the track you left earlier then climb away from the plain, towards the western reaches of the **Sierra de Baza**.

Reaching the top of a ridge, Charches comes into view to the east. Continue for 75 metres then angle 45 degrees right at a fence along an indistinct path. After running parallel to the fence, maintain your course down into a gully. The path becomes clearer, angles right then climbs close to another fence. Where the fence angles left, head straight on up through an olive grove. Pass right of a pylon to meet the track you left earlier. ◀

To your left you'll see farm buildings.

Turn right along the track for 50 metres until you reach a cairn with GR7 paint flashes; here, turn left down an indistinct track which descends to a small, fenced enclosure. Head straight across two fields on a southeasterly course towards a farm shed with green metal door.

The path becomes clearer then descends to a track. Bear left, cross a river bed then pass left of the shed with the green door along a narrow track through almond and olive groves. Cross another river bed to meet with a tarmac road. Turn left and follow the road up to **Charches**.

CHARCHES (ALTITUDE 1431M, POPULATION 427)

Charches is the third highest village in the province of Granada and the largest within the Sierra de Baza Natural Park. Its isolated position and harsh climate means that it sees few visitors and at present there is no accommodation in the village.

Food: Bar Espigares, tel 615 690 921. Simple tapas-style dining.

Transport: No buses. Taxi, tel 630 341 117 or in Guadix (15km), tel 616 547 488

Town hall: www.valledelzalabi.org, tel 958 698 085

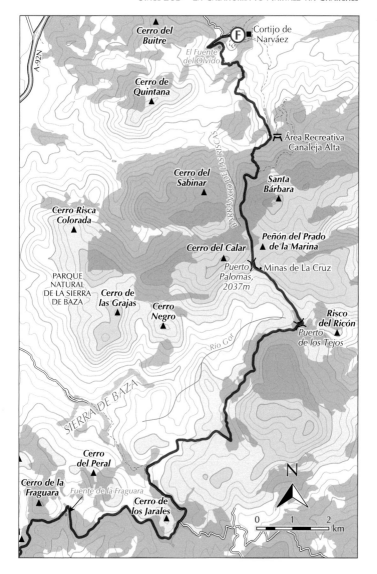

Charches to Narváez (33.5km/8hr 30min)

Keep right at the first fork and continue past the town hall, the church then the old washhouse to the east side of the village. Reaching the bed of the **Rambla de las Dehesas**, bear hard right (ignore a sign pointing straight on for Sendero Los Blanquizares) and at the next fork keep left. Views open out back across the plain to a wind farm and the solar plant. Brace yourself for a long but gradual climb.

Bearing left the track leads past a white hut as it climbs across the partially wooded hillside of Las Dehesas. Reaching a fork, keep left along the main track which enters stands of young pines. Ignore a sign off right for Rambla del Agua. The track levels, descends, then passes a stone corral to its right. Eventually bearing east it descends to forestry buildings and the **Fuente de la Fraguara**, a spring and water deposit left of the track. ◄

The spring water is excellent.

In 200 metres, the track loops right (ignore a track leading left) then climbs again. GR waymarking appears in abundance, which soon signs a path up to the left. Ignore this turn and continue along the main track. Pines begin to give way to evergreen oaks. The track contours round the **Cerro de los Jarales**. Ignore a track signed right, 'Casa Forestal El Raposo', to reach a junction with several signs. Here go left following a sign, 'Narváez 33km'. ◄

33km is the driving distance, 10km more than the route taken by the GR7.

The track runs in a northwesterly course with a *barranco* to its left. At the next fork turn right at a sign, 'Centro de Vistantes Narváez 21.8km'. The track climbs. Be ready to ignore GR waymarking cutting left but rather continue along the main track. After running almost due east it hairpins left, crosses a bridge then climbs past a viewing point, El Mirador de las Víboras. It shortly adopts a more level course, high above the **Río Gor**, which is down to your left. Reaching a junction at the **Puerto de los Tejos**, turn left following a sign for 'Narváez, 15km and Autovia A-92, 20km'.

From here the track climbs to reach the abandoned mining site of **Minas de la Cruz**. Beyond this, pass high above caves down to your left then bear right to reach the pass of **Puerto Palomas** (2037m). ◄ Walk a further 200 metres to reach a fork. Keep right, ignoring a sign for 'Collado El Resinero', sticking to the main track, passing east of the distinctive peak of **Cerro del Sabinar** and the deep gorge of **Barranco de las Riscas**.

This is the second highest point on the GR7.

The track soon loops hard right, and east. After 300 metres, leave the track to its left down a waymarked path, which loops steeply down with the Barranco del Ángulo to its left, eventually rejoining the track at **Área Recreativa Caneleja Alta**. There are springs in the picnic area that run all year.

Turn left along the track. Descend for 350 metres then turn left up a path via stone steps signed 'Narváez 1hr 30min'. A narrow path leads gently upwards before adopting a more level course. Reaching a firebreak turn down right then after 125 metres bear left to rejoin the path, which shortly merges with the firebreak once more, leaving it again to its left after 50 metres. The roof of Cortijo de Narváez comes into sight.

Rain clouds rolling in en route to Narváez

The path widens to become a track, which runs past a number of wooden and stone benches. After passing a spring, **El Fuente del Olvido**, ignore a sign pointing right for 'Cortijo de Narvaez 400m'. ▶ Bearing left the track runs away from Narváez to reach a GR7 sign, 'Narváez 760m', next to a water deposit. Here go right, descend past a spring then continue down the right side of the Barranco de Narváez to a tarmac road. Turn right and pass a track off left signed 'Baza 16km', then go left at a fork to reach the visitor's centre at **Cortijo de Narváez**.

You could take this path to save 750 metres of walking.

CORTIJO DE NARVÁEZ (ALTITUDE 1361M)

Situated at the foot of the Quintana massif, close to the confluence of El Barranco de Narváez and El Barranco del Peral, Cortijo de Narváez was once a farm before it became a centre for the forestry services then later a rural recreational area and visitor centre for the Sierra de Baza Natural Park.

Centro de Visitantes de Narváez: Contact via Baza tourist office (www. turismobaza.es, tel 958 861 325).

STAGE 29B
Narváez to Zújar

Start	Visitor centre, Cortijo de Narváez
Distance	24.2km
Ascent	270m
Descent	870m
Time	6hr
Highest point	1370m
Refreshments	In Baza

After a descent along forestry tracks and paths the GR7 passes through the sprawling town of Baza before reaching the cultivated plains and dry *ramblas* that lie northwest of the city.

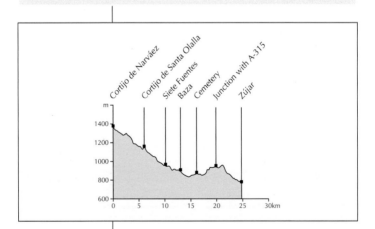

Narváez to Baza (14.3km/3hr 30min)
From the visitor centre, retrace your footsteps back to the tarmac road. Bear right for 70 metres then go right at a sign, 'Baza 16km'. Descend a gravel track then angle left, away from another entrance to **Cortijo de Narváez**. Some 25 minutes from Narváez turn right off the track at a GR7 post along

Zújar

F

A-315

warehouses

water
deposits

A-315

Arroyo del Carrizal

A-92N

A-92N

A-4200

Cerro
del Túnel

A-92N

Baza

Siete
Fuentes

PARQUE
NATURAL
DE LA SIERRA
DE BAZA

CAÑADA DEL CARRETÓN

Cortijo de
Santa Olalla

Dam

RAMBLA DE LOS PINOS

Cerro del
Tío Bardín

Cerrete
del Puerto

Cerro de
las Minillas

Cerro del
Buitre

S Cortijo de Narváez

Cerro de
Quintana

N

0   1   2
km

a rougher dirt track. After a few metres, at the next fork, keep left and continue past a barrel-roofed water deposit.

Pass through a swathe of low-growing pines to reach a fork. Keep left, still along a dirt track. ◀ The track narrows before descending to the **Rambla de los Pinos** where it loops to and fro across the streambed, running on an easterly course. Angling left it climbs away from the *rambla* passing above a dam across the streambed. Descending back to the *rambla* it narrows once again. Passing above a pan-tiled hut its bears back left before reaching a fork.

To your left an astronomical observatory comes into sight atop a ridge.

Keep left, uphill, then follow the track as it arcs right between the buildings of **Cortijo de Santa Olalla**. 80 metres beyond the farm it divides. Branch left then after a few metres right along a less distinct track, descending through pines. Reaching a fenced field go right along a path. With the fence to your left you soon reach the bed of **Cañada del Carretón**. Here keep right and continue down the dry *rambla*, crossing from bank to bank.

The plain beyond Baza comes into view.

Leaving the *rambla* you cross more rocky terrain. ◀ Descending, the path leads through a rusting metal gate. Turn right along the top of an almond grove then follow the path back left to return to the Cañada del Carretón. Here continue along a track with the river bed down to your right then maintain your course through a huge almond grove. The track turns to concrete then runs through the hamlet of **Siete Fuentes**.

Continue straight on down into **Baza** to Plaza San Marcos. Here, take the second turn right then cross a roundabout following a sign, 'Centro Urbano'. Descending across La Plaza de las Eras you pass an ornate fountain. Take the next left along Calle Alhondiga to reach the Plaza Mayor.

BAZA (ALTITUDE 853M, POPULATION 20,519)

Accommodation, restaurant/bar/café, food shop, ATM, PO, pharmacy, tourist info, transport

The plain surrounding Baza, El Hoyo de Baza, has long attracted settlers due to its rich soil and the abundant water at its fringes. Four centuries before Christ a sizeable Iberian settlement called Basti was in existence while during the Moorish period Baza's old quarter began to take on its present physiognomy. Its Arab baths are among the best preserved in Spain and worth a visit as is the archaeological museum. The town's sprawling suburbs are less attractive but you soon leave them behind as you follow the GR7 on towards Zújar.

Accommodation: Pensión los Hermanos €, www.hostalloshermanos.com, tel 958 701 880. Basic hostal with restaurant. Hotel-Restaurante Anabel €/€€, www.hotelanabelbaza.com, tel 958 860 998. Close to town centre, comfortable 2-star option with café downstairs. Cuevas al Jatib €€, www.aljatib.com, tel 958 342 248. A group of beautiful cave houses with pool, hammam, bar and restaurant reached in 10min by taxi from centre of Baza: great place for a first taste of troglodyte living. Cuevas de Ryder Loco €, www.facebook.com/cuevaderyderlocovwsusie/, tel 0044 7983 379987. Cave accommodation passed on your descent to Baza.

Transport: Bus to/from Granada and Almería. Taxi, tel 958 701 012

Town hall: www.ayuntamientodebaza.es

Tourist info: In the Museo Municipal de Baza, tel 948 861 325

Baza to to Zújar (9.9km/2hr 30min)

From the square by the church of Santa María turn right at a statue. Take the next left then turn once more right. Reaching a square, exit along Calle Barco then continue along Calle Granada to a roundabout. Here go right at a sign, 'Cementerio', and continue along the old drover's route of El Camino Real de Andalucía. A quiet tarmac road leads through olive groves to the **cemetery**. Here, bearing slightly left, the road's surface turns to dirt.

Reaching a fork by a water deposit, carry on straight ahead, pass beneath the **A-92N** then turn left and continue parallel to the motorway. Reaching a second underpass, follow the track steeply up right to a flat area. Here bear right, away from the track – there's no path – then climb WSW to a plateau and a field above the **Arroyo del Carrizal**. Continue west along the field's edge – twice you can cut corners where the field arcs in towards the Carrizal – to its far side, a few metres in from the A-315. Here, drop down to the old railway line, which looks like any other track. Follow it right, passing through a tunnel beneath the old Baza to Zújar road.

After 75 metres the track merges with the **A-315**. Follow the road for 275 metres then take a concrete track off left. Bearing right it crosses a bridge then reaches a junction. Turn left up a dirt track that crosses a rise then runs through a huge

The track running towards the Jabalcón peak

almond grove. Descending past a **water deposit**, you reach **warehouses** at the edge of Zújar. Bearing right at a mini-roundabout by a petrol station you come to a larger round-about and the A-315. Turn left and continue on through **Zújar** to Café Bar Torres. Here turn left, pass right of the town hall then descend two flights of steps to the Plaza Mayor.

ZÚJAR (ALTITUDE 769M, POPULATION 2597)

Accommodation, restaurant/bar/café, food shop, ATM, PO, pharmacy, tourist info, transport

The workaday village of Zújar, a mishmash of old and new beneath the Jabalcón peak (1492m), takes its name from the Moorish Sujayara (high mountain). It fell to the Christians at the tail end of the Reconquest and was repopulated with settlers from northern Spain.

The hot springs beside the Negratín reservoir, passed on Stage 30B, lie within the municipality and are worth a diversion. There are several cave houses in and around the village (see boxed text).

Accommodation: Hostal Restaurante Jaufil €, www.hostaljaufil.com, tel 958 716 191 Friendly hostel, its rooms with rather garish décor, just west of village beside the A-315. Hotel Balneario de Zújar €€, www.balneariodezujar.es, tel 958 191 000. Close to the point where you arrive at the Negratín reservoir on stage 30B of the GR7. Upmarket option with swish spa (paid as extra) and restaurant offering mix of traditional and fusion cuisine.

Food: Limited options. Restaurante Jaufil (see above) and a couple of tapas bars, including one on main square.

Transport: Bus to/from Baza. Taxi in Baza (11km), tel 958 701 012

Town hall: www.aytozujar.es, tel 958 716 017

CASAS CUEVAS OR CAVE HOUSES

Troglodyte dwellings dating back to the prehistoric times have been discovered on the vast plain of the Altiplano de Granada but it was during the Moorish period when cave houses became a defining feature of the region, dug out by hand from soft bands of sandstone.

Not only were the houses easy to build but, most importantly, they were inexpensive: most of the houses were dug out during the 19th and early 20th century at a time of grinding rural poverty.

The houses were also immensely practical being warm in winter and cool in summer with an ambient temperature of between 17 and 20 degrees.

Baza, Cúllar, Benamaurel, Orce, Galera and Huéscar all have several cave houses that are let on a self-catering basis while a growing number of ex-pats are choosing a *casa cueva* as their base for a new life in Spain.

STAGE 30B
Zújar to Benamaurel

Start	Plaza Mayor, Zújar
Distance	22km
Ascent	495m
Descent	540m
Time	5hr 30min
Highest point	885m
Refreshments	In season at Los Baños de Zújar
Notes	When open, Los Baños de Zújar make for an interesting break (tel 958 342 363).

After climbing across the western flank of the Jabalcón, a steep descent leads down to the Negratín reservoir. Here the route swings east past the Zújar hot springs then, after a second climb, crosses the cultivated plain west of Benamaurel.

Climbing towards El Jabalcón

Zújar to Benamaurel (22km/5hr 30min)

From the square head back past the town hall to Café/Bar Torres. Turn left along the **A-315R5** then, 20 metres before the km1 post, turn right. Passing the last village houses the road's surface turns to dirt. The track twists left and right through olive groves before adopting a northerly course as it climbs across the western flank of the **Jabalcón**, passing a number of electricity meter boxes. ◄

The Negratín reservoir comes into view to the north.

After running level the track descends through almond groves. Reaching a track that cuts hard down left, head straight on: there's GR waymarking and a green arrow on a rock. On clear days the Sierra Nevada is visible away to the south.

Passing beneath power lines the track runs up to the lower edge of a pine forest where it crosses a gully before swinging back north and descending steeply towards the **Negratín reservoir**. Looping right you pass beneath more power lines. Adopting a more level, northeasterly course the track passes above a greenhouse then reaches a junction where Tranco de Lobo is signed right. You should turn left and descend to the water channel of **El Canal de Jabalcón**, which you cross via a small, concrete bridge. A GR7 post here seems to suggest you should turn right.

To reach Hotel Balneario de Zújar (see accommodation) turn left then continue for 750 metres.

Continue down a steep track past a house with a line of palm trees. Reaching a road by the reservoir, turn right. ◄ Passing a metal building and a floating pontoon the road runs above the **Baños Termales de Zújar** then the grandiose **Monasterio La Granja**. Built in the 16th century the monastery is now a wedding venue.

284

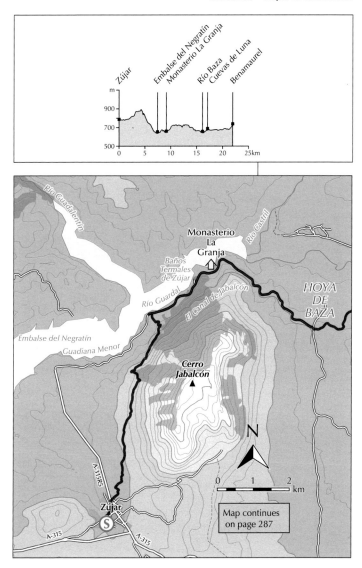

Map continues on page 287

285

Almond grove above the Embalse de Negratín

The road begins to climb away from the reservoir then runs just left of El Canal de Jabalcón. After 2 kilometres it angles left, away from the channel before bearing back up right to rejoin it. When you reach a three-way junction where a sign points back the way you've come, 'Zújar 11km', head straight on along a dirt track which descends through scrubby vegetation. Ignore tracks leading off right and left: stick to the main track. Passing beneath power lines head on towards the hamlet of Cuevas de Luna with polytunnel cultivation to either side as you cross the **Hoya de Baza**.

At a fork where a blue cabin is visible ahead on a ridge, keep right. Reaching the next junction go left then at the following one bear hard right. The track descends to reach yet another junction. Keep left and continue along a reed-lined track, which shortly crosses the **Río Baza**. Bearing right it climbs to the hamlet of **Cuevas de Luna** and a junction. Here go left along a tarmac road that runs across the plain through olive groves and cultivated fields. Crossing the **Río Cúllar**, continue past a *tanatorio* (funeral parlour) to reach **Benamaurel** and the A-4200. Turn left then follow signs for Centro Urbano up to the Plaza Mayor and the town hall.

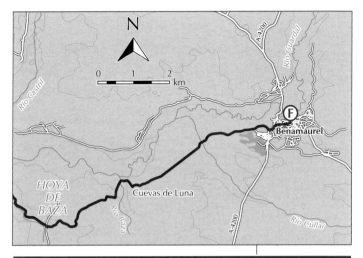

BENAMAUREL (ALTITUDE 722M, POPULATION 2328)

Accommodation, restaurant/bar/café, food shop, ATM, PO, pharmacy, tourist info, transport

Benamaurel spreads out along a low ridge just south of the Río Guardal. The green patchwork of irrigated plots that fill the river's alluvial plain stand in sharp contrast to the arid, semi-desert landscapes of the surrounding badlands of the Hoyo de Baza.

The village is famous for its cave houses. At the last census, more than 1900 *casas cuevas* were counted within the municipality, which embraces four other villages.

Benamaurel was once a centre for esparto crafts at a time when the grass was known locally as 'green gold'. Nowadays the local economy turns around cereal and olive farming while intensive, greenhouse cultivation is on the increase.

Accommodation: Apartamentos Turísticos Alhanda €€/€€€, www.alhanda. com, tel 958 104 271. Four top-notch apartments round a small pool. There are a number of cave houses a short drive from the village including Cuevas El Murallon €€, https://cueva-el-murallon-benamaurel.negocio.site, tel 627 350 650. One s/c house in village centre and another cave house 5km from village.

Transport: Bus to/from Baza. Taxi, tel 646 564 141

Town hall/tourist info: www.benamaurel.es, tel 958 733 011

STAGE 31B
Benamaurel to Cúllar

Start	La Plaza Mayor, Benamaurel
Distance	14.1km
Ascent	290m
Descent	120m
Time	3hr 20min
Highest point	905m
Refreshments	None on route

One of the GR7's shorter stages as you head east through the extraordinary, semi-desert landscapes of the Cañada del Caballo.

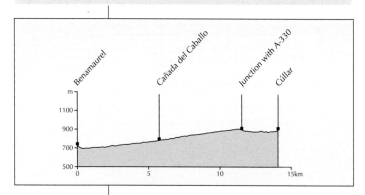

Benamaurel to Cúllar (14.1km/3hr)

Exit the square left of the town hall. Follow the road as it bears right then turn left to down Calle Bendo to reach the **GR-9108**. Turn left, continue past a pharmacy and supermarket then go left at signs for 'GR7 Cúllar 2hr 50min' and 'Puente Arriba, 8km'. Continue for 500 metres and when the road arcs left, maintain your course along a gravel track with cultivated fields to your right. Reaching a fork, carry on straight ahead and continue to climb gently along the left side of the valley floor of the **Cañada del Caballo**.

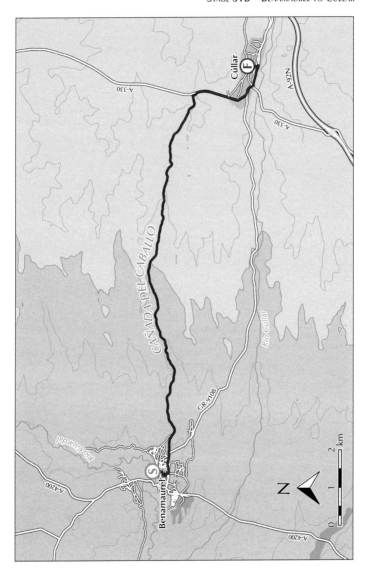

The Cañada del Caballo

After 8 kilometres the the track merges with one that runs in from the left. Bearing right, continue across more open farmland. The track's surface turns to tarmac before it passes right of a red-roofed warehouse and two white-and-blue towers. Reaching a road, turn right then at a Stop sign turn left and walk for 200 metres to reach the **A-330**. Turn right and follow the road down into **Cúllar**. Continue along the Avenida de Andalucía past Hostal Restaurante Montecarlo to a roundabout. Here bear left then after 500 metres turn up left at a sign Palacio Marqués del Condado to reach the Plaza de la Constitución and town hall.

CÚLLAR (ALTITUDE 895M, POPULATION 4898)

Accommodation, restaurant/bar/cafe, food shop, PO, pharmacy, tourist info, transport

If the present settlement of Cúllar dates from the Moorish period, the area surrounding the village has been settled since prehistoric times. Artefacts dating back to the Bronze Age have been found including an anthropomorphic figurine, El Ídolo de Malagón, which was unearthed close to the village.

In the mid 19th century the village lived a brief gold rush when 15 mines were dug close to the village by prospectors. No gold was discovered although small quanties were found in nearby Caniles.

There are dozens of *casas cuevas* in the village and its municipality, a few of them for rent.

Accommodation: Lunamar €, tel 958 731 120. Spruce little hotel down a quiet side street to one side of the GR7 as you enter village. No breakfast but café a few metres away. Hotel Montecarlo €, tel 958 73 08 26. Roadside restraurant with basic rooms passed as you arrive in village. Hostal Ventas del Peral €, www.ventadelperal.com. tel 958 730 288. Small but comfortable rooms above a rather garish roadside restaurant. There are also a number of *casas cuevas* close by that can be rented close to the village (see www.granadaaltiplano.org).

Food: Casa Dolos Venta Alegre, tel 958 730 160, offers traditional home cooking as well as barbecued meats, along the road from Hotel Lunamar.

Transport: Bus to/from Baza and Granada. Taxi, tel 619 034 471

Town hall/tourist info: www.cullar.es, tel 958 730 225

STAGE 32B
Cúllar to Orce

Start	Plaza de la Constitución, Cúllar
Distance	23.9km
Ascent	330m
Descent	290m
Time	5hr 30min
Highest point	1063m
Refreshments	None on route

A beautiful day of gentle walking via farm tracks, the bed of a *rambla* and a final section of road as the GR7 adopts a northerly course towards its end point.

Cúllar to Orce (23.9km/5hr 30min)

Exit the square to the left of the town hall then climb via El Parque Infantil de las Eras (a children's play area) to the top of the village and Carretera Vieja. Follow the road east past two red-and-white radio masts. Walk 150 metres beyond the masts and, reaching a farm shed at the northeastern tip of Cúllar, turn left along a track that runs across scrubby, open ground. Looping right then left it descends to merge with another track where, maintaining your course, you reach a

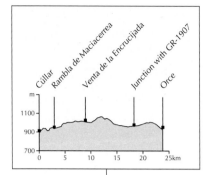

fork. Branch left, looking for GR flashes on a rock. The track climbs then levels as it crosses a high plateau. At the next fork, keep left.

The track descends to reach the dry bed of the **Rambla de Maciacerrea**. Here, turn right along a track following the broom-lined *rambla*. After briefly leaving the streambed the track rejoins it before crossing the streambed and climbing past a GR post. Cross the streambed a second time to come to a track where, up left, a fence

Views open out to the north and back towards the Jabalcón as you pass along the northwestern flank of the Sierra de la Torrecica.

encloses a former landfill site. Turn up left then after 200 metres turn right, following the fence. ◄ The track eventually merges with another then bears left before passing between the buildings of **Cortijo de Luís Pichón**.

Continuing in a northerly direction you reach the farm of **Venta de la Encrucijada** and a crossroads. Head straight on. Passing right of the farm, follow the track as it bears left past a fenced enclosure. After adopting a northwesterly course the track bears right, parallel to the southwestern slopes of **La Sierra de Orce**.

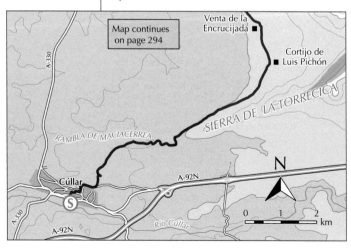

Map continues on page 294

Passing the gates of Cortijo el Periate you reach a fork. Keep right, looking for waymarking on a rock. Continue past a greenhouse then at the next crossroads walk straight on to reach the **GR-1907**. Turn right and continue along the road to **Orce** where, following signs for Centro Urbano you come to Plaza Vieja, between a tower and the village church.

Heading northeast towards the Cortijo de Luis Pichón

ORCE (ALTITUDE 932M, POPULATION 1198)

Accommodation, restaurant/bar/café, food shop, pharmacy, ATM, tourist info, transport

Orce brands itself 'la cuna de los primeros pobladores de Europa' or 'home of Europe's earliest settlers' and lies at the centre of a remarkable series of archaeological sites dating as far back as 1.4 million years. A part of the skull of an early hominin known as 'El hombre de Orce' was unearthed close to the village (although some paleontologists say it comes from a horse).

Two buildings not to be missed are El Palacio de los Segura (home to the tourist office) and the Alcazaba de las Siete Torres, an imposing Nasrid fortress with seven high towers.

Accommodation: Pensión La Morata €, tel 660 550 816. Small, friendly hostel in village centre offering B&B but no other meals. Alojamientos Cuevas en Orce €/€€, reservations via Booking.com, tel 626 192 136. Group of comfortable cave houses in town centre with open fires. There are also several other cave houses (www.orce.es/donde-alojarse).

Transport: Bus to/from Baza and Granada. Taxi, tel 676 572 042

Town hall/tourist info: www.orce.es, tel 958 746 101. Tourist office: In El Palacio de Los Segura, tel 958 746 171

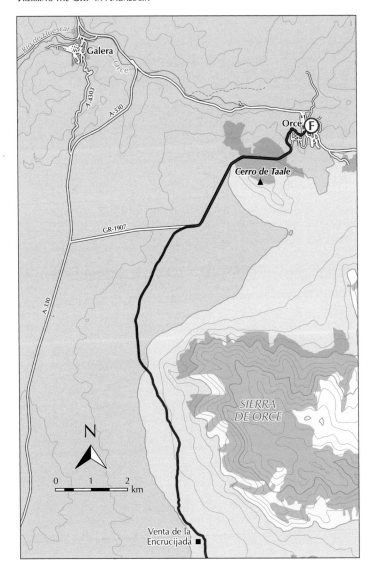

STAGE 33B
Orce to Huéscar

Start	Plaza Vieja, Orce
Distance	17.7km
Ascent	260m
Descent	230m
Time	4hr 10min
Highest point	960m
Refreshments	In Galera
Notes	In spite of scant waymarking, this is an easy stage to follow which coincides in part with the newly-created footpath of La Gran Senda de los Primeros Pobladores.

Another wonderful day of walking leads on across the semi-arid plain of La Vega, one of Europe's oldest inhabited areas, passing numerous cave houses.

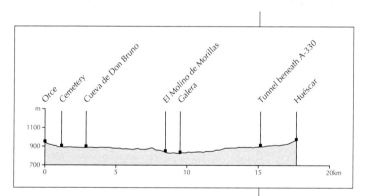

Orce to Galera (9.4km/2hr 10min)

Following the wall of the Castillo de las Siete Torres, leave Plaza Vieja along Calle Carrera. Keep right at a fork to exit the village before passing the Chapel of San Sebastián. At the next junction carry on straight ahead following a sign, 'Cementerio'. The track winds down into the fertile plain north of Orce to the village **cemetery**, beyond which you

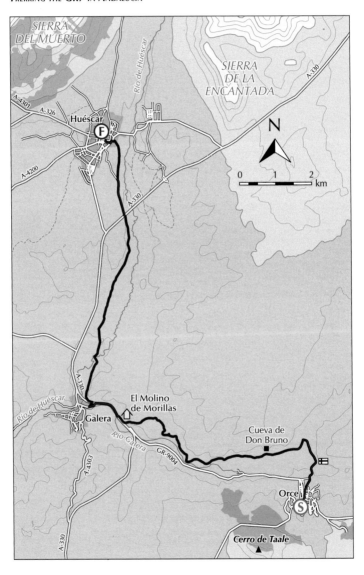

arrive at a fork. Keep left along a track, which leads out into the plain known locally as La Vega. Reaching a crossroads and a sign, 'Camino Rural', turn left.

Soon a water channel runs left of the track. Heading west you pass the imposing farm of **Cueva de Don Bruno** then an abandoned cave house. ▶ Reaching a fork keep left, sticking to the main track which runs beneath a cliff face as it approaches the **GR-9004**.

Passing another abandoned cave house the track passes between farm buildings before running close to the cliff face once again where you should ignore a track cutting left towards the GR-9004. The track narrows to become a path which leads to another group of farm buildings. Keep left of the buildings along the edge of a field then, climbing past a small house, join the farm's access track. Looping left the track passes beneath the porticoed façade of a once grandiose cave house, beyond which it narrows to become a path.

Bearing right the path widens as it runs past a fenced group of cave houses then crosses an almond grove to reach a junction. Turn left and follow the track over a ridge then descend towards the valley floor of the **Río Galera**. Stick to the main track with cultivated fields and the A-330 to your left. Approaching the road, just beyond more cave houses, you come to a fork. Keep left to pass **El Molino de Morillas** (see box on Galera) where the track arcs left to reach the **A-330**.

Here turn right. Carry on for 750 metres, just past a sign for **Galera**, then turn left towards the village.

It's worth climbing up to have a look inside the cave house: there are a dozen rooms carved out of the hillside behind its modest façade.

GALERA (ALTITUDE 836M, POPULATION 1090)

Accommodation, restaurant/bar/café, food shop, ATM, transport

At the centre of the Altiplano de Granada, several prehistoric archaeological sites close to Galera attest to this being one of Spain's oldest areas of human habitation. Tombs from the Bronze Age were discovered at Castellón Alto, while the remains of the Iberian settlement of Tutugi from the 5th and 6th century BC are a national heritage site. Artefacts from both sites can be seen in the town's archaeological museum.

In 1569 one of the bloodiest incidents of the Morisco uprising took place when, after a two-month siege, more than 2500 *moriscos* (Moors who adopted the Christian faith) were slaughtered by Christian troops. Like Orce, the village has dozens of cave houses.

Inside an abandoned cave house

Accommodation: El Molino de Morillas €€, www.molinodemorillas.es, tel 608 459 645. Plush s/c apartments in a converted millhouse with gardens and pool (covered in winter), which you pass just before Galera on stage 33B. Hotel Restaurante Galera €€, www.hotel-galera.com, tel 958 739 555. A beautiful boutique hotel with stunning views across the village and restaurant/bar serving award-winning tapas. Several cave houses to rent in and around the village: El Mirador de Galera €/€€, www.elmiradordegalera.com, tel 639 600 264. Award-winning cave houses, all beautifully furnished, sleeping from 2–6.

Food: Best eats at Restaurante Galera (see above).

Transport: Bus to/from Granada. Taxi in Huéscar, tel 661 642 304

Town hall/tourist info: www.ayuntamientogalera.es, tel 958 739 071

*The reed-lined track
en route to Huéscar*

Galera to Huéscar (8.3km/2hr)

After leaving the A-330 continue for 200 metres then take the first right. The road climbs steeply then crosses a bridge over the A-330. Immediately beyond the bridge turn left along a track, parallel to the road, which arcs right in 100 metres. You're now on El Camino Viejo de Galera a Huéscar, the cart track that once linked the two villages. Passing beneath a solitary pantiled hut atop a rise, keep left at a fork. The track shortly loops right and crosses a bridge. ▶

*A few metres to the
left there's a spring.*

Stick to the reed-lined track, which shortly passes right of a house surrounded by a thick hedge. Continue past another building lined with cypress trees then a group of cave openings fronted by a group of pines. Passing a farm shed with a green metal roof you reach a fork. Here, go right. The track soon merges with a narrow lane then, bearing right, runs past a poplar plantation then a solar farm.

The road, running parallel to the **Río de Huéscar** – which is to your right – passes through a tunnel beneath the A-330. As you head north, just past a farm shed, a track runs in from the right to merge with yours. After 75 metres, at a pylon, turn right along a dirt track whose surface soon changes to tarmac.

At the next junction, at a house fenced with cypresses, keep right. Passing the first houses of **Huéscar** the road arcs left then right before reaching a Stop sign and the A-330. Turn left, carry on for 70 metres, then turn right at a traffic light to arrive at the Plaza Mayor and its gaily-tiled bandstand.

HUÉSCAR (ALTITUDE 960M, POPULATION 7367)

Accommodation, restaurant/bar/café, food shop, ATM, PO, pharmacy, tourist info, transport

Like neighbouring Galera, Huéscar – the easternmost village of the province of Granada – lies in the midst of one of Spain's earliest areas of human settlement.

The town lay on the frontier between Moorish and Christain Spain, being definitively reconquerted in 1488.

In 1981 a local historian discovered that the village had remained officially at war with Denmark since the French invasion of 1809. A peace treaty was hastily signed even though a shot had never been fired during the 172-year 'war'.

Accommodation: Hostal Ruta del Sur €, www.hostalrutadelsur.com, tel 958 741 289. Roadside hotel with threes stories of clean, balconied bedrooms with restaurant offering standard Spanish fare. Hotel Rural Patri €€, www.hotelpatri.com, tel 958 742 504. Superb small hotel and restaurant at the centre of town with 18 spick-and-span bedrooms. Hotel El Maño €€, www.grupohem.es, tel 958 740 422. Another excellent choice with nicely decorated bedrooms above a restaurant/café.

Transport: Bus to/from Baza, Granada and Jaén. Taxi, tel 661 642 304

Town hall: www.aytohuescar.es, tel 958 740 036

Tourist info: www.huescar.org

STAGE 34B

Huéscar to Puebla de Don Fadrique

Start	Plaza Mayor, Huéscar
Distance	26km
Ascent	580m
Descent	375m
Time	6hr 45min
Highest point	1481m
Refreshments	None on route

A long section of quiet road walking leads you due north into the Sierra de Jorquera. After swinging east on forestry tracks, you descend to the GR7's end point in Andalucía.

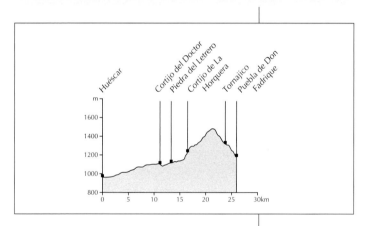

Huéscar to Puebla de Don Fadrique (26km/6hr 45min)
Exit the square along Calle Nueva. At the end of the road turn left then right along Calle Mayor following a sign, 'Paraje Las Santas'. Leaving the village continue along a road lined by cypress trees, running close to the eastern flank of the **Sierra del Muerto**, **Sierra Bermeja** and the **Sierra de Montilla** with a cultivated plain to your right. ▶

You're following the ancient drover's route of El Camino de Huéscar a Las Santas.

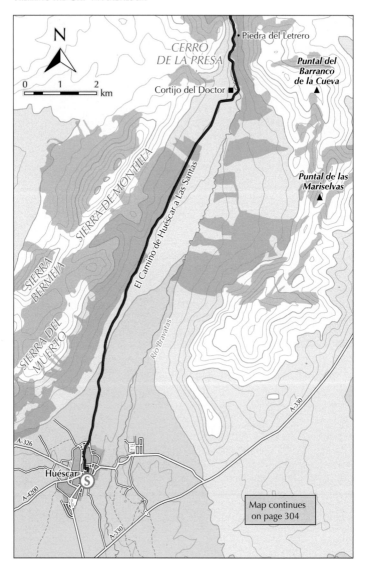

N

0 1 2 km

CERRO
DE LA PRESA

Piedra del Letrero

Puntal del
Barranco
de la Cueva
▲

Cortijo del Doctor ■

Puntal de las
Mariselvas
▲

SIERRA DE MONTILLA

El Camino de Huéscar a Las Santas

Río Bravatas

SIERRA
BERMEJA

SIERRA DEL
MUERTO

A-326

Huéscar
Ⓢ

A-4200

A-330

A-330

Map continues
on page 304

The cypress-lined Camino de Huéscar a Las Santas

After 9.5 kilometres the cypress trees end before you cross a vast almond grove. Running level, the road loops left then right before descending on an easterly course. Angling back north it passes the **Cortijo del Doctor**, crosses a bridge then climbs gently up the gorge of the **Río Bravatas**. The gorge narrows as the road enters pine forest, looping to and fro across the river before passing the archaeological site of **Piedra del Letrero**.

The **cave** and its paintings is a UNESCO World Heritage site. It was officially 'discovered' in 1915 and investigated by the French archaeologist Henri Breuil. Viewings are no longer possible.

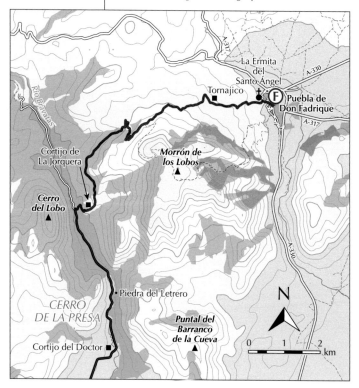

The road continues to climb on a gentle gradient. Reaching the top of a rise and a yellow inspection hut with a green door, go right up a track signed 'GR7 Puebla de Don Fadrique 3hr 45min'. The track zigzags steeply up past the ruins of **Cortijo de la Jorquera**, beyond which you should ignore a smaller track cutting down left: stick to the main track. ▶ Passing a water deposit and picnic bench the track runs up to a junction. Here turn right. A GR7 post to the left seems to suggest that you turn left because its X (not this way) is hidden from sight.

The track zigzags up to another junction. Turning left and east you shortly come to a fork and the highest point on the stage (1487m). Take the left turn, waymarked with orange paint on a rock, and begin a long and steep descent. Passing a farm marked **Tornajico**, follow the track on to the east, ignoring a track cutting up right after 600 metres. **Puebla de Don Fadrique** comes into sight as you enter more barren terrain. Pass two high aerial masts and descend to a chapel, **La Ermita del Santo Ángel**. Bearing right, continue down into the village to a junction. Here drop down a flight of steps then take the second left to reach La Plaza de la Constitución.

Lavender fields on the descent towards Don Fadrique

There are now panoramic views to the north and the Cuerda del Pozanco.

APPENDIX A
Facilities table

Mid-stage towns and villages are shown in *italics*

Town	Distance from previous town	Time from previous town	Accommodation	Camp site	Restaurant/Café/Bar	Drinking fountain	Food shop
The common route							
Tarifa	0	0	X	X	X	X	X
Los Barrios	47.1km*	12hr 30min	X	X	X	X	X
Castellar de la Frontera	26.5km	7hr 40min	X		X	X	X
Castillo de Castellar	6.8km(*)	2hr	X		X	X	X
Jimena de la Frontera	21.3km	6hr 15min	X	X	X	X	X
Ubrique	37.7km*	10hr 30min	X		X	X	X
Benaocáz	4.5km	1hr 10min	X		X	X	X
Villaluenga del Rosario	6.1km	1hr 30min	X		X	X	X
Montejaque	17.6km	5hr	X		X	X	X
Ronda	10.8km	3hr 15min	X	X	X	X	X
Arriate	9km	2hr 15min	X		X	X	X
Serrato	20.2km	5hr 20min	X		X	X	X
Ardales	14.3km	4hr 10min	X	X (+7km)	X	X	X
El Chorro	16km	5hr	X	X	X	X	X
Valle de Abdalajís	10.6km	3hr	X		X	X	X
Antequera	19.5km	5hr 40min	X		X	X	X
Villanueva de Cauche	16.8km	4hr 40min	X		X	X	X
The northern variant							
Villanueva del Rosario	11.7km	3hr	X		X	X	X

Villanueva del Trabuco	4.9km	1hr 15min	X		X	X	X
Villanueva de Tapia	31.2km(*)	8hr 45min	X		X	X	X
Villanueva de Algaidas	17.2km	4hr 45min	X		X	X	X
Cuevas Bajas	10km	2hr 50min	X		X	X	X
Cuevas de San Marcos	8.8km	2hr 20min	X		X	X	X
Rute	13.6km	3hr 40min	X		X	X	X
Priego de Córdoba	25.9km	7hr 30min	X		X	X	X
Almedinilla	12.1km	3hr 10min	X		X	X	X
Alcalá La Real	25km	7hr	X		X	X	X
Frailes	10.2km	2hr 30min	X		X	X	X
Carchelejo	35.2km	10hr	X		X	X	X
Cambil	13km	3hr 45min	X		X	X	X
Torres	27.7km	8hr 30min	X	X	X	X	X
Albanchez de Mágina	5.4km	1hr 30min	X	X	X	X	X
Bedmar	11km	3hr 15min	X		X	X	X
Jódar	9.2km	2hr 50min	X		X	X	X
Quesada	35.3km	9hr 45min	X		X	X	X
Cazorla	18.1km	4hr 50min	X	X	X	X	X
Vadillo de Castril	16km	5hr 30min	X	X	X	X	X
Coto Ríos	33.8km	8hr 30min	X	X	X	X	X
Pontones	30.3km	8hr	X		X	X	X
Santiago de la Espada	13.4km	3hr 45min	X		X	X	X
Puebla de Don Fadrique	34.3km	8hr 15min	X		X	X	X

Town	Distance from previous town	Time from previous town	Accommodation	Camp site	Restaurant/ Café/Bar	Drinking fountain	Food shop
The southern variant							
Riogordo	23.8km	5hr 30min	X		X	X	X
Guaro	20.2km	5hr 15min	X		X	X	
Ventas de Zafarraya	8.4km	2hr 15min	X		X	X	X
Alhama de Granada	20.4km	5hr 45min	X		X	X	X
Arenas del Rey	22.3km	6hr	X (+7km)	X (+7km)	X	X	X
Jayena	17.2km	6hr	X	X (+4km)	X	X	X
Albuñuelas	31km(*)	8hr 30min	X		X	X	X
Restábal	5.5km	1hr 30min	X		X	X	X
Nigüelas	9.4km	3hr	X		X	X	X
Lanjarón	18.8km	5hr 15min	X		X	X	X
Cáñar	8km	2hr 40min	X		X	X	X
Soportújar	4.7km	1hr 30min	X		X	X	X
Pampaneira	6.5km	2hr	X		X	X	X
Bubión	1.3km	25min	X		X	X	X
Pitres	4.8km	1hr 20min	X	X	X	X	X
Pórtugos	3.5km	1hr	X		X	X	X
Busquístar	1.9km	40min	X		X	X	X
Trevélez	12km	4hr	X	X	X	X	X
Juviles	10km	2hr 30min	X		X	X	X
Tímar	2.5km	40min				X	
Lobras	2.6km	40min			X	X	
Cádiar	5.4km	2hr	X		X	X	X
Narila	1.7km	30min				X	
Bérchules	3.2km	1hr	X		X	X	X
Mecina Bombarón	6km	2hr	X		X	X	X

308

Yegen	6.2km	1hr 40min	X		X	X	X
Válor	5.2km	1hr 20min	X		X	X	X
Nechite	2km	40min				X	
Mairena	4.1km	1hr 15min	X		X	X	X
Júbar	1.4km	20min					
Laroles	5.2km	1hr 40min	X	X	X	X	X
Bayárcal	4.6km	1hr 30min	X		X	X	X
Puerto de la Ragua	11.6km	4hr 30min				X	
Ferreira	7.8km	2hr 15min			X	X	X
La Calahorra	3.8km	1hr 5min	X		X	X	X
Charches	21.1km	5hr 30min				X	
Narváez	33.5km*	8hr 30min				X	
Baza	14.3km	3hr 30min	X		X	X	X
Zújar	9.9km	2hr 30min	X		X	X	X
Benamaurel	22km	5hr 30min	X		X	X	X
Cúllar	14.1km	3hr 20min	X		X	X	X
Orce	23.9km	5hr 30min	X		X	X	X
Galera	9.4km	2hr 10min	X		X	X	X
Huéscar	8.3km	2hr	X		X	X	X
Puebla de Don Fadrique	26km	6hr 45min	X		X	X	X

* It is recommended that you split these stages into two days either by leaving the route or by camping. (An asterisk in brackets indicates an optional two-day section.)

APPENDIX B
Spanish–English glossary

Spanish	English
acequia	water channel
alameda	park or promenade in town centre
alberca	water tank
albergue	hostel
alcázar	fortress
aljibe	water deposit
alquería	from the Arab al-qairia: a mountain farm or hamlet
arroyo	stream
ayuntamiento	town hall
bandolero	a highway brigand/smuggler
barranco	gulley or gorge
barrio	district /quarter of town or village
bruja/brujo	witch
calera	lime kiln
calzada	footpath, originally cobbled
cañada/colada/cordel	drovers' track or transhumance route
capilla	chapel
casa cueva	cave house
castillo	castle
cerro	hill or low mountain
consultorio	doctor's surgery
cordillera	mountain range
cortijo	farmhouse/farm
coto	hunting reserve
dehesa	forest that has been partially cleared to leave select species such as evergreen, deciduous and cork oak
embalse	reservoir
era	threshing floor
ermita	chapel
espeleología	caving

Spanish	English
frontera	border
fuente	spring
ganadería	livestock
huerta/huerto	cultivated plot where fruit and veg are grown
lavandería	wash house
llano	plain, flat extension between mountains
majanos	piles of stones
mesón	restaurant
mirador	viewpoint
molino	mill
monte bajo	low growing, shrubby vegetation
morisco	Moors who adopted the Christian faith
nacimiento	source of spring, river or stream
nava	flat area between outcrops of rock
pantano	reservoir
parador	a hotel group owned and managed by the state
paseo	park or promenade in town centre
prohibido el paso	no entry
puerto	pass
ración	whole plate of any particular tapas
rambla	causeway of river, often dry, synonymous with wadi
rió	river
sendero	footpath
sierra	mountain range (less extensive than cordillera)
taha	district
tajo	gorge or cliff face
tanatorio	funeral parlour
tapa	small saucer/dish of food to accompany drink
tinao	roof or room spanning street in Las Alpujarras
venta	restaurant
vereda	footpath
vía pecuaria	drovers' track
vía verde	former railway line converted to walk/cycle path

APPENDIX C
Further information

Transport

Bus travel

Local bus companies and relevant services are detailed in the introductions to each province and the village boxes.

Umbrella websites to view connections from most villages, with tickets bookable online
www.omio.com
www.busbud.com

Train travel

www.renfe.com
www.raileurope.com
www.seat61.com

The route

For more information on the GR7
www.andalucia.org/es/rutas/sendero-europeo-peloponeso-tarifa-gr-7-e-4/

European hiking

The European Ramblers Association
www.era-ewv-ferp.org

Maps and navigation

To download Basecamp
https://www.garmin.com/en-GB/software/basecamp/

For lists of all IGN 1:50,000 maps required for route with info on villages on route
www.fedamon.com
(Andalucían Mountaineering Federation's website with GPX downloads, route overview in Spanish)

Other

For information about El Caminito del Rey, as well as tickets
www.caminitodelrey.info/en/

Apps

Weather

Eltiempo.es
Yr.no

Transport

Renfe Ticket
Omio (book trains, buses and flights)
Busbud
Alsa

Mapping

Wikiloc Outdoor Navigation GPS
Maps.me (offline maps)
Google Earth
Google Maps

Accommodation

Booking.com (travel deals)
Airbnb

APPENDIX D
Further reading

Plants and wildlife

Botanical Guides

A Field Guide to the Wild Flowers of Southern Europe, Davies and Gibbons

Flowers of Southwest Europe: A Field Guide, Oleg, Polunin and Smythies

Wildflowers of the Mediterranean, Marjorie Blamey and Christopher Grey-Wilson

Ornithological Guides

A Field Guide to the Birds of Britain and Europe, Peterson, Mountfort and Hollom

Birds of Europe, Svensson

Collins Bird Guide, Svensson

Accounts of living in the areas through which the GR7 passes

Driving Over Lemons, Chris Stewart

Factory of Light, Michael Jacobs

South from Granada, Gerald Brennan

The Road from Ronda, Alastair Boyd

The Sierras of the South, Alastair Boyd

Cicerone walking guides covering areas through which the GR7 passes

Coastal Walks of Andalucía, Guy Hunter-Watts

The Mountains of Nerja, Jim Ryan

The Mountains of Ronda and Grazalema, Guy Hunter-Watts

Walking and Trekking in the Sierra Nevada, Richard Hartley

Walking in Andalucía, Guy Hunter-Watts

NOTES

NOTES

DOWNLOAD THE ROUTES
IN GPX FORMAT

All the routes in this guide are available for download from:

www.cicerone.co.uk/995/GPX

as GPX files. You should be able to load them into most formats of mobile device, whether GPS or smartphone.

When you go to this link, you will be asked for your email address and where you purchased the guide, and have the option to subscribe to the Cicerone e-newsletter.

www.cicerone.co.uk

LISTING OF CICERONE GUIDES

BRITISH ISLES CHALLENGES, COLLECTIONS AND ACTIVITIES

Cycling Land's End to John o' Groats
The Big Rounds
The Book of the Bivvy
The Book of the Bothy
The C2C Cycle Route
The Mountains of England and Wales: Vol 1 Wales
The Mountains of England and Wales: Vol 2 England
The National Trails
Walking The End to End Trail

SCOTLAND

Backpacker's Britain: Northern Scotland
Ben Nevis and Glen Coe
Cycle Touring in Northern Scotland
Cycling in the Hebrides
Great Mountain Days in Scotland
Mountain Biking in Southern and Central Scotland
Mountain Biking in West and North West Scotland
Not the West Highland Way
Scotland
Scotland's Best Small Mountains
Scotland's Mountain Ridges
Skye's Cuillin Ridge Traverse
The Ayrshire and Arran Coastal Paths
The Borders Abbeys Way
The Great Glen Way
The Great Glen Way Map Booklet
The Hebridean Way
The Hebrides
The Isle of Mull
The Isle of Skye
The Skye Trail
The Southern Upland Way
The Speyside Way
The Speyside Way Map Booklet
The West Highland Way
The West Highland Way Map Booklet
Walking Ben Lawers, Rannoch and Atholl
Walking in the Cairngorms
Walking in the Pentland Hills
Walking in the Scottish Borders
Walking in the Southern Uplands
Walking in Torridon
Walking Loch Lomond and the Trossachs
Walking on Arran
Walking on Harris and Lewis
Walking on Jura, Islay and Colonsay
Walking on Rum and the Small Isles
Walking on the Orkney and Shetland Isles

Walking on Uist and Barra
Walking the Cape Wrath Trail
Walking the Corbetts
   Vol 1 South of the Great Glen
   Vol 2 North of the Great Glen
Walking the Galloway Hills
Walking the Munros
   Vol 1 – Southern, Central and Western Highlands
   Vol 2 – Northern Highlands and the Cairngorms
Winter Climbs Ben Nevis and Glen Coe
Winter Climbs in the Cairngorms

NORTHERN ENGLAND TRAILS

Hadrian's Wall Path
Hadrian's Wall Path Map Booklet
The Coast to Coast Walk
The Coast to Coast Map Booklet
The Dales Way
The Dales Way Map Booklet
The Pennine Way
The Pennine Way Map Booklet
Walking the Dales Way
Walking the Tour of the Lake District

NORTH EAST ENGLAND, YORKSHIRE DALES AND PENNINES

Cycling in the Yorkshire Dales
Great Mountain Days in the Pennines
Mountain Biking in the Yorkshire Dales
St Oswald's Way and St Cuthbert's Way
The Cleveland Way and the Yorkshire Wolds Way
The Cleveland Way Map Booklet
The North York Moors
The Reivers Way
The Teesdale Way
Trail and Fell Running in the Yorkshire Dales
Walking in County Durham
Walking in Northumberland
Walking in the North Pennines
Walking in the Yorkshire Dales: North and East
Walking in the Yorkshire Dales: South and West

NORTH WEST ENGLAND AND THE ISLE OF MAN

Cycling the Pennine Bridleway
Cycling the Reivers Route
Cycling the Way of the Roses
Hadrian's Cycleway
Isle of Man Coastal Path

The Lancashire Cycleway
The Lune Valley and Howgills
Walking in Cumbria's Eden Valley
Walking in Lancashire
Walking in the Forest of Bowland and Pendle
Walking on the Isle of Man
Walking on the West Pennine Moors
Walks in Silverdale and Arnside

LAKE DISTRICT

Cycling in the Lake District
Great Mountain Days in the Lake District
Joss Naylor's Lakes, Meres and Waters of the Lake District
Lake District Winter Climbs
Lake District: High Level and Fell Walks
Lake District: Low Level and Lake Walks
Mountain Biking in the Lake District
Outdoor Adventures with Children – Lake District
Scrambles in the Lake District – North
Scrambles in the Lake District – South
The Cumbria Way
Trail and Fell Running in the Lake District
Walking the Lake District Fells –
   Borrowdale
   Buttermere
   Coniston
   Keswick
   Langdale
   Mardale and the Far East
   Patterdale
   Wasdale

DERBYSHIRE, PEAK DISTRICT AND MIDLANDS

Cycling in the Peak District
Dark Peak Walks
Scrambles in the Dark Peak
Walking in Derbyshire
Walking in the Peak District – White Peak East
Walking in the Peak District – White Peak West

SOUTHERN ENGLAND

20 Classic Sportive Rides in South East England
20 Classic Sportive Rides in South West England
Cycling in the Cotswolds
Mountain Biking on the North Downs

Mountain Biking on the
  South Downs
Suffolk Coast and Heath Walks
The Cotswold Way
The Cotswold Way Map Booklet
The Great Stones Way
The Kennet and Avon Canal
The Lea Valley Walk
The North Downs Way
The North Downs Way Map Booklet
The Peddars Way and Norfolk
  Coast path
The Pilgrims' Way
The Ridgeway National Trail
The Ridgeway Map Booklet
The South Downs Way
The South Downs Way Map Booklet
The Thames Path
The Thames Path Map Booklet
The Two Moors Way
The Two Moors Way Map Booklet
Walking Hampshire's Test Way
Walking in Cornwall
Walking in Essex
Walking in Kent
Walking in London
Walking in Norfolk
Walking in the Chilterns
Walking in the Cotswolds
Walking in the Isles of Scilly
Walking in the New Forest
Walking in the North Wessex Downs
Walking on Dartmoor
Walking on Guernsey
Walking on Jersey
Walking on the Isle of Wight
Walking the Jurassic Coast
Walking the South West Coast Path
Walking the South West Coast Path
  Map Booklets:
    Vol 1: Minehead to St Ives
    Vol 2: St Ives to Plymouth
    Vol 3: Plymouth to Poole
Walks in the South Downs
  National Park

WALES AND WELSH BORDERS

Cycle Touring in Wales
Cycling Lon Las Cymru
Glyndwr's Way
Great Mountain Days in Snowdonia
Hillwalking in Shropshire
Hillwalking in Wales – Vols 1&2
Mountain Walking in Snowdonia
Offa's Dyke Path
Offa's Dyke Path Map Booklet
Ridges of Snowdonia
Scrambles in Snowdonia
Snowdonia: 30 Low-level and
  easy walks – North

Snowdonia: 30 Low-level and
  easy walks – South
The Cambrian Way
The Ceredigion and Snowdonia
  Coast Paths
The Pembrokeshire Coast Path
The Pembrokeshire Coast Path
  Map Booklet
The Severn Way
The Snowdonia Way
The Wales Coast Path
The Wye Valley Walk
Walking in Carmarthenshire
Walking in Pembrokeshire
Walking in the Forest of Dean
Walking in the Wye Valley
Walking on Gower
Walking on the Brecon Beacons
Walking the Shropshire Way

**INTERNATIONAL CHALLENGES,
COLLECTIONS AND ACTIVITIES**

Canyoning in the Alps
Europe's High Points

AFRICA

Kilimanjaro
The High Atlas
Walking in the Drakensberg
Walks and Scrambles in the
  Moroccan Anti-Atlas

ALPS CROSS-BORDER ROUTES

100 Hut Walks in the Alps
Alpine Ski Mountaineering
    Vol 1 – Western Alps
    Vol 2 – Central and Eastern Alps
Chamonix to Zermatt
The Karnischer Hohenweg
The Tour of the Bernina
Tour of Monte Rosa
Tour of the Matterhorn
Trail Running – Chamonix and the
  Mont Blanc region
Trekking in the Alps
Trekking in the Silvretta and
  Ratikon Alps
Trekking Munich to Venice
Trekking the Tour of Mont Blanc
Walking in the Alps

**PYRENEES AND FRANCE/SPAIN
CROSS-BORDER ROUTES**

Shorter Treks in the Pyrenees
The GR10 Trail
The GR11 Trail
The Pyrenean Haute Route
The Pyrenees
Walks and Climbs in the Pyrenees

AUSTRIA

Innsbruck Mountain Adventures
The Adlerweg
Trekking in Austria's Hohe Tauern
Trekking in the Stubai Alps
Trekking in the Zillertal Alps
Walking in Austria
Walking in the Salzkammergut:
  the Austrian Lake District

EASTERN EUROPE

The Danube Cycleway Vol 2
The High Tatras
The Mountains of Romania
Walking in Bulgaria's National Parks
Walking in Hungary

**FRANCE, BELGIUM AND
LUXEMBOURG**

Chamonix Mountain Adventures
Cycle Touring in France
Cycling London to Paris
Cycling the Canal de la Garonne
Cycling the Canal du Midi
Mont Blanc Walks
Mountain Adventures in
  the Maurienne
Short Treks on Corsica
The GR20 Corsica
The GR5 Trail
The GR5 Trail – Benelux
  and Lorraine
The GR5 Trail – Vosges and Jura
The Grand Traverse of the
  Massif Central
The Loire Cycle Route
The Moselle Cycle Route
The River Rhone Cycle Route
The Way of St James – Le Puy to
  the Pyrenees
Tour of the Queyras
Trekking in the Vanoise
Trekking the Robert Louis
  Stevenson Trail
Vanoise Ski Touring
Via Ferratas of the French Alps
Walking in Provence – East
Walking in Provence – West
Walking in the Ardennes
Walking in the Auvergne
Walking in the Briançonnais
Walking in the Dordogne
Walking in the Haute Savoie: North
Walking in the Haute Savoie: South
Walking on Corsica

GERMANY

Hiking and Cycling in the
  Black Forest
The Danube Cycleway Vol 1

The Rhine Cycle Route
The Westweg
Walking in the Bavarian Alps

HIMALAYA
Annapurna
Everest: A Trekker's Guide
Trekking in Bhutan
Trekking in Ladakh
Trekking in the Himalaya

IRELAND
The Wild Atlantic Way and
    Western Ireland
Walking the Wicklow Way

ITALY
Italy's Sibillini National Park
Shorter Walks in the Dolomites
Ski Touring and Snowshoeing in
    the Dolomites
The Way of St Francis
Trekking in the Apennines
Trekking in the Dolomites
Trekking the Giants' Trail:
    Alta Via 1 through the Italian
    Pennine Alps
Via Ferratas of the Italian Dolomites
    Vols 1&2
Walking and Trekking in the
    Gran Paradiso
Walking in Abruzzo
Walking in Italy's Cinque Terre
Walking in Italy's Stelvio
    National Park
Walking in Sicily
Walking in the Dolomites
Walking in Tuscany
Walking in Umbria
Walking Lake Como and Maggiore
Walking Lake Garda and Iseo
Walking on the Amalfi Coast
Walking the Via Francigena
    pilgrim route – Parts 2&3
Walks and Treks in the
    Maritime Alps

JAPAN, ASIA AND AUSTRALIA
Hiking and Trekking in the Japan
    Alps and Mount Fuji
Hiking the Overland Track
Japan's Kumano Kodo Pilgrimage
Trekking in Tajikistan

MEDITERRANEAN
The High Mountains of Crete
Trekking in Greece
Treks and Climbs in Wadi Rum,
    Jordan
Walking and Trekking in Zagori

Walking and Trekking on Corfu
Walking in Cyprus
Walking on Malta
Walking on the Greek Islands –
    the Cyclades

NORTH AMERICA
The John Muir Trail
The Pacific Crest Trail

SOUTH AMERICA
Aconcagua and the Southern Andes
Hiking and Biking Peru's Inca Trails
Torres del Paine

SCANDINAVIA, ICELAND
AND GREENLAND
Hiking in Norway – South
Trekking in Greenland – The Arctic
    Circle Trail
Trekking the Kungsleden
Walking and Trekking in Iceland

SLOVENIA, CROATIA, SERBIA,
MONTENEGRO AND ALBANIA
Mountain Biking in Slovenia
The Islands of Croatia
The Julian Alps of Slovenia
The Mountains of Montenegro
The Peaks of the Balkans Trail
The Slovene Mountain Trail
Walking in Slovenia: The Karavanke
Walks and Treks in Croatia

SPAIN AND PORTUGAL
Camino de Santiago:
    Camino Frances
Coastal Walks in Andalucia
Cycle Touring in Spain
Cycling the Camino de Santiago
Mountain Walking in Mallorca
Mountain Walking in
    Southern Catalunya
Portugal's Rota Vicentina
Spain's Sendero Historico: The GR1
The Andalucian Coast to Coast Walk
The Camino del Norte and
    Camino Primitivo
The Camino Ingles and Ruta do Mar
The Camino Portugues
The Mountains of Nerja
The Mountains of Ronda
    and Grazalema
The Sierras of Extremadura
Trekking in Mallorca
Trekking in the Canary Islands
Trekking the GR7 in Andalucia
Walking and Trekking in the
    Sierra Nevada
Walking in Andalucia

Walking in Menorca
Walking in Portugal
Walking in the Algarve
Walking in the Cordillera Cantabrica
Walking on Gran Canaria
Walking on La Gomera and El Hierro
Walking on La Palma
Walking on Lanzarote and
    Fuerteventura
Walking on Madeira
Walking on Tenerife
Walking on the Azores
Walking on the Costa Blanca
Walking the Camino dos Faros

SWITZERLAND
Switzerland's Jura Crest Trail
The Swiss Alpine Pass Route –
    Via Alpina Route 1
The Swiss Alps
Tour of the Jungfrau Region
Walking in the Bernese Oberland
Walking in the Engadine –
    Switzerland
Walking in the Valais
Walking in Zermatt and Saas-Fee

TECHNIQUES
Fastpacking
Geocaching in the UK
Map and Compass
Outdoor Photography
Polar Exploration
The Mountain Hut Book

MINI GUIDES
Alpine Flowers
Navigation
Pocket First Aid and
    Wilderness Medicine
Snow

MOUNTAIN LITERATURE
8000 metres
A Walk in the Clouds
Abode of the Gods
Fifty Years of Adventure
The Pennine Way – the Path,
    the People, the Journey
Unjustifiable Risk?

For full information on all our guides,
books and eBooks,
visit our website:
www.cicerone.co.uk

CICERONE

Trust Cicerone to guide your next adventure,
wherever it may be around the world...

Discover guides for hiking, mountain walking, backpacking,
trekking, trail running, cycling and mountain biking, ski touring,
climbing and scrambling in Britain, Europe and worldwide.

Connect with Cicerone online and find inspiration.

- buy books and ebooks
- articles, advice and trip reports
- podcasts and live events
- GPX files and updates
- regular newsletter

cicerone.co.uk